NAMING THE POWERS

OTHER FORTRESS PRESS BOOKS
BY WALTER WINK

The Bible in Human Transformation:
Toward a New Paradigm for
Biblical Study
(1973)

THE POWERS SERIES

Unmasking the Powers:
The Invisible Forces That
Determine Human Existence
(1986)

Engaging the Powers:
Discernment and Resistance in
a World of Domination
(1992)

WALTER WINK

NAMING THE POWERS

The Language of Power
in the New Testament

FORTRESS PRESS   PHILADELPHIA

COPYRIGHT 1984 BY FORTRESS PRESS

Cover design: Terry Bentley
Cover art: Pomona Hallenbeck

Library of Congress Cataloging in Publication Data

Wink, Walter.
  Naming the powers.

  (The Powers; v. 1)
  Includes bibliographical references.
  1. Powers (Christian theology)—Biblical teaching.
  2. Power (Christian theology)—Biblical teaching.
  3. Bible. N.T.—Criticism, interpretation, etc.
  I. Title. II. Series: Wink, Walter. Powers.
  BS2545.P66W56 vol. 1   235 s [235]   83–48905
  ISBN 0–8006–1786–X

Printed in the United States of America   1-1786

96   95   9   10

To June
Where the tongues
of flame
are in-folded

Contents

3

Interpreting the Powers

Preface

This book was not intended. I had almost finished what is now one of its companion volumes and had gone to Latin America on a sabbatical leave, hoping to complete the writing while experiencing life under military dictatorship. During that four-month leave, most of it spent in Chile but also including Argentina, Brazil, Bolivia, Peru, Costa Rica, and Nicaragua, my wife June and I observed the churches' responses to human rights violations and hunger. We stayed in barrios and favelas, talking with priests and nuns struggling with the everyday crush of oppression. We interviewed a lawyer who represented the families of people who had "disappeared." We spent an excruciating evening in dialogue with a woman who had been tortured.

This kind of exposure went on week after week. Finally I had had more than I could stomach. Instead of expressing the pain of so much evil in tears, I tried to stop the avalanche. I wanted simply to escape it. I became angry with the oppressors, angry with the oppressed, unaware of the grief tearing at my heart.

At the end of the trip I became ill. I had planned to spend the last bit of unbroken time writing, but now I was so weak and underweight that I could scarcely function. Worse, I was overwhelmed by despair. I had gone to Latin America hoping that what we experienced there would help me write a book that could make a difference. The evils we encountered were so monolithic, so massively supported by our own government, in some cases so anchored in a long history of tyranny, that it scarcely seemed that anything could make a difference.

Since I was unable to mobilize my energies for creative writing, I started working through a book that had come out while we were gone: Wesley Carr's *Angels and Principalities* (1981). It was largely in error, I felt, but it was persuasively argued. I could at least rally for a book review. That written, I still felt unsatisfied. Perhaps an article would be better. When that exceeded fifty pages and was scarcely begun, I realized that I simply had to jettison my own itinerary and run with the wind.

What Carr had done was force me to abandon the relative consensus that I thought existed on the issue of the Powers and to reexamine every scrap of evidence from scratch. That kind of detailed work was good therapy for someone who still had not cried. It was like assembling a telephone book. For three days I would look up all the references to a single word in Philo or Josephus, then write perhaps a sentence. I am an impatient person; in good health I would never have submitted to such tedium. I was—how shall I put this—tricked into it.

Then one day, after plowing through all the data (Part One) and having completed virtually all the exegesis (Part Two), suddenly, just the way the books on scientific method say it is supposed to happen, the mass of data crystallized into a simple pattern. For the first time I sensed that I understood what the biblical language of power was about. Often our research begins with a clear hypothesis that we test by research; there was something elating about having the hypothesis emerge *from* the research.

During all this time I had also been struggling with my despair. How could the writers of the New Testament insist that Christ is somehow, even in the midst of evil, sovereign over the Powers? I wrestled with this assertion with all my might. Gradually an answer began to shape itself. What I found may not strike anyone else as amounting to much, but for me it was the thin margin of hope, and I clung to it desperately.

And somewhere in the midst of the writing and the wrestling, I was given the gift of my tears.

Perhaps it may seem strange to say now, but I am profoundly grateful for all that: to Carr for writing a book that, however wrong, forced me to a task I would never have taken up voluntarily; for the despair, since I have tried to avoid it all my life—now I know it can be endured; also for June, who suffered with me through all that and a great deal more, and to whom this book is lovingly dedicated; and to God, because I now know, in a way that I had not before, that "neither death, nor life, nor angels, nor principalities . . . will be able to separate us from the love of God in Christ Jesus."

This volume, which is more technical than the two to follow, attempts to comprehend the language of power in the New Testament. Part One is a thoroughgoing examination of the use of the terms for power in all the relevant literature of the period and in the New Testament. Part Two applies the guidelines developed in Part One to the more problematic passages dealing with the principalities and powers—what I have called "the disputed passages." Part Three attempts a consistent interpretation of the meaning of the biblical language of power for human existence, then and now.

Fundamental research is necessarily laborious, and despite all my efforts to pare it down to a minimum, may still make for laborious reading. You should therefore feel free to skim or skip Part One, and even the early sections of Part Two, or proceed directly to Part Three, and then work backward if you are so inclined.

The companion volumes will each appear in successive years. Volume Two, *Unmasking the Powers*, will take a long look at the phenomena dubbed "spiritual" in the New Testament—demons, Satan, angels of the churches, angels of the nations, angels of nature, gods, the elements of the universe—and try to make contemporary sense of them, working from the hypothesis developed in this volume. Volume Three, *Engaging the Powers*, will address practical issues: what does it mean, in down-to-earth terms, to confront the Powers with the fact that they exist to serve the human purposes of the Cosmic Christ?

I initially conceived this study in 1964 under the impetus of William Stringfellow's *Free in Obedience*, which for the first time awakened me to the relevance of the Powers for comprehending institutional evil. In 1973 I began researching in earnest, with frequent interruptions and precious little leisure to write. These friends helped guard my words and stretch my comprehension: John Pairman Brown, Andrew Canale, Burton Cooper, Robert A. Evans, James A. Forbes, Robert T. Fortna, Ethné Gray, Dwayne Huebner, Morton Kelsey, George A. Riggan, Sharon Ringe, William Stringfellow, Caroline Usher, Barbara Wheeler, and Thomas Wieser. A word of thanks also to Norman Hjelm and John Hollar of Fortress Press.

Abbreviations

Ancient documents with their abbreviations and dates are listed at the back of the book in the Index of Passages.

AAA	*Apocryphal Acts of the Apostles*, trans. W. Wright (London: Williams & Norgate, 1871), vol. 2
A&P	Wesley Carr, *Angels and Principalities*, SNTSMS 42 (New York and Cambridge: Cambridge University Press, 1981)
ANRW	*Aufstieg und Niedergang der römischen Welt*, ed. H. Temporina and W. Haase (New York and Berlin: Walter de Gruyter)
APOT	*Apocrypha and Pseudepigrapha of the Old Testament*, ed. R. H. Charles, 2 vols. (Oxford: Clarendon Press, 1912)
BAG	Walter Bauer, *A Greek-English Lexicon of the New Testament*, trans. W. F. Arndt and F. W. Gingrich (Chicago: University of Chicago Press, 1957; rev. ed. 1979)
B.C.E.	Before the Common Era
BDF	F. Blass, A. Debrunner, *A Greek Grammar of the New Testament*, trans. and ed. R. W. Funk (Chicago: University of Chicago Press, 1961)
Bib Sac	*Biblia Sacra*
C.E.	Common Era
CGTC	The Cambridge Greek Testament Commentary
DSSE	*The Dead Sea Scrolls in English*, trans. Geza Vermes (Baltimore: Penguin Books, 1975)
ExpTim	*Expository Times*
HibJ	*Hibbert Journal*
HSM	Harvard Semitic Monographs

HTR	*Harvard Theological Review*
ICC	International Critical Commentary
IDB	*Interpreter's Dictionary of the Bible,* ed. G. A. Buttrick (Nashville: Abingdon Press, 1962)
Int.	*Interpretation*
JAAR	*Journal of the American Academy of Religion*
JB	Jerusalem Bible
JES	*Journal of Ecumenical Studies*
JNES	*Journal of Near Eastern Studies*
JRS	*Journal of Roman Studies*
JTS	*Journal of Theological Studies*
KJV	King James Version of the Bible
LCL	Loeb Classical Library
LSJ	H. G. Liddell, R. Scott, and H. S. Jones, *A Greek-English Lexicon* (Oxford: Clarendon Press, 1958)
LXX	The Septuagint (Greek translation of the Hebrew Bible)
M.	*The Mishnah,* ed. Herbert Danby (Oxford: Clarendon Press, 1933)
NEB	New English Bible
NHL	*The Nag Hammadi Library,* ed. James M. Robinson (New York: Harper & Row, 1981)
NPNF	*Nicene and Post-Nicene Fathers,* ed. Philip Schaff (Grand Rapids: Wm. B. Eerdmans, 1956)
NT Apoc.	*New Testament Apocrypha,* 2 vols., ed. Edgar Hennecke and Wilhelm Schneemelcher (Philadelphia: Westminster Press, 1965)
NTS	*New Testament Studies*
PGM	Karl Preisendanz, *Papyri Graecae Magicae* (Leipzig: B. G. Teubner, 1928)
Phillips	J. B. Phillips paraphrase of the New Testament
RechSR	*Recherches de Science Religieuse*
RSR	*Religious Studies Review*
SBL	Society of Biblical Literature
SJT	*Scottish Journal of Theology*
SNTSMS	Society for New Testament Studies Monograph Series
ST	*Studia Theologica*
Str-B	H. L. Strack and P. Billerbeck, *Kommentar zum*

	Neuen Testament aus Talmud und Midrasch, 6 vols. (Munich: Beck, 1922–61)
T.B.	Babylonian Talmud
TDNT	*Theological Dictionary of the New Testament,* ed. G. Kittel and G. Friedrich, trans. G. W. Bromiley (Grand Rapids: Wm. B. Eerdmans, 1964–74)
ThR	*Theologische Rundschau*
USQR	*Union Seminary Quarterly Review*
WUNT	Wissenschaftliche Untersuchungen zum Neuen Testament
ZNW	*Zeitschrift für die Neutestamentliche Wissenschaft*
ZThK	*Zeitschrift für Theologie und Kirche*

NAMING THE POWERS

1

IDENTIFYING THE POWERS

1. Introduction

Power in Its Mythological Context

The reader of this work will search in vain for a definition of power. It is one of those words that everyone understands perfectly well until asked to define it. Sociologists and political scientists generally complain that no one (prior to their writing) has ever provided an adequate definition, but the definitions they offer are in turn rejected by others. This is all quibbling. The dictionary definitions of power will do quite well, as long as the word is not pressed to answer for the myth with which it presently keeps company.

Our use of the term "power" is laden with assumptions drawn from the contemporary materialistic worldview. Whereas the ancients always understood power as the confluence of both spiritual and material factors, we tend to see it as primarily material. We do not think in terms of spirits, ghosts, demons, or gods as the effective agents of powerful effects in the world. When the typewriter jams, I do not suspect a jinni of having jimmied with it, though I sometimes *behave* as if I did, nor do I lay on hands and pray for it, though I confess to having friends who do. No, most of us, if we are truly "modern," look for nonspiritual, material causes. What happens then when we moderns examine the biblical understanding of the Powers? Will we not tend to assume that what the ancients called "Powers" were merely little-understood manifestations of material power: the laws of physical power, institutionalized forms of corporate power, psychological forms of power, perhaps even various forms of psychic power? And whatever residue we cannot force into our material categories, we will tend to regard as "superstition." The ancients could not help it if they did not understand the physical laws of the universe uncovered by our science. They could deal with these invisible, unknown forces only by personifying them and treating them as if they were conscious, willing beings.

There is a fine irony here. We moderns cannot bring ourselves by any feat of will or imagination to believe in the real existence of these mythological entities that traditionally have been lumped under the general category "principalities and powers." We naturally assume that the ancients conceived of them and believed in them the same way we conceive of and disbelieve them. We think they thought of the Powers quite literally as a variety of invisible demonic beings flapping around in the sky, occasionally targeting some luckless mortal with their malignant payload of disease, lust, possession, or death. This view of their view finds its way into even the best modern translations of the Bible, where words like "spiritual" and "spirits" are constantly being added to the text gratuitously in order to make it clear that spiritual, not material, or material/spiritual, entities are involved. When we read the ancient accounts of encounters with these Powers, we can only regard them as hallucinations, since they have no real physical referent. Hence we *cannot* take seriously their own descriptions of these encounters—as long as our very categories of thought are dictated by the myth of materialism.

In short, our eyes and minds are themselves captive to a way of seeing and thinking that can only regard such entities as mere fantasies conjured up by the prevailing belief system. It is as impossible for most of us to believe in the real existence of demonic or angelic powers as it is to believe in dragons, or elves, or a flat world. For us the intermediate realm—what Henry Corbin has called the "imaginal" realm—is virtually unknown. We simply do not have categories for thinking of such Powers as real yet unsubstantial, as actual spirits having no existence apart from their concretions in the world of things. We play a double trick on ourselves, first personifying spiritual entities that are in fact not "persons," and then dismissing the creations of our own personifying as improbable, nonempirical, unscientific superstitions.

Thus a gulf has been fixed between us and the biblical writers. We use the same words but project them into a wholly different world of meanings. What they meant by power and what we mean are incommensurate. If our goal is to understand the New Testament's conception of the Powers, we cannot do so simply by applying our own modern sociological categories of power. We must instead attend carefully to the unique vocabulary and conceptions of the first century and try to grasp what the people of that time might have meant by power, within the linguistic field of their own worldview and mythic systems.

It is a virtue to disbelieve what does not exist. It is dangerous to disbelieve what exists outside our current limited categories. The three volumes comprising this study are themselves the record of my own pilgrimage away from a rather naive assurance that the "principalities and powers" mentioned in the New Testament could be "demythologized," that is, rendered without remainder into the categories of modern sociology, depth psychology, and general systems theory. The Powers, I thought, could be understood as institutions, social systems, and political structures. They would provide a means for developing a Christian social ethic from within the language of the New Testament.

Much of that proved true. But always there was this remainder, something that would not reduce to physical structures—something invisible, immaterial, spiritual, and very, very real. Perhaps the reader would be helped by knowing briefly where I came out in the concluding section of this volume. I will argue that the "principalities and powers" are the inner and outer aspects of any given manifestation of power. As the inner aspect they are the spirituality of institutions, the "within" of corporate structures and systems, the inner essence of outer organizations of power. As the outer aspect they are political systems, appointed officials, the "chair" of an organization, laws—in short, all the tangible manifestations which power takes. Every Power tends to have a visible pole, an outer form—be it a church, a nation, or an economy—and an invisible pole, an inner spirit or driving force that animates, legitimates, and regulates its physical manifestation in the world. Neither pole is the cause of the other. Both come into existence together and cease to exist together. When a particular Power becomes idolatrous, placing itself above God's purposes for the good of the whole, then that Power becomes demonic. The church's task is to unmask this idolatry and recall the Powers to their created purposes in the world—"so that the Sovereignties and Powers should learn only now, through the Church, how comprehensive God's wisdom really is" (Eph. 3:10, JB).

This hypothesis, it seems to me, makes sense of the fluid way the New Testament writers and their contemporaries spoke of the Powers, now as if they were *these* centurions or *that* priestly hierarchy, and then, with no warning, as if they were some kind of spiritual entities in the heavenly places. In order to try to distinguish the material from the spiritual pole I will refer to the latter as the "spiritual aspect of the Powers." By that means I hope to make it clear that the Powers generally are only encountered as corporealized in some form. The implications of this view for healing the split between one-sided materialism and one-sided spiritualism are, I believe, extremely far-reaching. But I leave that for Part Three and the subsequent volumes. Enough has been said, at least, to provide the reader with a way to test the data to see if they do, in fact, support the hypothesis. Let us then consider the evidence.

Preliminary Guidelines
for Analyzing
the Data

Despite several excellent studies of the "principalities and powers" over the last fifty years,[1] there has been no comprehensive treatment of the theme. Most studies have focused on the epistles attributed to Paul, or even an aspect of Paul (such as Romans 13), ignoring or overlooking the pervasiveness of the language of power throughout the New Testament. This has led to preoccupation with the question whether these Powers are evil spirits or social institutions and whether they are good or evil, leaving aside the broader and more significant question of how power was conceived by people in the first century and by the New Testament authors in particular.

Now liberation and political theologians are attempting to undergird their social ethics by appealing to the biblical notion of the Powers, reducing them almost entirely to social institutions and structures. At the other extreme, Wesley Carr has recently argued that the Powers are good altogether, and not the demonic forces they have been pictured to be; hence they cannot be made to serve the needs of Christian social ethics.[2] Carr's thesis is fundamentally in error, as I have tried to show briefly elsewhere.[3] Nevertheless it usefully opens the whole subject for a complete reassessment of the precise field of meanings that the language of power manifested in the New Testament era.

1. Heinrich Schlier, *Principalities and Powers in the New Testament* (New York: Herder & Herder, 1961); H. Berkhof, *Christ and the Powers* (Scottdale, Pa.: Herald Press, 1962); Clinton Morrison, *The Powers That Be* (London: SCM Press, 1960); G. B. Caird, *Principalities and Powers* (Oxford: Clarendon Press, 1956); E. Gordon Rupp, *Principalities and Powers* (London: Epworth Press, 1952); G. H. C. MacGregor, "Principalities and Powers: The Cosmic Background of Paul's Thought," *NTS* 1 (1954): 17–28; James S. Stewart, "On a Neglected Emphasis in New Testament Theology," *SJT* 4 (1951): 292–301; John Howard Yoder, *The Politics of Jesus* (Grand Rapids: Wm. B. Eerdmans, 1972), 135–214; William Stringfellow, *Free in Obedience* (New York: Seabury Press, 1964) and *An Ethic for Christians and Other Aliens in a Strange Land* (Waco, Tex.: Word Books, 1973); W. A. Visser't Hooft, *The Kingship of Christ* (New York: Harper & Brothers, 1948); A. H. van den Heuvel, *These Rebellious Powers* (New York: Friendship Press, 1965).
2. Wesley Carr, *Angels and Principalities: The Background, Meaning, and Development of the Pauline Phrase "Hai Archai kai hai Exousiai,"* SNTSMS 42 (New York and Cambridge: Cambridge University Press, 1981), hereafter referred to as *A&P*; idem, "The Rulers of this Age—I Corinthians II.6–8," *NTS* 23 (1976): 20–35.
3. See my review in *USQR* 39 (Spring 1984).

A word about method is in order here. Because the language of power pervades the New Testament, not so much as a consciously articulated set of doctrines but as a background belief held almost universally by the age, I have chosen to treat the terms synthetically, drawing on usage found anywhere in the New Testament, rather than analytically, writer by writer. While the latter would have introduced more precision, it would also have complicated an already complex discussion, and with very little return. What we are dealing with here is not so much the conscious reflections of a discrete author (or even a community or set of communities) but the unconscious presuppositions and worldview of an entire era. I am, in short, trying to reconnoiter what Michel Foucault called the "epistemological space specific to a particular period"[4] as it touches on the way the Powers were experienced and described. I will, however, try to indicate when differences of usage exist among writers.

To aid in the analysis of the data, let me propose a series of preliminary observations as guidelines:

1. *The language of power pervades the whole New Testament.* No New Testament book is without the language of power. The phrase *archai kai exousiai* ("principalities and powers") is but one of many paired expressions for power and should not be singled out as of unique significance. Other such pairs are:

Rulers (*archontes*) and great men (Matt. 20:25)

Those who supposedly rule (*hoi dokountes archein*) and great men (Mark 10:42)

Kings (*basileis*) and those in authority (*hoi exousiazontes*) (Luke 22:25)

Chief priests (*archiereis*) and rulers (*archontes*) (Luke 24:20)

Authorities (*archontōn*) and Pharisees (John 7:48)

Rulers (*archontes*) and elders (Acts 4:8)

Kings and rulers (*archontes*) (Acts 4:26)

Angels and principalities (*archai*) (Rom. 8:38)

Power (*dynamei*) and name (*onomati*) (Acts 4:7)

Power (*dynamin*) and wisdom (*sophian*) (1 Cor. 1:24)

Power (*dynamin*) and authority (*exousian*) (Luke 9:1; Rev. 17:13)

Authority (*exousias*) and commission (*epitropēs*) (Acts 26:12)

Authority (*exousia*) and power (*dynamei*) (Luke 4:36)

Half of these (7) are found in the Gospels, 4 in Acts, and only 2 in Paul.

Of the 10 times *archai kai exousiai* are paired, 2 instances refer ex-

---

4. *The Order of Things* (New York: Vintage Books, 1973), xi. For the hermeneutical method employed in this study, see Walter Wink, *The Bible in Human Transformation* (Philadelphia: Fortress Press, 1973).

plicitly to human agents or institutions: Luke 12:11 ("And when they bring you before the synagogues and rulers [*archas*] and the authorities [*exousias*]") and Luke 20:20 ("[they] sent spies, who pretended to be sincere, that they might take hold of what he said, so as to deliver him up to the authority [*archē*] and jurisdiction [*exousia*] of the governor [*hēgemonos*]"). Both passages have a political focus, but one uses the terms under discussion to refer to human officeholders, the other to refer to the structures of authority.

Of the other 8 pairs of *archai kai exousiai*, 1 is found in 1 Cor. 15:24, 3 in Colossians (1:16; 2:10, 15), 3 in Ephesians (1:21; 3:10; 6:12), and 1 in Titus 3:1. If one holds that at least Ephesians and possibly also Colossians are by Paul's disciples and not Paul himself, then this most "Pauline" of phrases appears possibly as little as once in Paul![5] Around these 8 pairs most of the debate has focused. I will call them the "disputed passages" and postpone their assessment, and that of other similarly problematic passages, until Part Two of this volume.

Not only do expressions for power tend to be paired, they also attract each other into series or strings, as if power were so diffuse and impalpable a phenomenon that words must be heaped up in clusters in order to catch a sense of its complexity. One need only scan this list of phrases to get a sense of their variety and frequency:

Chief priests, captains, elders (Luke 22:52)

Chief priests, rulers (*archontas*), people (Luke 23:13)

Rulers (*archontas*), elders, scribes (Acts 4:5)

Synagogues, rulers (*archas*), and authorities (*exousias*) (Luke 12:11)

Death, life, angels, principalities (*archai*), present, future, powers (*dynameis*), height, depth, any other creature (Rom. 8:38)

Rule (*arches*), authority (*exousias*), power (*dynameōs*), dominion (*kyriotētos*), name (*onomatos*) (Eph. 1:21)

Principalities (*archas*), powers (*exousias*), world rulers (*kosmokratoras*), spirits of wickedness (*pneumatika tēs ponērias*) (Eph. 6:12)

Thrones (*thronoi*), dominions (*kyriotētes*), principalities (*archai*), authorities (*exousiai*) (Col. 1:16)

Angels, authorities (*exousiōn*), powers (*dynameōn*) (1 Pet. 3:22)

---

5. The earliest instance of the couplet *archai kai exousiai* is in Plato (*Alc.* 1.135AB), where the reference is clearly to the civil government (*A&P*, 42). The fact that the phrase is not taken up by later writers suggests that Plato was in no sense using a technical phrase, that it was merely a chance pairing of two of the terms for "power."

Power (*dynamin*), throne (*thronon*), authority (*exousian*) (Rev. 13:2)

Salvation, power (*dynamis*), kingdom, authority (*exousia*) (Rev. 12:10)

Glory, majesty, dominion (*kratos*), authority (*exousia*) (Jude 25)

Of these strings, the first four decidedly consist of human agents, the last two run more to attributes of one who has power. The remainder appear to be at least heavenly, perhaps also earthly, powers; for now that question, which will remain one of the chief preoccupations of this study, must remain open.

In the lists above I have had to transliterate the Greek for key terms because the English translations constantly shift (I am following the RSV); this shifting is unavoidable because the terms themselves are fluid. This leads to our second observation:

2. *The language of power in the New Testament is imprecise, liquid, interchangeable, and unsystematic.* An author uses the same word differently in different contexts, or several different words for the same idea. In a single chapter, only six verses apart, Luke uses *exousia* in reference to the "power" of Satan (12:5) and to human "authorities" (12:11). In the same book he uses *archē* to mean "rulers" (12:11) and the more structural principle of power, "jurisdiction" (20:20). In one chapter Matthew uses *archōn* both of a Jewish leader or "ruler" (9:18) and of the "prince" of demons (9:34, although a few manuscripts omit this sentence). John does likewise; in 12:31 *archōn* designates Satan as the "ruler" of this world, yet only verses later it means the Jewish "authorities" who believed in Jesus (12:42). So it goes throughout the New Testament: *archē* refers twice to human rulers, perhaps as many as 8 times to divine powers; 24 times *archōn* refers to human rulers, 9 times (at least) to divine powers. This same shift of meaning is found in other documents of the period.[6]

6. Daniel uses *archōn* 21 times of human captains, rulers, officials, chiefs, commanders, and 1 (LXX) to 7 (Theodotion) times for angelic spirits (10:13, 20–21; 12:1). *Asc. Isa.* 3:11 speaks of the human "princes" (*archontōn*) of Judah, yet uses the same term in 10:11–12 and 11:16 for heavenly powers. *Test. Abr.* 9 uses a form of *archō* to speak of Michael as the "commander-in-chief (*archistratēgos*) of the upper powers (*dynameōn*)," yet later speaks of human "kings and rulers (*archontas*)" (19, both Recension A). In *Test. Job* 21:2b and 40:8–9, *archontōn* is used of human rulers, while in 33:8a and 34:4b a different word is used for such rulers, *hēgoumenoi;* then in 49:2 *archontōn* designates angels. And *3 Enoch*, which refers repeatedly to heavenly "princes" (*sar*, a word usually translated by *archōn* in the LXX), nevertheless also lists a string of earthly "rulers of each generation," which includes heads, court officers, chiefs, presidents, magistrates, princes, and nobles, at least some of which would be rendered into Greek by *archontes* (45:1–5). And no one reading this passage would infer that these were anything but human leaders.

Not only do we find an author using the same word to mean different things, we also find an author using different words for the same thing. *Exousia* and *archē* can both be used for "authority" (Luke 20:20; 10:19); *exousia* and *dynamis* can both denote "power" (Eph. 6:12; 1:21). (In Rom. 13:3 *archōn* and *exousia* are used as synonyms, through common association with the word "good.") *Archōn* always means an incumbent-in-an-office or role, whereas *archē* might be expected to denote the office or role itself (on the basis of the usage of the LXX and Josephus). Yet in the New Testament, *archē* often usurps its place and denotes an incumbent; this is the case in 10 of its 12 nontemporal uses in the New Testament. "Thrones" is the one term that remains stable in its usage, thanks to its clear image. But *kyriotēs* is so imprecise that no one is quite sure how to translate it in Jude 8. It wobbles between "lordship" and "dominion," but the latter term can also be preempted by *thronos* and *exousia*.[7]

3. *Despite all this imprecision and interchangeability, clear patterns of usage emerge.* *Archōn* (always, without exception in the LXX, Josephus, and the New Testament) refers to an incumbent-in-office. *Archē* can indicate the office itself, or an incumbent, or the structure of power (government, kingdom, realm, dominion). *Exousia* denotes the legitimations and sanctions by which power is maintained; it generally tends to be abstract. *Dynamis* overlaps with *exousia* in the area of sanctions; it refers to the power or force by which rule is maintained. *Kyriotēs* may point to that over which the *kyrios* reigns—the dominion, realm, territory—although in later usage it collapses toward equivalence with *kyrios*. *Thronos* designates the seat of power, the locus or centralization of rule. And *onoma* is a metonym in which the part ("name") stands for the whole (the person), usually a person or power of celebrity or rank.[8]

4. *Because these terms are to a degree interchangeable, one or a pair or a series can be made to represent them all.* It is the demands

7. Josephus amply illustrates this phenomenon. In *Jewish War* 1.512 he speaks of Herod and his "nobles," for which we would expect the usual *archontōn* but which here is *dynatōn*. And in *Ant.* 18.326 he uses *archē* for "realm" where we might have expected *kyriotēs*, and *dynamei* for "authority" where we might have expected *exousia*. And just to keep us alert, in *Ant.* 18.345 he uses *archē* for "authority" and *exousia* for "dominion." Even though some of this confusion is due to the translators, the fact is that the translators were prevented from being consistent by the sliding nuances of the terms.

8. Other terms belong here as well: *basileia, basileus, theoi, hēgemōn, angelos, daimonion, daimōn,* and all the terms for Satan. They require little lexical clarification, however, and some of them will be featured in later discussion.

of rhetoric, not the requirements of precision, that drive Paul to the long list of Rom. 8:38–39:

> For I am sure that neither death, nor life, nor angels, nor principalities, nor things present, nor things to come, nor powers, nor height, nor depth, nor anything else in all creation, will be able to separate us from the love of God in Christ Jesus our Lord.

Elsewhere the same realities can be indicated just as well by three terms—

> Then comes the end, when he delivers the kingdom to God the Father after destroying every rule and every authority and power (1 Cor. 15:24);

by two terms—

> And you have come to fulness of life in him, who is the head of all rule and authority (Col. 2:10);

or by one term—

> If with Christ you died to the elements of the universe, why do you live as if you still belonged to the world? (Col. 2:20; au. trans.).

So too the reader is clear that I am referring to the same thing whether I say "the Principalities and Powers" or simply "the Powers."

5. *These Powers are both heavenly and earthly, divine and human, spiritual and political, invisible and structural.* The clearest statement of this is Col. 1:16, which should have been made the standard for all discussions of the Powers: "For in him [the Son] all things were created, in heaven and on earth, visible and invisible, whether thrones (*thronoi*) or dominions (*kyriotētes*) or principalities (*archai*) or authorities (*exousiai*)—all things were created through him and for him." The parallelism of the Greek, ably rendered here by the RSV,[9] indicates that these Powers are themselves both earthly *and* heavenly, visible *and* invisible. We would expect them to include human agents, social structures and systems, and also divine powers. The reiteration of "whether on earth or in heaven" in v. 20 connects back to v. 16 and suggests that the cosmic reconciliation which God is bringing about through Christ will specifically include these powers, human and divine, and that no reconciliation would be complete without them.

9. The NEB translation presupposes the exegetical conclusion that these powers could only be heavenly and clearly violates the Greek syntax of the sentence. It reads, "In him everything in heaven and on earth was created, not only things visible but also the invisible orders of thrones, sovereignties, authorities, and powers."

Indeed, it is only because scholars have narrowed the focus to just the occurrences of *archai kai exousiai* in the Pauline or Paulinist corpus that the full scope of the Powers has gone unrecognized.[10] We have already seen that they are found in every book of the New Testament; much more evidence waits its turn. The theme of the Powers encompasses every concentration of power in any authorized agent or actor. If a worldview includes spiritual beings, then they naturally will be covered by the vocabulary of power. But they do not exhaust it or even have first call on it. The vast preponderance of uses of the terms for power is for its human bearers or the social structures that manifest it.

6. *These Powers are also both good and evil.* Recently Carr has challenged this assertion, arguing that all the Powers mentioned in Paul, and indeed in the whole New Testament, are good and that there is no evidence for a belief in demonic forces of any stature, apart from Satan, until almost the end of the second century. He is able to make this sweeping assertion only by regarding Eph. 6:12 as an interpolation and by a consistently tendentious exegesis of every text that would seem to controvert his thesis. Nevertheless he has done us the service of forcing a rigorous discussion of the issue. In each of the subsequent sections, then, we will deal with the question whether the Powers referred to by the New Testament are good or evil.

The six observations above will prove indispensable for evaluating the mass of data that must now be examined in order to establish how the Powers were regarded in the first-century world and in the New Testament in particular.

10. Oscar Cullmann argued that although over 80 of the uses of *exousia* have the ordinary meaning of "any power that someone has," the only significant usage for a study of the Powers is the *plural* form and the pluralistic use of the singular (*pasa exousia:* "all authority"). See Cullmann's *Christ and Time: The Primitive Christian Conception of Time and History* (Philadelphia: Westminster Press, 1950), 194–95. This approach cut off at the outset 85 percent of the data.

2. The Powers

Archē and Archōn

For the purposes of this discussion the two terms *archē* and *archōn* may be taken together, since *archē* so often verges on the sense of *archōn* in the New Testament.[1] The normal use of both terms is for human power arrangements. Apart from four passages in Philo, in the LXX, Philo, and Josephus, *archōn* is used exclusively for an incumbent-in-office and, with the sole exception of Daniel 10 and 12, for human agents. *Archē* is a more abstract term for power, the presociological word for the institutionalization and continuity of power through office, position, or role, although occasionally (as in the New Testament) it is used, like *archōn*, of incumbents-in-office. And as the data in Appendix 1 shows, both terms were most certainly used of evil spiritual forces.

The LXX, Josephus, and Philo are consistent with classical and Hellenistic usage generally. *Arch-* simply denotes the organization of power. It was compounded with other terms to form the title of virtually every conceivable office. Most frequently it denotes the role or position which an incumbent (*archōn*) filled, such as town clerk (*archigrammateus*) or head jailer (*archidesmophylax*, Gen. 39:21, LXX); occasionally it could extend to the place where the role was played, such as a local court of record (*archeiōtika*) or the town hall or mayor's office (*archeion*). *Archōn*, as usual, specifies the actual incumbent, from the emperor to the mayors of Greek cities[2] to the chairperson (*archithronos:* note the use of "throne") of a club. The Liddell-Scott-Jones *Greek-English Lexicon* lists more than two hundred positions of power just with *archi-* as a prefix; scores of

---

1. Ten out of 12 times (Luke 12:11; Rom. 8:38; 1 Cor. 15:24; Eph. 1:21; 3:10; 6:12; Col. 1:16; 2:10, 15; Titus 3:1); its other two uses denote "office" (Luke 20:20; Jude 6).

2. See William Bell Dinsmoor, *The Archons of Athens in the Hellenistic Age* (Cambridge: Harvard University Press, 1931) and *The Athenian Archon List in the Light of Recent Discoveries* (New York: Columbia University Press, 1939). These massive volumes simply list all the known *archontes* (mayors) of Athens by name.

other words use it as a suffix (e.g., *gymnasiarchai, chiliarchai, heka-tontarchai*).

It is necessary to survey the full sweep of this usage in order to make clear that the expression "principalities and powers" did not exist in a vacuum. The normal, daily use of the terms described the political, religious, and economic structures and functionaries with which people had to deal. This language was known even within Palestine itself, which during the reign of the Ptolemies had been subdivided into districts under *hyparchoi*.[3] The Jews themselves called the civil governor of the district of Jerusalem under the rule of Antiochus IV Epiphanes a *meridarchēs* (1 Macc. 10:65). Galilee was sectioned by the *tetrarchēs* Herod Antipas into five *toparchoi*,[4] and Tiberias, which Herod the Great founded, had an *archōn* as mayor,[5] in imitation of the Greek cities of the Decapolis.[6] Jesus and his disciples must have been familiar with these titles, even in their Greek forms; the sarcasm in Mark 10:42 par. and Matt. 11:8 par. is directed precisely against such "so-called rulers" who live "in kings' houses."[7]

The fact that almost every extant pre-Christian use of *archē* and *archōn* refers to the role played by some human agent in the exercise of office should caution us against assuming too quickly that their use in the New Testament implies exclusively angelic or demonic powers. Neither Paul nor any other New Testament writer ever feels compelled to explain what

3. W. W. Tarn, *Hellenistic Civilization* (London: E. Arnold & Co., 1927), 121.
4. Harold W. Hoehner, *Herod Antipas* (New York and Cambridge: Cambridge University Press, 1972), 45–46.
5. A. H. M. Jones, *The Cities of the Eastern Roman Provinces* (Oxford: Clarendon Press, 1937), 277. *Hyparchoi* assisted in administrative details (Hoehner, *Herod Antipas*).
6. Gerasa had as its "executive officials" *archontes* (Carl H. Kraeling, *Gerasa, City of the Decapolis* [New Haven, Conn.: American Schools of Oriental Research, 1938], 44).
7. It is likely that, even in Judea, Zacchaeus was known by his Greek title, "Commissioner of Taxes" (*architelōnēs*, Luke 19:2). Other Greek terms in the New Testament compounded with *archi-* include *archiereus* (103 times), *archisynagōgos* (8 times), *architekton* (1 Cor. 3:10), *archipoimēn* (1 Pet. 5:4), *archieratikos* (Acts 4:6), *archēgos* (4 times), *archaggelos* (2 times), *politarchai* (Acts 17:8), and *asiarchai* (Acts 19:31).
   Qumran used similar power-terms, and while we can only speculate as to what would have been their equivalents had they been translated into Greek, our speculations are given considerable weight by the evidence already cited. Words like chief (17 times), head (5), leader (8), office (5), and rulers (1) clearly denote the same human agents that we have found designated by *archōn* and *archē* in other documents from the period, as would even more certainly have been the case with prince (23 times), which is used not only of humans (9 times) or the messiah of David (3), but also of God (1), angels (9), and Satan (1) (following the English translation of Vermes, *DSSE*). For the Hebrew or Aramaic terms, see K. G. Kuhn et al., *Konkordanz zu den Qumrantexten* (Göttingen: Vandenhoeck & Ruprecht, 1960).

is meant by these terms. Every commentator qualified to judge has agreed that the biblical authors assume a content for these words which is familiar to the readers as a part of the background beliefs of the epoch, held almost universally by the age.[8]

It is within this language-world that *archē* and *archōn* were occasionally used to designate spiritual powers, good or evil. It was far from the case that these terms primarily referred to spiritual entities; to the contrary, these terms could be extended to take in spiritual powers because they were the normal terms for power in all its manifestations. The world of the ancients was not a physical planet spinning in empty space in rotation around a nuclear reactor called the sun; it was a single continuum of heaven and earth, in which spiritual beings were as much at home as humans. There is thus no distinctive pattern in the use of these terms for human or for spiritual beings, apart from the vast preponderance being human (see Observation 2, above, and Appendix 1). The language of power in the New Testament is far too rich and complex to reduce either to the human structures and institutions of the liberation theologians or to the spiritual beings of traditional theology. What is needed is an interpretive framework that can do justice to the loose way the ancients could refer to these powers as now human, now structural, now heavenly, without feeling any apparent need to indicate specifically which they had in mind.

Exousia

We find in the use of *exousia* the same general pattern that held for *archē* and *archōn*. The vast majority of references are to human arrangements of power, with an occasional use to designate spiritual beings. In the LXX, Philo, and Josephus, *exousia* is never used of spiritual Powers, apart from a handful of references to the authority of God. The term usually bears the sense of the right or authorization to exercise power, or else refers to that body or person so authorized (see Appendix 2). "Legitimation" comes closest to catching its meaning.

The New Testament uses *exousia* 102 times, 87 of them for the impersonal capacity for action which is bestowed by an office. Most studies on the Powers simply bracket that impressive figure and rush on to hypostatized *exousiai*—those regarded as spiritual beings—as being more significant. But the single most significant fact about *exousia* as a term for power is that 85 percent of its uses refer to *a structural dimension of*

---

8. See esp. Clinton Morrison's excellent survey of the first-century worldview in *The Powers That Be* (London: SCM Press, 1960).

existence, that permission or authorization provided by some legitimate authorizing person or body. In other words, the *exousiai* in the New Testament are, in the vast majority of cases, not spiritual beings but ideological justifications, political or religious legitimations, and delegated permissions.

It is a modern bias to single out just the supernatural Powers as if they alone were of significance. For the ancients, heaven and earth were a seamless robe, a single interacting and continuous reality. To read the literature on the subject, one would never have suspected that the spiritual Powers comprised only 15 percent of the uses of the term. *We* are fascinated with the supranatural forces the ancients described; *they* seem to have taken them for granted and to have been much more preoccupied with that more amorphous, intangible, indefinable something that makes it possible for a king to command subjects to voluntary death in war or for a priest to utter words that send a king to his knees. Perhaps they lacked the systematic precision of modern sociological analyses of power, but that does not mean they lacked experience of what our modern analyses describe or a vocabulary for designating it. And they may have been in touch with dimensions of power which our more materialistic point of view scarcely glimpses.

The material surveyed in Appendix 2 also shows how arbitrary was Oscar Cullmann's assertion that *exousiai* in its plural form (or the collective usage of the singular, *pasa exousia*, "all authority") in the New Testament always has "no other sense than that which it always has for Paul, that is, the meaning of 'angelic powers.' "[9] Not only does the risen Jesus use the pluralistic singular of his own authority in Matt. 28:18 ("All authority in heaven and on earth has been given to me"), but Luke 12:11 and Titus 3:1 use the plural for undeniably *human* rulers:

> And when they bring you before the synagogues and the rulers (*archas*) and the authorities (*exousias*), do not be anxious. . . .

> Remind them to be submissive to rulers (*archais*) and authorities (*exousiais*). . . .

As Appendix 2 shows, both the LXX and Josephus are also familiar with the plural use of *exousia* for human agents of power.

On the other hand, there is not a single instance of the use of *exousia* for angels, demons, or spirits prior to the New Testament. *First Enoch* 61:10 offers the only possible exception, but the Parables section in which it appears is now regarded by most scholars as contemporary with or

9. See Cullman's *Christ and Time* (Philadelphia: Westminster Press, 1964), 194.

postdating most of the New Testament.[10] Paul seems to have launched the phrase *archai kai exousiai* on its peculiarly Christian voyage as denoting spiritual entities. It is easy to see how *exousia* could be extended to spiritual beings,[11] but its main use, even in the New Testament, continued to be in reference to the legitimations, sanctions, and permissions that undergird the everyday exercise of power.

Dynamis

In Jewish sources of the period, *dynamis* is most often used of military or political power or forces (a "host" or army, military might, or political clout). (See Appendix 3.) By extension it was applied to the angelic "army" or "host" of God. God was "Lord of the Powers" (*dynameōn*). As "heavenly hosts," the Powers were identified in the LXX with angels (Ps. 103:21), stars (Isa. 34:4), and even gods (Ps. 29:1; 89:5–8). The term is often used by Philo of angels, a use probably also paralleled in at least some of our disputed texts (Rom. 8:38; 1 Cor. 15:24; Eph. 1:21; 1 Pet. 3:22). In contrast to Philo, however, the Powers in at least some of these disputed texts would appear to be evil.

With the exception of Rev. 13:2 and 17:12–13, the New Testament ignores the military, political, and economic uses of the term, so frequent in the LXX and Josephus, focusing instead on the spiritual dimension of power in its capacity to determine terrestrial existence for weal or for woe "from above." Consequently we encounter the term as denoting evil spirits, the spirits of the dead, stars, spiritual powers, Godhead, and delegated authority (Appendix 3). In the New Testament, and increasingly in later Christian writers, both orthodox and gnostic, the "Powers" are no longer so much God's agents as God's enemies. The "Lord *of* the Powers" now is engaged in a cosmic struggle to assert lordship *over* the Powers.

10. The term used in the Greek version of *1 Enoch* 61:10 may not even be *exousia* but rather *dynamis*. On the dating of the Similitudes section of *Enoch* (chaps. 37–71), see J. T. Milik, "Problèmes de la littérature Hénochique à la lumière des fragments araméens de Qumrân," *HTR* 64 (1971): 333–78; J. C. Hendley, "Towards a Date for the Similitudes of Enoch," *NTS* 14 (1968): 551–65; and the collected essays in *SBL Seminar Papers* 13, ed. P. J. Achtemeier (Missoula, Mont.: Scholars Press, 1978), and *Religious Studies Review* 7 (1981).
11. See, e.g., the frequency with which it has been employed in Coptic as a loan-word to denote spiritual entities: *Gos. Eg.* 63:8; *Soph. Jes. Chr.* 91:6; 94:6–9; 95:24; *Eugnostos* 71:15–17; 73:5; *Dial. Sav.* 123:2; 145:16; *Apoc. Paul* 19:3; 23:22, 28; *Auth. Teach.* 25:34; 26:28; *Paraph. Shem* 31:34; 34:5; *Treat. Seth* 58:19; *Apoc. Peter* 77:4; *Ep. Pet. Phil.* 135:4; *Melch.* 2:9; *Testim. Truth* 32:5; 65:4; *Interp. Know.* 6:30–37; 20:23; *Trim. Prot.* 41:25; 43:4. In most of these instances the *exousiai* are evil and are paired with *archai,*

Thronos

In the LXX, "throne" is used 123 times of kings and dynasties, emphasizing the continuity and legitimacy of royal office. Here "throne" indicates not so much the actual seat but "a symbol of government . . . which transcends the present occupant of the throne."[12] By analogy, God has a throne (29 times), and Wisdom sits beside God (Sir. 24:4). This use is continued by Josephus (27 of the seat of kings, 2 of the high priest's chair, 1 of God's throne). In most of these cases the term "throne" is used structurally to represent all the paraphernalia and power resident in the "chair" and its incumbent.[13]

One obscure reference in Dan. 7:9 set in motion a whole new extension of the term, however. In a vision whose impact for Jewish merkabah mysticism and Christian theology is incalculable, Daniel saw:

thrones were placed
   and one that was ancient of days took his seat . . .
his throne was fiery flames. . . .

The plurality of thrones around a central throne suggests the "sons of God" (*bene elohim*) of the heavenly council, but no further reference is made to them. No surviving documents allude to these thrones again prior to the New Testament. Those that have been cited by some scholars are all late.[14]

But some kind of speculative ferment must have existed almost from

12. Otto Schmitz, "Thronos," *TDNT* 3 (1965): 160–67, esp. 162. *Thronos* occasionally appears in clusters of power-terms, especially with *basileia* but also with *archē* and *dynasteia*—Jer. 49:38 (LXX 25:17); 1 Macc. 10:52–53; Wisd. of Sol. 5:23.

13. Philo uses *thronos* but once, of "the emblems of sovereignty, the throne, the sceptre, the diadem . . ." (*De congr.* 118). In *Leg.* 87 he uses *archēs* as a virtual equivalent of *thronos*.

14. *Test. Levi* 3:8 reads, "And in heaven next to this [the angels of the presence] are thrones and dominions, in which always they offer praise to God," but this reading is lacking in one manuscript (A²), and other manuscripts have been variously interpolated in order to bring an earlier three-heavens view into line with a seven-heavens concept. *Second Enoch* 20:1 refers to "thrones" as if they were an order of angels, but only in a much embroidered list in manuscript A; manuscript B, which contains the preferred reading, omits "thrones" altogether, and even then is probably second century at the earliest (Ernst Bammel, "Versuch Col. 1¹⁵⁻²⁰," *ZNW* 52 [1961]: 90–91; *A&P*, 49). *Asc. Isa.* 7:14—8:28 describes Isaiah's ascent through the seven heavens, the first five of which have "thrones" and their occupants, with angels to the right and to the left. In the seventh heaven are God and the Elect One, "to whose voice all the heavens and thrones give answer" (8:8; the two Latin texts read "the heavens and *angels*"). So even this manuscript tradition is uncertain, and it could not at any rate be dated earlier than toward the end of the first century.

the publication of Daniel, for what crops up in the Book of Revelation is a full-blown and mature picture of God's throne surrounded by twenty-four thrones, on which were seated twenty-four elders with golden crowns (Rev. 4:4 [twice]; so also 4:2; 11:16; 20:4). We are given little data for deciphering the identity of these heavenly "elders"; by analogy they are "advice-givers" and possibly represent the heavenly council. But in this book they give no advice, only praise.

Other than that, and the enigmatic reference to "thrones, dominions, principalities, and authorities" in Col. 1:16, the New Testament uses *thronos* of God's throne (42 times), of earthly rulers (3 times), of the disciple's future place in heaven (3 times), the throne of Satan or his agents (3 times), of the Son of man's throne in heaven (2 times), and once of Christ's throne in heaven.[15]

The use of "thrones" in Col. 1:16 is puzzling; are these spiritual, personalized beings, or are they impersonal structures of power? Perhaps *Asc. Isa.* 7–8 offers a clue. In each of the first five heavens, Isaiah is shown a "throne"; each time the text adds the qualifying phrase "he who sat on the throne" (7:19, 29, 31, 33, 35, 37). Isaiah and other righteous persons have thrones laid up for them in heaven (7:22; 8:26). In short, *someone always occupies these thrones*. The term is simply metonymy for a "throne-prince" or "throne-angel," one of the highest of the heavenly orders.[16] We find a revealing case of double metonymy in 8:8—"For it is He alone to whose voice all the heavens and thrones give answer." By "heavens" the author clearly means the heavenly hosts in each of the seven heavens; by "thrones," then, he must mean those seated on them (so also 7:27). The fact that the chair could supplant its incumbent as a symbol for authority is an indication that the *structure* of power, and not the personality of the one exercising it, is the central focus. The "thrones" in Col. 1:16, by inference, would not be spiritual beings then but symbols of authority stretching through time. Like the

15. How then can Carr (*A&P*, 49) say, "It is impossible that the term [*thronos*] could be used of evil powers or angels or even of civil governments"? It is used of evil powers in Rev. 2:13; 13:2; and 16:10, and of civil governments in Luke 1:32, 52 and Acts 2:30. Carr's whole discussion of *thronos* in the New Testament is confusing. He argues that it "refers exclusively to the throne of God or of Christ," a position we have just seen to be in error. But he himself follows that sentence with this non sequitur: "Whenever it refers to some other throne it is qualified and the reference is explained." Does he mean that only the *absolute* use refers to God or Christ? That would be equally wrong (see Rev. 4:2).

16. So also Carr, *A&P*. In *2 Enoch* 48:2 the sun even "has two thrones on which he rests," and another 364 "thrones" or world-stations (see *1 Enoch* 75:2) which it occupies each of the 364 days of the year in the Jewish reckoning. The sun is not a throne; it "has" thrones which it occupies.

scepter, the crown, the robes, and the ring, the throne represents the continuity of power which may be assumed by a series of incumbents but transcends each individual personality. Only much later, by the time of Pseudo-Dionysius (ca. 500), was the object of this metonymy forgotten, and "thrones" began their medieval career as a curious kind of praise-singing, animated, heavenly musical chairs.[17]

Kyriotēs

There is no evidence of pre-Christian use of *kyriotēs*. Its principal sense seems to be "dominion," "lordship," "ruling power"; later it blurs to become synonymous with *exousia* in the sense of "authority." The image is that of the realm or expanse of territory over which a *kyrios* rules. There are pre-Christian sources that use "dominion,"[18] but it is not clear whether the Greek terms used in *1 Enoch* and *Jubilees* were *kyriotēs* or *exousia* (Col. 1:13) or *hēgemonia* (Josephus *War* 6.330) or even *archē* (Deut. 17:20, LXX). *Kyriotēs* appears in Jude 8 and 2 Pet. 2:10 meaning "authority" or possibly "limit." Col. 1:16 and Eph. 1:21 use it in series. Some later Christian exegetes tended to regard these series as heavenly beings (*Epist. Apost.* 13; *NHL Treat. Res.* 44:35–38), but others used the term in the sense of a human "ruling power" (Hermas, *Sim.* 5.6.1).

17. Post–New Testament references to "thrones" prior to Pseudo-Dionysius as the shortened form of "throne-princes" or "throne-angels" are not frequent. Apart from the interpolated or late instances already mentioned (in *Test. Levi* 3:8; *2 Enoch* 20:1; and *Asc. Isa.* 7–8), they are found in *Apoc. Elij.* 1:10–11; 4:10; the *NHL: Orig. World* 102:16 and the *Gos. Eg.* 50:6; 53:20; 54:21—55:1; 62:9. But even as late as *Eugnostos* 88:16, "thrones" still figure not as personified powers but as the chairs on which such powers sit. So also *Apoc. Paul* 22:27; *Great Pow.* 45:11; *Teach. Silv.* 89:23, 33; 92:7; 117:1; *Trim. Prot.* 43:15; *Apoc. Elij.* 2:3, 5; 18:2 (P. Chester Beatty 2018, reflecting an earlier tradition than the Elijah apocalypse cited above); and *Pistis Sophia* 96 (*NT Apoc.* I, 257).

Perhaps we should also note in this connection a parallel tendency to hypostatize thrones in Jewish merkabah mysticism, since it developed in apparent isolation from Christianity. See, e.g., the curious hymn of praise sung by the "throne of glory" to its king, in the Greater Hekhaloth (in G. G. Scholem, *Major Trends in Jewish Mysticism* [New York: Schocken Books, 1941, 1965], 61). On "throne" in Roman religion, A. D. Nock, "The Emperor's Divine Comes," *JRS* 37 (1947): 116.

18. *Jub.* 5:6; *1 Enoch* 82:10, 16, 17, 20; Dead Sea Scrolls—the dominion of God, 1QH 20; of the angels of light, 1QS 10; 1QM 10; 13; 1QH 1; of the stars, 1Q 34bis; of Satan, 1QS 1 (twice); 2; 1QM 14; 18; 4Q 286–87 (twice); of Satan's demonic hosts, 1QH 24; of Wisdom as an evil power, 4Q 184; of the community of the saints, 1QM 1; 1QH 19; of the teacher of righteousness, 1QH 11; of Israel, 1QM 12; of nations generally, 1QH 19; of sinners, 4Q 169.2; of Rome, 1QM 1; 1QpHab 2. This usage confirms preliminary observation 5 ("These Powers are . . . both heavenly and earthly, divine and human, spiritual and political, invisible and structural").

Thus only the context can help determine the meaning of the term in Colossians and Ephesians (see Part Two).

Onoma

The "name" (*onoma*) is once more a case of metonymy, the part representing the whole.[19] In the older sections of the Old Testament the "name of Yahweh" (*shem Yahweh*) stands for Yahweh as such. This gives way later to its being hypostatized as a distinguishable though not separate agent of God's will and work. Thus Ps. 54:1 (LXX, 53:2) reads: "Save me, O God, by thy name (*onómati*), and vindicate me by thy might (*dynamei*)." Here both "name" and "might" are virtually hypostatic forces acting on God's behalf.[20] The name is thus a transcendent entity at work on Yahweh's behalf in the world. This tendency toward hypostatization was characteristic of developing Judaism generally; as God's transcendence was heightened it became necessary to transfer God's working in the world to intermediate beings.[21] *Jub.* 36:7 goes so far as to state that the earth itself and all the cosmos were created by the "name" of Yahweh (see also *1 Enoch* 69:13–21). Thus in Acts 8:18–19, Simon Magus is depicted as thinking that the "Holy Spirit" is a magical, miracle-working name of "power" (*exousia*) which can be transferred to him on payment of a fee.[22]

Angels have power, according to the rabbis, because God has shared his name with them: Micha*el*, Gabri*el*, Uri*el*. God's *shem* ("name") is inscribed over their hearts (*Pesiq. R.* 21:10; 46:3). They are thus only "powers" or "names" in a derivative sense; there can be no thought of independent action.

As a term of power, *onoma* in the New Testament is used most often of Jesus as Lord or Christ (97 of 226 uses). It is also associated with God's name 44 times, always with the sense of the totality of God's power and being. In one place "name" designates the office, dignity, or rank of Christ as opposed to that of angels: "having become as much

19. In Rev. 11:13, e.g., the toll of a great earthquake is "seven thousand names" ("people," RSV); in *1 Enoch* 70:1, Enoch is translated to heaven solely by means of his name: "his name during his lifetime was raised aloft to that Son of Man and to the Lord of Spirits."
20. See also Ps. 89:24; 20:1, 5; 44:5; 54:6; 118:10–12; Jer. 10:6; Prov. 18:10; Isa. 30:27–28; Mal. 1:11.
21. Hans Bietenhard, "Onoma," *TDNT* 5 (1967): 257–58; Walther Eichrodt, *Theology of the Old Testament* (Philadelphia: Westminster Press, 1967), 2:40–45.
22. The use of magical names in the magical papyri is commonplace; see Bietenhard, ibid., 269–70.

superior to angels as the name he has obtained is more excellent than theirs" (Heb. 1:4). Seven times "name" represents the essence of satanic evil, all in Revelation. Used of the beast or harlot (Rev. 13:1, 17; 14:11; 15:2; 17:3, 5) it crystallizes the inner reality, the moral degeneracy and political brutality of the Roman Empire; used of the king of the locusts, it encompasses etymologically his function: he is the "angel of the bottomless pit; his name in Hebrew is Abaddon, and in Greek he is called Apollyon," that is, Destroyer (Rev. 9:11). The names of evil powers are sought by Jesus ("Legion," Mark 5:9) and by the "rulers (*archontes*) and elders and scribes," who ask Peter and John, "By what power (*dynamei*) or by what name (*onomati*) did you do this?" In defense, Peter responds, "There is no other name under heaven given among [humanity] by which we must be saved" (Acts 4:7, 12). Before this name demons quail, as the disciples (Luke 10:17) and even outsiders (Mark 9:38; Acts 19:13-16) discover. Jesus' name, in short, has become the Name of names; "on his thigh he has a name inscribed, King of kings and Lord of lords" (Rev. 19:16).

When in the disputed passages Jesus is given "a name which is above every name," that is, *kyrios* (Phil. 2:9-11), and is exalted far "above every name that is named" (Eph. 1:21), this is all but verbally identical to the statements just examined in Acts 4:12 and Rev. 19:16. Since both the disputed passages use the qualifier "every" (see Acts' "no other") and couch the claim in utterly comprehensive spatial and temporal categories ("in heaven and on earth and under the earth," "not only in this age but also in that which is to come"), we cannot limit those named to heavenly or angelic powers. They must include every power with a title, every authority invested with an office, every incumbent with a role, whether divine, diabolical, or human. Like Col. 1:16, then, the term *onoma* points us toward the most expansive understanding of the Powers possible.

Angels

Angels are, of course, the Powers in their "heavenly" form par excellence. But even this term is subject to the same imprecision we found with other terms for power. *Aggelos* can be used of a human "messenger" or prophet even in books where heavenly angels are rife (Mal. 1:1; 3:1; Hag. 1:13; Isa. 44:26; Luke 7:24; 9:52; James 2:25);[23] or "angel" can be substituted for "the Holy Spirit" or used where the Holy Spirit would

---

23. Both prophet and angel could also be called "man of God" (1 Kings 17:18; Judg. 13:6, 8, respectively).

have been expected (Mark 13:32; Luke 9:26; Matt. 24:36; Rev. 3:5). In the *Ascension of Isaiah* the expression "the angel of the Holy Spirit" is even used (3:16; 4:21; 7:23; 9:36, 39, 40; 11:33). We find angels spoken of as *archai, archontes, exousiai, dynameis, thronoi, onomata,* and possibly *kyriotētes*. But the most common synonym, especially in the Pseudepigrapha, is the word *pneumata,* "spirits." The evidence for this is too extensive to list; just the title of Yahweh in *1 Enoch* ("Lord of Spirits") is clue enough.

Angels could be good or evil ("fallen"). By virtue of their exclusion from heaven, the latter become a category all their own.

Fallen Angels, Evil Spirits, Demons

The problem of theodicy has obsessed Jewish writers from the time of the exile right down to the present. Israel's misfortunes were too great to ascribe purely to human sin. Adam and Eve could not bear the weight of all human tragedy. The ancient myth of the fall of the "sons of God" in Gen. 6:1–4 was enlisted to explain the presence of an evil that emanates not from humanity alone but from something higher as well: not divine, but transcendent, suprahuman, that persists through time, is opposed to God and human faithfulness, and seeks our destruction, damnation, illness, and death. The fall, mischief, and judgment of the angels is one of the chief preoccupations of intertestamental Jewish literature, its most striking innovation and most lasting contribution to theodicy.

Carr, however, insists that the terms for power are used in Jewish literature not to refer to evil spirits, demons, or Satan but only to obedient angelic powers whose activity and presence confirm the status of Yahweh, that the world into which the gospel came was not a world which longed for release from powers, and that the Christian message was not one of a cosmic battle in which Christ rescued humanity from the domination of such forces. Indeed, Carr states, there was nothing in Judaism from which such a myth could be constructed. Further, Carr claims that there is no evidence for a belief in demonic forces of any stature, apart from Satan, until toward the end of the second century C.E., and nothing in Pauline writings that refers to a battle between Christ and hostile powers.[24]

But the evidence points in almost the opposite direction from everything Carr asserts. Ecclus. 16:7 (which Carr dismisses as a book with "almost no reference" to angels or demons[25]) happens to contain one of the earliest indications of new interest in the myth of the Watchers and Giants. The

24. *A&P*, 174ff.
25. Ibid., 26.

Hebrew reads "He forgave not the princes (*nasik*) of old who revolted in their might." For "princes," the LXX reads "giants." Wisdom of Solomon, which Carr also dismisses with the same expression, alludes to the same myth in 14:6. But by far the densest concentration of references to the fallen-angels myth is found in the oldest sections of *1 Enoch*. Add to that the evidence from *Jubilees*, Daniel, and Qumran, and we have ample grounds for dismissing Carr's ʰelief that angels in Jewish literature are on⅂ᵛ good.[26] These defecting angels sired giants, who were drowned in the flood; their spirits live on as demons, evil spirits, or "the powers of Mastema."[27] Their leader is variously called Semjaza,[28] Azazel,[29] Mastema,[30] Satan,[31] and Beliar.[32] Idol-worshipers in fact worship these demonic powers,[33] and the language of power is most certainly used of them,[34] whatever the precise Greek terms. The sheer weight of these data renders unintelligible Carr's assertion that in Jewish literature, "compared with the number of names and terms for angels, . . . the terminology for the demonic is notably limited."[35] In fact, fallen angels and demons receive as much attention as the good angels.[36] The world that produced *Jubilees* and *1 Enoch* very much believed in evil powers. And it was a world that sought redemption from these Powers: "Deliver me from the hands of evil spirits who have dominion over the thoughts of men's hearts, and let them not lead me astray from thee, my God," cries Abraham on behalf of himself and all who, through him, will subsequently believe.[37] It was in precisely such a spiritual climate that 1 John 3:8 declares, "The reason the Son of God appeared was to destroy the works of the devil."

26. *1 Enoch* 6:1–8; 7:1–6; 8:1–4; 9:1–11; 10:1–22; 12:1–6; 13:1–10; 14:1–8; 15:1–12; 16:1–4; 18:13–16; 19:1–3; 21:1–10; 23:1–4; 84:4; 86:1–6; 87:1–4; 88:1–3; 91:15; 100:4; 102:2–3; *Jubilees* 4:15, 21–22; 5:1–12; 7:21; 8:3; 10:1–13; 20:5; Dan. 8:10; Qumran 1QapGen 2:16; 4Q180 1:7–8; 1QH 16. Carr says that the fallen angels play no part in the Enoch Similitudes (*A&P*, 28), but they are very much present there too: 39:1; 64:1–2; 65:1–6, 11; 67:4–7, 11–12; 68:2–5; 69:1–14, 27–28, only without the title "Watchers."

27. *1 Enoch* 10:15; 15:8–12; 16:1–4; 19:1; 99:7; *Jub.* 7:27; 10:1–3, 5, 8, 13; 11:4, 5; 12:20; 19:28; 22:17; 48:16; 49:2.

28. *1 Enoch* 6:3; 8:3; 9:7; 10:11.

29. *1 Enoch* 8:1; 9:6; 10:4, 8; 13:1; *Apoc. Abr.* 13, 20, 23, 29.

30. *Jub.* 10:7; 11:5, 11; 17:16; 18:9, 12; 19:28; 48:2–3, 9, 12, 15, 18; 49:2.

31. *Jub.* 10:11; 23:29; 40:9; 46:2; plural in *1 Enoch* 40:7; 65:6.

32. *Jub.* 1:20; 15:33.

33. *1 Enoch* 19:1; 80:7; 99:7; *Jub.* 1:11; 11:4; 12:20; 22:17.

34. *1 Enoch* 9:7; 72:3; *Jub.* 1:29; 15:32; 49:2, 4.

35. *A&P*, 42.

36. The seven archangels are named in *1 Enoch* 20:1–8 (in 9:1 there are but four), while twenty "chiefs of tens" of fallen angels are named in 6:7–8. In *1 Enoch* 69:1–14

First Enoch and *Jubilees* do not hold the franchise for the language of fallen angels and evil powers. One of the earliest allusions to the myth of the fallen angels is Ps. 82:6–7: "I say, 'You are gods, sons of the Most High, all of you; nevertheless, you shall die like [human beings], and fall like any *prince*'" (LXX, *archontōn*). The myth appears frequently in Jewish literature of the period.[38] It is alluded to in the New Testament in 1 Cor. 6:3; 11:10; Jude 6; and 2 Pet. 2:4.[39]

twenty-one chiefs of the fallen angels are named, showing that interest in such speculative matters continued into the late first or early second century c.e.

Carr comments that apart from chap. 10 little prominence is given to supernatural beings in *Jubilees* (*A&P*, 29), but as I have shown above, *Jubilees* is packed with them. The writer is essentially retelling the history of the patriarchs through the exodus from Egypt, a story that in its canonical form features few angels and no demonic powers whatever. Every reference to evil spirits has had to be interpolated by the writer into his sources. That he has done so with such consistency and inventiveness shows how central demonology is to his system of beliefs. Angelology was equally dear to the heart of the author of *Jubilees*. He refers to angels roughly forty times, most of them added to his source; many of these are in the form of the "I" or "we" of the angelic narrator. The entire book is dictated by an angel! The Book of Revelation and the three Hermas books are also dictated by angels.

37. *Jub.* 12:20; see also 1:20; 10:3–8; 23:29; *1 Enoch* 8:4; 9:2–3, 10.

38. Fallen angels are featured in the pre-Christian period in *Test. Napht.* 3:5; *Test. Reub.* 5:6; *Test. Benj.* 3:3 (lacking in ms. A); and *Fragment of the Book of Noah* 106:13–14. The motif is continued in the first century and later by Philo, *De gig.* 6; Josephus, *Ant.* 1.73; *1 Bar.* 3:26; *2 Bar.* 56:11–13; *Life of Adam and Eve* 12–17; *2 Enoch* 7:1–5; 18:1–9; *Acts Thom.* 32; *Pirke R. El.* 26; *NHL Apoc. Adam* 83:17; *NHL Zost.* 4:28; 130:10.

Evil spirits are found in pre-Christian Tobit 3:8, 17; 6:8, 14–18; *Test. Reub.* 2:1—3:8; *Test. Sim.* 2:7; 3:1, 5; 4:7, 9; *Test. Levi* 3:2–3; 4:1; 9:9; 18:12; *Test. Jud.* 13:3; 14:2, 8; 16:1; 20:1; 23:1; 25:3; *Test. Iss.* 4:4; 7:7; *Test. Zeb.* 9:7 (βAS), 8 (bdg); *Test. Dan* 1:6–8; 2:1, 4; 3:6; 4:5; 5:5–6; 6:1; *Test. Napht.* 3:3; *Test. Ash.* 1:9; 6:2, 5; *Test. Benj.* 3:3–4; 5:2; at Qumran, 1QS 3 (2 times); CD 12 (2 times); 1QM 1 (5 times); 11; 13 (5 times); 14; 15 (2 times); 18 (2 times); 1QH 24; 1QapGen 20 (2 times); 4Q 286–87 (4 times); 11QMelch; and the "Account of David's Poems" found in col. 27 of the Psalms Scroll (*DSSE*, 265); and in Philo, *De gig.* 6–17. Evil spirits appear in the post-Christian *Apoc. Abr.* 14:5–6; 20:5; 22:6; *1 Bar.* 4:7, 35; *Asc. Isa.* 10:12, 15; Josephus, *War* 1.556, 613, 628; 4.41; 7.185; *Ant.* 6.166, 168, 211, 214, 223; 8.45–48; 14.291; 16.76; *Life* 402; the Similitudes section of *1 Enoch* (40:7; 55:4; 65:6); Hermas, *Mandate* 5,1,3; 5,2,6–8; Chrysostom, *Hom. on Eph.*, 22; the *NHL: Thom. Cont.* 144:12–13; *Gos. Eg.* 57:16–22; *Apoc. Adam* 79:4–5; *Auth. Teach.* 34:28; *Great Pow.* 42:17; *Paraph. Shem* (31 times); *Apoc. Pet.* 75:4; 82:23; *Zost.* 43:12; 113:2; *Testim. Truth* 33:7; 42:25; 70:1–30; *Sent. Sextus* 348–49; *Trim. Prot.* 35:17; 39:21; 40:4; 41:6; and almost every other Christian writer (see, among others, Pseudo-Clementine *Recog.* 4.26; *Hom.* 8.13; Tertullian, *De Idol.* 4; *De Orat.* 23; *De Virg.* 7; Justin, *Dial.* 79; Methodius, *On the Resur.* 7; Theodotus, *Excerpts* 53; *Book of Elkasai* (in Hippolytus, *Ref.* 9.16.1); *Barn.* 18:1).

39. The judgment of angels (1 Cor. 6:3) implies that some at least deserve judgment and therefore "sinned" and are fallen. Rom. 8:38 may also refer to these evil angels who try to separate us from the love of God. 1 Cor. 11:10 is best explained by reference to *Test. Reub.* 5:5–6, which also associates the head of woman with the lust of the Watchers or fallen angels.

In the early church, Christians were instructed in the art of discerning the good spirits from the evil spirits.[40] The use of "demons" and "evil spirits" in the New Testament is too extensive to review here;[41] it must suffice simply to note that Jesus regards his healings and exorcisms as an assault on the kingdom of Satan and an indication that the kingdom of God is breaking in.[42] The gospel is very much a cosmic battle in which Jesus rescues humanity from the dominion of evil powers.

Angels of the Nations

The fascinating notion of angels of the nations is quite ancient. Our first evidence for it is Deut. 32:8–9, but even there (v. 7b) it is described as a piece of primordial tradition. Verses 8–9 read: "When the Most High gave to the nations their inheritance, when he separated the sons of men, he fixed the bounds of the peoples according to the number of *the sons of God.* For the Lord's portion is his people, Jacob his allotted heritage."[43]

---

40. 1 Cor. 12:1–3, 10; 14:12; 1 John 4:1. E. Earle Ellis has demonstrated that these spirits are in fact a category of angels, as elsewhere in all our sources ("'Spiritual' Gifts in the Pauline Community," *NTS* 20 [1974]: 128–44). M. Dibelius (*Die Geisterwelt im Glauben des Paulus* [Göttingen: Vandenhoeck & Ruprecht, 1909], 73–76) notes that the plural *pneumata* in 1 Cor. 14:12 refers to discernment. Christians must distinguish between the divine *pneuma* and demonic *pneumata.*

41. Briefly, *daimonion* is used 63 times in the New Testament; in the Gospels it refers to possession, in Acts, Paul, and Revelation it refers to demons worshiped as gods. *Daimōn* is used but once, exactly like *daimonion.* Josephus also uses the terms interchangeably (see below, n. 42). The verb *daimonizomai* appears 13 times, all in the Gospels. "Evil spirit," "unclean spirit," "demonic spirit," etc., appear 51 times, 32 of them in the synoptic Gospels.

42. Matt. 12:28 ‖ Luke 11:20 (Q); Mark 3:22–30 par.; Luke 10:17–20; Mark 6:7, 13 par. Carr avoids these passages entirely; they do not conform to his thesis.

Some scholars have objected that the demons of the Gospels seem a bit local alongside the more cosmic demons of *1 Enoch* and *Jubilees.* But *1 Enoch* expressly lists the causing of illnesses and possession as among the activities of the demons that came forth from the dead giants (15:11–12; 16:1), and Jesus connects them with Satan as their archon (Mark 3:23 par.). Their knowledge of Jesus' divine attributes show that they were conceived of as privy to secret cosmic knowledge. Josephus makes no distinction between "daemon" in the Greek sense (Socrates' "daemon," e.g.) and the Jewish understanding of demons as evil spirits. He uses *daemōn* 3 times for the former, 6 times for the latter; and he employs *daimonion* both for evil spirits and—specifically—for Socrates' "daemon." He regards demons as not only troublesome (they trip his horse in battle, *Life* 402) and agents of possession (*Ant.* 6.168), but also as capable of killing people (*War* 1.556; 7.185) and dethroning kings (*War* 1.628; *Ant.* 6.168, 211, 214, etc.). Whatever the separate tributaries in which the Greek "daemons" and the Jewish "demons" may have first arisen, they have in first-century Jewish sources largely run together into a single channel of united opposition to God.

43. The Hebrew text reads "sons of Israel" (where the LXX has "angels of God"), alluding perhaps to Exod. 1:5—"All the offspring of Jacob were seventy persons." But

The idea that God had appointed an angel or god over each of the pagan nations finds its most notable development in Daniel 10. According to the Book of Daniel, in the third year of Cyrus, king of Persia, an angel appears to Daniel, delayed for twenty-one days because "the prince of the kingdom of Persia[44] withstood me." But Michael, "one of the chief princes (archontōn)," came to the angel's aid. "So I left him there with the prince (archōn) of the kingdom of Persia and came. . . ." Hastily he finishes his message, then: "But now I will return to fight (polemēsai) against the prince (archontos) of Persia; and when I am through with him, lo, the prince (archōn) of Greece will come. . . . There is none who contends by my side against these except Michael, your prince (archōn)" (Dan. 10:13, 20, 21).

This connection between the angels or "princes" of the nations and the "sons of God" is also reflected by Isaiah 41–46 and 48, where Yahweh, in a "divine lawsuit" (rib) before the heavenly council, addresses the pagan nations, calling them to hear his case. The real suit, however, is not with the nations as such but with their idol-gods. Since Israelite tradition had already long since identified the "sons of God" or "sons of gods" with the heavenly council, and the heavenly council with angels, it was perfectly natural and inevitable that early on these gods of the pagan nations would be understood as the guardian angels appointed over

---

the discovery at Qumran of a Hebrew version of Deut. 32:8 reading "sons of God" confirms the tradition represented by the LXX and has been adopted by most translations as the more probable reading. See D. S. Russell, The Method and Message of Jewish Apocalyptic (Philadelphia: Westminster Press, 1964), 248, esp. 244–49, for a helpful survey of this theme. The idea that the "seventy" were sons of Israel was simply not available to the LXX or the Qumran text of Deut. 32:8, because their Hebrew exemplar of Exod. 1:5 numbered seventy-five sons of Israel that went down to Egypt. See Geza Vermes, The Dead Sea Scrolls: Qumran in Perspective (Philadelphia: Fortress Press, 1981), 204–5. This is a strong indication that the earlier tradition understood the seventy as nations and their angels.

The Palestinian Targum reflects knowledge of both readings and synthesizes them into one: The Most High divided humanity "among the seventy angels, the princes of the nations" at the time of the dispersion at the Tower of Babel; at the same time "He established the limits of the nations according to the sum of the number of the seventy souls of Israel who went down" into Egypt (Targum Onkelos follows the Masoretic text here). The Targum has done more than combine two variant readings, however. It also has amalgamated them with Dan. 10:13, 20, 21, where the guardian angels of Persia, Greece, and Israel (Michael) are called "princes" (archontes). Theodotion uses archōn seven times in Daniel 10, of all three guardians; the LXX uses it only of Michael, reserving stratēgos for the angels of Persia and Greece. The Targum is thus further evidence that Theodotion's version of Daniel is closer to the original (see Appendix 2, n. 1).

44. LXX, "the commander of the king of Persia."

them. What we find in Daniel 10, the Jerusalem Targum, and the Dead Sea Scrolls had thus already had a long prehistory.[45] The notion of angels appointed over each nation, devoted to that nation's well-being and responsible for its fate, represents a kind of systems-view of international politics under the aspect of God's final sovereignty. Daniel's vision pictures two of the highest angels of God virtually held to a standoff for twenty-one days by the archon of Persia. This scarcely moves in the smooth channel of a simple monotheism, where God directly causes all that happens (Isa. 45:7). This is rather a complex, antagonistic henotheism[46] in which, under the sole sovereignty and permission of God, vying forces are able to prevail against one another to determine the unfolding of history. The power of the prince of Persia here reflects the actual power of the Persian Empire and Israel's experience of the difficulty of praying in the face of such monolithic power. Not even God, it appeared, could easily prevail against such forces.[47] We must not regard these angels of the nations as necessarily evil; they merely represent the interests of their own people, which would not evidently be served by Israel's ascendency over them.

God grants each empire a certain time and judges it for what it does within that time. Only tiny Israel's guardian, Michael, takes the part of the messenger sent from God to Daniel (earlier tradition had reserved that task for God alone). No other angels in the heavenly council rush to their side. Even in the celestial sphere, Israel experienced itself iso-

---

45. Frank M. Cross, Jr., "The Council of Yahweh in Second Isaiah," *JNES* 12 (1953): 274 n. 3. Isa. 34:1–5 seems to indicate that Yahweh's wrath against all the nations involves the stars as well; when the nations are given over to slaughter, the heavenly hosts will also be struck down. "For my sword has drunk its fill in the heavens; behold, it descends for judgment upon Edom" (v. 5). Is there here an early instance of the view so often encountered later, that the judgment of earthly powers is preceded by the judgment of their heavenly counterparts? See *Mekilta* to Exod. 15:1—"In the future the Holy One, blessed be He, will punish the kingdoms only after He has first punished their guardian angels, as it is said: 'And it shall come to pass in that day, that the Lord will punish the host of the high heaven on high, and only afterwards the kings of the earth upon the earth'" (Isa. 24:21). So also *Exod. Rab.* 21:5—"God does not cast down a nation before He destroys their guardian angel first."

46. "Henotheism" is defined below, p. 132 n. 27.

47. Thus the Seleucid king Antiochus IV Epiphanes "shall destroy many; and he shall even rise up against the Prince of princes" (*sar-sarim*, Dan. 8:25). The textual tradition is a tangle; the underlined phrase does not appear in the Greek versions. On the basis of 8:11 and 10:13, 20–21, we should identify the "princes" here as the heavenly host and not earthly rulers (see also 2:47—"God of gods"). The "one like a son of man" in Dan. 7:13 may even represent the angelic representative of the people of God and not a heavenly messiah. So Christopher Rowland, *The Open Heaven: The Study of Apocalyptic in Judaism and Early Christianity* (New York: Crossroad, 1982), 178–83.

lated—or, put in the terms of the worldview we are describing, Israel experienced itself isolated on the plane of world affairs *because* it was isolated in the celestial sphere.[48]

Jub. 15:31–32 adds a surprising twist:

> . . . For there are many nations and many peoples, and all are His, and over all hath He placed spirits in authority *to lead them astray from Him.* But over Israel He did not appoint any angel or spirit, for He alone is their ruler, and He will preserve them and require them at the hand of His angels and His spirits, and at the hand of all His powers in order that He may preserve them and bless them. . . .

Why would God want the nations led astray? Is this merely hindsight that treats what happens in history as the determined plan of God? In any case, this inevitably casts the angels of the nations in a negative light. The step from this to their demonization is very short.

In a most important passage, *1 Enoch* 89–90, we can watch that step being taken. Seventy shepherd-angels are appointed to punish Israel. They are not commissioned to protect Israel or defend its interests. Their sole task is to punish, either directly (through pestilence, plague, famine) or by means of the Gentile nations (through war, occupation, oppression) (89:63). A seventy-first angel is appointed to keep track of their overkill: "for they will destroy more than I have commanded them" (89:61). The allegory covers the period from the decline of the two kingdoms until

---

48. A quaint "explanation" for Gabriel's twenty-one-day delay in reaching the fasting Daniel is provided by T.B. *Yoma* 77a. Gabriel had been disobedient and so "was led ou. behind the curtain and received forty fiery strokes"; thereupon "Dubbiel, the guardian angel of the Persians, was brought in and placed in his stead, and he officiated for twenty-one days" (see Dan. 10:13). (The Talmud's identification of the angel in Dan. 10:5–7 with Gabriel would appear to be correct; see Dan. 8:15–17.)

Ecclus. 17:17 alludes to the older notion that Yahweh alone was Israel's guardian:

> For every nation He appointed a ruler,
> But Israel is the Lord's portion.

This verse may be misplaced, or even added. Carr (*A&P*, 31) argues that it refers to earthly rulers set over the nations, not to the angels of the nations. He notes the later use of *hēgoumenos* in 41:17, where it undoubtedly means a human prince. But we saw earlier (Observation 2) that a book frequently uses the same word for earthly powers and spiritual powers. Had the author meant earthly rulers, we would have expected a plural: "For every nation He appointed rulers," that is to say, a succession of governors. Rulers die; the fact that "ruler" here is singular implies permanence. Its parallelism with God suggests that it is a spiritual power. We know in any case that the manuscript tradition interpreted this ruler as angelic, since manuscripts 70 and 248 insert here the phrase "at the separation of the peoples of the whole earth," a reference back to Deut. 32:8–9, when God first placed heavenly guardians over each nation.

the Hasmonean renewal, all of which time, except the very first years, Israel had languished under foreign dominion (the devouring "beasts"). The issue is one of theodicy: how can God allow the elect to suffer under foreign oppressors? The answer is a variation on the theme of Assyria as the rod of God's anger: God is punishing Israel for its sins by means of foreign oppression, which is admittedly excessive and will be avenged on the last day (90:20–27).[49]

When the Maccabees rise up to throw off the foreign yoke, the shepherd-angels actually join with the "beasts" in trying to crush the resistance (90:13), which would be unthinkable if the shepherds were Israel's guardians. These shepherds seem to be none other than the spiritual aspect of the hostility Israel experienced from the nations. They are not here called the angels of the nations, but their being seventy in number certainly presses in that direction. Later exegesis was to make that connection explicit, as we shall see.

We can easily trace the threads leading from these early witnesses to their later developments. One thread completes their demonization. Even in *1 Enoch* 90:20–27 the shepherd-angels will be punished with the fallen Watchers of Gen. 6:1–4; by virtue of their excesses they have become evil. The demonic motif becomes explicit in Luke 4:6, where Satan speaks of the authority and glory of the kingdoms of the world having been "delivered" to him, or in *3 Enoch,* where Sammael, or Satan, is described as the angel of Rome and the head of the seventy princes of the kingdoms of the world.[50] Even here, however, Satan and the angels of the nations remain members in good standing in the heavenly court: "Every day Satan is sitting, together with Sammael, the Prince of Rome, and with Dubbiel, the Prince of Persia, and they write the iniquities of Israel on writing tablets which they hand over to the *Seraphim,* in order that they may present them before the Holy One, blessed be He, so that He may destroy Israel from the world," that is, so that they might be permitted, as the rod of God's judgment, to let *their nations* devour Israel. But the Seraphim, true to their name, burn (*saraph*) the accusations before they can reach God's throne (*3 Enoch* 26:12).[51]

49. *1 Enoch* 56:5 describes the angels hurling themselves on the Parthians and Medes: "They shall stir up the kings . . . and they shall go up and tread under foot the land of His elect ones."

50. *3 Enoch* 14:2; 26:12; see also T.B. *Sota* 10b.

51. Here Satan is the Prince (*sar* = *archōn*) of Accusers, with Sammael and Dubbiel as his assistants. This function devolves more and more on Sammael, however, who as the representative of Rome, head of the Gentile nations, naturally is seen as the chief supraterrestrial enemy of Israel. So in *3 Enoch* 14:2 he is named "Prince of the Accusers."

Another thread from *1 Enoch* 89–90 leads to the full identification of the seventy shepherds with the seventy angels of the seventy nations. This identification may have already been intended by *1 Enoch,* since the idea of seventy nations was as old as Genesis 10. The Hebrew *Testament of Naphtali* 8, whose antiquity has now been confirmed by the discovery of fragments at Qumran, tells of the time when "the Lord . . . came down from His highest heavens, and brought down with Him seventy ministering angels, Michael at their head. He commanded them to teach the seventy families which sprang from the loins of Noah seventy languages."[52]

One last thread drawn out from the tradition in *1 Enoch* 89–90 is the idea that whatever happens on earth is the result of events in heaven which it simultaneously mirrors. In *1 Enoch,* the Gentile nations are able to ravage Israel only when their angelic shepherds permit them to do so. This connection is developed further in *3 Enoch* 17:8 (A), where the "seventy-two princes[53] of the kingdoms on high corresponding to the 72

52. See also 9:1–5, where the seventy "families" are explicitly called "the seventy nations." So also *3 Enoch* 48C:9; 29:1–2. The same motif of seventy angels over the seventy nations and tongues is reflected in the Jerusalem Targum I of Gen. 11:7–8, where every nation has its own guardian angel who pleads the cause of the nation under its protection in the heavenly council.

The Dead Sea Scrolls also bear witness to the concept of nation-angels. The *War Scroll* promises redemption to Israel by "the princely Angel [= Michael] of the kingdom of Michael [= Israel]. . . . He will raise up the kingdom of Michael in the midst of the gods [= the angels of the Gentile nations in the heavenly council], and the realm of Israel in the midst of all flesh" (1QM 17:5ff.). The *Melchizedek* text equates Melchizedek with Michael as judge over the "gods" of the heavenly council, with special authority to punish "Satan and the spirits of his lot." Here Satan appears to be the chief of the rebellious gods or angels of the nations, a theme granted much prominence in later writing. Likewise, in the *War Scroll,* the "hordes of Satan" are clearly Rome (the Kittim—1; 11; 13; 14; 15; 17; 18). See Vermes' note, *DSSE,* 123.

See also Jerusalem Targum I of Deut. 32:8–9. *Mass. Hek.* 5:70 speaks by metonymy of "seventy thrones of the Holy One, blessed be He, corresponding to the nations of the world." Likewise, in various ways, *3 Enoch* 2:3; 3:1–2; 4:1; 48D:1; T.B. *Sabbat* 32a; T.B. *Yoma* 77a; T.B. *Sukka* 29a; T.B. *Makkot* 12a; *Gen. Rab.* 44; 47; 77:3; *Exod. Rab.* 21:5; 32; *Lev. Rab.* 21:4; 29:2; *Cant. Rab.* on 2:1; *Pesiq. R.* 21:8; *Schemoth Rabba* 32; *Midr. Ps.* 78 § 6 (174a); *Mekilta* to Exod. 15:1; *Ruth Rab.* Proem 1; *Pirqe R. El.* 45 Bi–46Ai; *Zohar* 1:173b. Some of these are as late as medieval times, but the persistence of this theme in Jewish thought indicates the vitality of the concept. Carr (*A&P,* 34) dismisses the idea of the angels of the nations as unimportant in Judaism and focused not on politics but on God's care for Israel. For the Jews, of course, politics were inseparable from the question of God's care for Israel. (Jewish references are from Odeberg, *Third Enoch;* Werner Foerster, "Diabolos," *TDNT* 2 (1964): 76 n. 20; Str-B. 3, 48–51.)

53. Some texts in *3 Enoch* and elsewhere give "seventy-two" as the number of the nations, possibly under the influence of the size of the Sanhedrin; since what is below reflects what is above, the great Sanhedrin in heaven (the heavenly council) should be

tongues of the world" who ride on royal horses holding royal scepters in their hands, with royal servants running before them, are precisely mirrored at that very moment on earth by human princes traveling in chariots with horsemen and great armies and in glory and greatness. This motif is developed in more detail below (pp. 131–40).

Given the prominence of the notion of angels of the nations in Judaism and its popularity among the early Christian theologians, it is surprising that we find so little clear evidence for it in the New Testament. The chief controversy surrounds Rom. 13:1—are the "higher authorities" angels of the nations or merely human rulers? We will return to that question in Part Two; here we merely present the data for such a discussion.[54]

Luke shows familiarity with the idea of seventy Gentile nations when he describes the sending of the seventy disciples, ostensibly symbolic of the later mission to the Gentile nations (10:1). But he makes no mention of their angels. Again, in Luke 4:6 Satan offers Jesus all the kingdoms of the world but says nothing about their angels. When he says, "To you I will give all this authority and their glory; for it has been delivered to me, and I give it to whom I will," he is not lying, as some theologians allege. Insofar as the nations have turned away from the purposes of God to their own narrow interests, they and, possibly by implication, their angels are in effect "delivered to" and made bondservants of Satan.

Dibelius finds a reference to the angels of the nations in 1 Cor. 4:9. We apostles, Paul complains, "have become a spectacle (*theatron*) to the world, to angels and to [humanity]." Since the image of the Roman theater conjures up hostile and jeering crowds oblivious to the sufferings of the victim, Dibelius sees the angels here as the heavenly representatives of the Gentile nations and peoples, who watch, not without malicious glee, the tribulations endured by the apostle to their peoples.[55]

First Timothy 3:16 may be another instance of the angels of the nations. In the hymn quoted, Christ was "seen by angels, preached among the nations." The angels are apparently ignorant of God's plan of salvation through Christ and need revelation. Their coming to knowledge of Christ as Lord is juxtaposed, then, to the preaching to the nations. It may be

---

seventy-two. That this figure is secondary is proven by the statement just quoted, however, since Genesis 10 lists only seventy nations/tongues.

54. The motif of angels of the nations will also be developed in its contemporary meaning in the second volume of this work.

55. *Die Geisterwelt*, 28–30, with references to hostile angels in Jewish tradition.

that an awareness of the relation between the good will of the angel and the responsiveness of a people to preaching is what later led Father Peter Faber, a colleague of Ignatius Loyola, to pray to the angel of a region before entering it.[56] Origen interpreted Acts 16:9 in a similar way. When Paul saw in a vision a "man of Macedonia" beseeching him, "Come over and help us," Origen understood this to be the angel of Macedonia appealing to Paul for help in bringing the people under its care into alignment with the purposes of God.[57]

Dibelius thinks the angels of the nations are alluded to offhandedly in 1 Cor. 6:3 also: "Do you not know that we are to judge angels?"[58] The idea that the saints will be the agents of judgment was commonplace;[59] the judgment of angels was a constituent part of the world judgment.[60] Paul assumes that his hearers all know that they are to judge angels ("Do you not know?"); otherwise his appeal from the lesser to the greater ("how much more") has no support. But the judgment of angels requires that they have sinned. Satan and his angels come first to mind. But much tradition identified Satan as the angel of Rome, thus adapting the angels-of-the-nations idea to the situation of Roman world-hegemony. Since Rome had conquered the entire Mediterranean region and much else besides, its angel-prince had become lord of all other angel-princes of the vanquished nations. This identification was already explicit at Qumran, where Rome and the Romans (the "Kittim" of the *War Scroll*) are made the specific allies and agents of Satan and his host.[61] Similarly in the New Testament, Satan as the "archon of this world" (John 12:31; 14:30; 16:11) or "god of this aeon" (2 Cor. 4:4) could scarcely avoid

---

56. This tradition was told to me by a Jesuit missionary in Chile.

57. Origen, *Homily on Luke*, 12. "Man" is frequently used in the Bible to refer to angels: Gen. 18:1–33; 19:5–16; 32:24; Judg. 13:6; Zech. 2:1; Mark 16:5.

58. Dibelius, *Die Geisterwelt*, 7–13; so also Oscar Cullmann, *Christ and Time* (Philadelphia: Westminster Press, 1950), 193.

59. Ps. 149:5–9; Dan. 7:22, LXX—reading "to" not "for"; Wisd. Sol. 3:8; Matt. 19:28; Luke 22:30.

60. See above, p. 25 n. 39. Later midrashim make the judgment of the angels of the nations explicit: "Wait until I sit in judgment over the mountains, that is, over the guardians of the peoples, who are with me in heaven" (*Cant. R.* 8:14, cited by Dibelius, *Die Geisterwelt*, 12).

61. So also the rabbis. See *Pes. RK* 151a; *3 Enoch* 26:12; 14:2; *Gen. Rab.* 77; and elsewhere (Hans Bietenhard, *Die himmlische Welt im Urchristentum und Spätjudentum*, WUNT 2 [Tübingen: J. C. B. Mohr (Paul Siebeck), 1951], 108–16). We have seen already how Sammael, the angel-prince of Rome, fuses with Satan in *3 Enoch* (above, p. 30, n. 51).

being identified as the special patron of Rome. In 1 Cor. 6:3, Paul probably is still thinking in more general terms of all fallen or disobedient angels, those of the nations possibly included. But by the time of the Apocalypse of John (12–17), the connection had been made explicit: Satan (the "Dragon") is the lord and master of the Empire (the "Beast from the sea") and its entire cultic and propaganda apparatus (the "Beast from the land").

Michael's role in Revelation 12 is inexplicable apart from the angels-of-the-nations motif. The problem Michael poses in a Christian work is that it is he, and not Christ, who overthrows Satan and casts him down to earth with his angels. This victory has been made possible somehow by the blood of the Lamb and the witness of the martyrs on earth (v. 11); as the heavenly guardian of the elect, Michael is thus empowered to act against his ancient enemy (v. 9). The usual causal sequence ("as above, so below") is here reversed, breaking the heavenly deadlock. Now "as below, so above"; the suffering of Christ and the martyrs makes possible the expulsion of Satan from heaven. The Dragon and his angels (identified as Satan and his hosts in v. 9) are the heavenly counterpart to the beast and the kings of earth who "are of one mind and give over their power and authority to the beast" (17:12–13). This is a virtual signature of the belief in angels of the nations, who are here subordinated to the prince of this world, Satan, just as the kings of their nations are subjugated to the empire. Revelation 12–17 thus recurs to all the themes of *1 Enoch* 89–90. The "angel" of the nation has now been fully demonized; it is completely identified with a hostile nation which, in the freedom of God, "is allowed"[62] to make war on the saints and to conquer them; and what happens on earth is simply a mirror of the activity of spiritual forces in the transcendent realm.[63]

In summary, the angels of the nations are far better attested immediately before and after the New Testament period than within the New Testament itself. The motif is fairly explicit in Revelation 12–17. It may also be presupposed in Acts 16:9 and 1 Cor. 6:3, and possibly also in 1 Cor.

---

62. Rev. 13:5, 7, 14, 15.
63. In the Nero *redivivus* myth of Rev. 13:3, 18, and 17:9–14, the angel of Rome incarnates not only in the empire but also in the successive rulers who preside over it. The same motif appears also in *Asc. Isa.* 4:2–4, where Beliar is identified with the returning Nero, and possibly also in *Sib. Or.* 3:63–92, where Beliar the Antichrist is called the "stock of Sebaste," which Charles takes as a reference to the Augustan line of emperors and specifically Nero *redivivus*. But H. C. O. Lanchester believes the allusion is to Simon Magus (*APOT* 2:380 n. 63).

4:9, 1 Tim. 3:16, and Luke 4:6 and 10:1 as well. Whether Rom. 13:1 is a further example of the angel of the nation must be determined in Part Two.

In biblical studies, word studies are the equivalent of field exploration and mineral classification in geology. Very little may seem to have been revealed in the field, yet when all the finds have been plotted, it is possible to view the whole map and predict where oil, or copper, or iron might be discovered. Our explorations in the language of power in this volume are indispensable for establishing a firm basis for the entire study. Because no comprehensive study of the Powers has been undertaken before, previous works have tended to depend on word studies isolated from the entire language-field and on a thin selection of texts (almost always only the "disputed texts"), and have thus been more impressionistic than exhaustive. On the whole our more extensive exploration has served to confirm the findings of the pioneers in this field—Schlier, Berkhof, Stewart, Caird, Morrison, Stringfellow, Yoder—and to map in the areas passed over in their earlier sweeps through the territory.

Mapmakers have one privilege denied most explorers, however: the chance to become so engrossed with the contours and characteristics of an environment that its total configuration begins to emerge as a single entity. The sheer comprehensiveness of this survey of data makes it possible to attempt such a total view of our subject. Such a synthetic interpretation of the Powers cannot proceed without an analysis of the disputed passages, and that will be our concern in Part Two. But now the topography has been charted. We are in a better position to see the disputed passages within the larger cosmological framework through which people perceived, encountered, and suffered from the Powers.

2

THE DISPUTED
PASSAGES

3. The New Testament Evidence

Throughout Part One I have postponed treating those passages in the New Testament in which the identity of the Powers is uncertain. Now we must reckon with them, attempting, on the basis of our preceding analysis of the general use of the language of power, to specify who or what the Powers are in these more clouded texts.[1]

The analysis in Part One has already yielded several important clues for unraveling the identity of the Powers in the more ambiguous passages. One of these emerged in the use of "all" in Col. 1:16 and of "name" (*onoma*) in Phil. 2:9–10 and Eph. 1:21–22. This clue can be formulated as an additional observation and added to the set developed at the beginning of our study: *Unless the context further specifies* (and some do), *we are to take the terms for power in their most comprehensive sense,* understanding them to mean both heavenly *and* earthly, divine *and* human, good *and* evil powers. No other conclusion would be consistent with the results of our word studies, which have demonstrated that every term for the Powers is used in each of these ways. The ancient writers never offer any explanation for their varied uses of the terms. We must conclude, then, that the original hearers of the New Testament, whether Jewish or Gentile, understood this language to be the comprehensive vocabulary for power in general and took the meaning from the context. Where the meaning is left ambiguous, it is just that, as Roland Barthes reminds us: *ambo,* "both."

In some texts where the language of power is used, the meaning of the terms is not ambiguous at all. We have already seen that *archai kai exousiai* in Luke 12:11 and 20:20 refer without question to human au-

1. The order in which passages are dealt with in this part is largely arbitrary. On the whole I have attempted to begin with the Pauline passages and work chronologically, but to avoid needless repetition I have juxtaposed texts that deal with the same theme, even if it meant violating chronological order or introducing a different author.

thorities ana the structures of government respectively. To these we can now add from among the disputed texts, Titus 3:1: "Remind them to be submissive [or subject] to rulers and authorities (*archais exousiais*)."[2] The rest of the advice in Titus 3:1-7 is thoroughly mundane, aimed at impressing outsiders through honest work, a placid temperament, and perfect courtesy toward everyone. These powers must include local magistrates, mayors, police officials, and the like. And 3:1 follows on 2:15, "Exhort and reprove with all authority. Let no one disregard you." Following that, 3:1 is nothing less than a command to the church to be submissive to "Titus" and all such ecclesiastical leaders as well.[3]

The rest of the disputed passages are more ambiguous. It is this very feature which has made their identity the focus of such endless and inconclusive debate. We will examine each in turn, beginning with what is one of the most hotly contested texts of all.

1 Corinthians 2:6-8

Yet among the mature we do impart wisdom, although it is not a wisdom of this age or of the rulers of this age, who are doomed to pass away. But we impart a secret and hidden wisdom of God, which God decreed before the ages for our glorification. None of the rulers (*archontes*) of this age understood this; for if they had, they would not have crucified the Lord of glory.

The arguments in favor of reading these *archontes* as human beings are very powerful, but a strong case can be made for regarding them as demonic powers as well. Let us examine each in order.

First: the brief for interpreting the *archontes* here as human. An early and repeated refrain in Christian preaching was the culpability of the "chief priests (*archiereis*) and rulers (*archontes*)" who "delivered him up to be condemned to death, and crucified him" (Luke 24:20). "And now, brethren, I know that you acted in ignorance [in delivering Jesus to death], as did also your rulers (*archontes*)" (Acts 3:17). "Can it be that the authorities (*archontes*) really know that this is the Christ?" (John 7:26; see also Luke 23:13, 35; Acts 4:8-10, 26; 13:27-28, all using *archontes* for those who had Jesus crucified). At the very least, then, the

2. On the textual evidence for asyndeton, see Bruce M. Metzger, *A Textual Commentary on the Greek New Testament* (London and New York: United Bible Societies, 1971), 655.

3. See Ignatius, *Trall.* 2: "Therefore it is necessary . . . that you should do nothing without the bishop, but also be in subjection [*hypotassesthai*—identical to Titus 3:1] to the presbytery."

archontes in 1 Cor. 2:6–8 include religious leaders, the military procurator, soldiers, and accomplices ("spies," Luke 20:20), who were the physical agents of Jesus' death.[4]

As Schniewind shows, the context supports this conclusion. Paul has already spoken of the "wise person" (*sophos*), the "scribe" (*grammateus*) (1:20), the "powerful" (*dynatoi*), and the "well-born" (*eugeneis*) (1:26), whom God is bringing to nothing (1:28). These are the "powers" of this age (*tou aiōnos*, 1:20), and they are all human. The wisdom of this age in 2:6 is the same as that in 1:20. It is humanity, symbolized by the term "the world," which opposes God here, not demonic forces (1:26, 27, 28). Hence it is human wisdom that prevents knowledge of God (2:5, 13), not heavenly powers. Matt. 11:25 reminds us who Jesus' own opponents had been: the wise (*sophoi*) and understanding (*synetoi*). These brought Jesus to death.[5]

Furthermore, the antithesis in 1 Corinthians 1–2 is not between saved humans and lost angels but between two groups of humans. The structure is "we—they":

WE		THEY
Our glorification (2:7)	vs.	Rulers of this age (2:6)
Those who love him (2:9)	vs.	Those who crucified the Lord of glory (2:8)
The Spirit of God (2:12)	vs.	The spirit of the world (2:12)
The spiritual person (2:15)	vs.	The unspiritual person (2:14)

Paul, continues Schniewind, no doubt believed that Jesus' opponents, like his own, were devil-inspired (2 Cor. 4:4; 11:14–15; see James 3:15). But such a view, if pressed, would put Paul at odds with the synoptic tradition, which holds that Satan (Matt. 4:1–11 par.) and the demons (Mark 1:21–28; 3:11 par.) did recognize and even reveal to others Jesus' real identity.[6] But this last point is quite weak, since Paul is not to be held accountable for what the synoptic writers were to say later.[7] And

4. So Chrysostom, *I Corinthians*, Hom. 7.
5. Julius Schniewind, *Nachgelassene Reden und Aufsätze* (Berlin: A. Töpelmann, 1952), 104–9.
6. Ibid.
7. Martin Werner (*The Formation of Christian Dogma* [London: A. & C. Black, 1957], 97) argues that 1 Cor. 2:8 was originally interpreted as referring to angelic powers who did not know who Jesus was and that the early Christian exegetes, when they realized that this stood in contradiction to the Gospels, were driven to reinterpret 1 Cor. 2:8 as referring to earthly rulers.

Paul elsewhere regards people as culpable even for their ignorance (Rom. 1:18–23; 10:16–19; 2 Thess. 1:8; see Mark 4:11–12). Wesley Carr buttresses Schniewind's case with additional arguments. In Rom. 13:3, whatever the interpretation of *exousiai* in v. 1, the *archontes* must be human magistrates, since they bear the sword and levy taxes (vv. 4, 6). The word cannot yet be regarded as a technical term of gnosticism, since Paul is describing his own message, not that of his opponents.[8]

The case that the archons of 1 Cor. 2:6–8 are human is very persuasive, but an appealing brief can be made for the opposite opinion as well. Dibelius rightly protests that Herod, Pilate, and the Jewish authorities cannot possibly be made to bear the weight of the phrase "rulers of this aeon."[9] At the time Paul writes, none of them is still in office; Herod has indeed "passed away," but every mortal must, and his death had no eschatological significance. The statement is extravagant applied to humans, but sensible if it refers to powers considered by his hearers to be *athanatoi*, immortal. Greek gods were by definition *athanatoi*, and it was one of their appellations—the Immortals. Once Jewish apologetics had identified the gods as demons, however, their eternity became problematic. Here and in 1 Cor. 15:24–25—on this interpretation—Paul declares them to belong only to "this aeon" which is passing away.

8. "The Rulers of This Age," *NTS*. Others of Carr's arguments are of less value, and some are simply wrong, skewed by his tendency to explain away every text that features demons in the first-century world. What, for example, are we to make of his claim that Ignatius, *Smyr.* 6:1, "refers to the angels of heaven and not obviously in any evil sense" (*A&P*, 28)? Ignatius, speaking of "*archontes* visible and invisible," says that "even for them there is a judgment if they do not believe in the blood of Christ." How can an angel be judged unless it is evil? And the very mention of such judgment is gratuitous unless Ignatius thought such defections had happened. Or how can we evaluate Carr's contention that "Ignatius shows very little interest in angelic or demonic beings" (ibid.), when Ignatius refers to heavenly *archontes* in *Trall.* 5 and *Smyr.* 6; to Satan as the *archōn* of this world in *Eph.* 17; 19; *Mag.* 1; *Trall.* 4; *Rom.* 7; *Phil.* 6; to the devil in *Eph.* 10; 13 (*hai dynameis tou Satana*); *Trall.* 4 (?); 8; *Rom.* 5; *Smyr.* 9; and to "war in heaven and on earth" (*Eph.* 13), which presupposes a whole host of evil powers? Ignatius himself provides what may be one of the earliest commentaries on 1 Cor. 2:8 when he says that the death of the Lord was "hidden from the Prince (*archonta*) of this world" (*Eph.* 19). Marcion is not, then, the first to suggest that the archons were demonic, as Carr asserts; indeed, Appendix 1 demonstrates that this association is to be found in pre-Christian, apocalyptic Judaism.

9. M. Dibelius, *Die Geisterwelt im Glauben des Paulus* (Göttingen: Vandenhoeck & Ruprecht, 1909), 89. The phrase appears to be structurally similar to 2 Cor. 4:4, where Satan is called "the god of this aeon." See also John 14:30–31, where the "coming" of Satan would appear to refer to the crucifixion. This would imply that Satan was the real architect of Jesus' death.

As for the ignorance of these Powers, the seed of that is already planted in *1 Enoch* 16:1–3. The spirits of the giants, "'having gone forth, shall destroy without incurring judgment—thus shall they destroy until the day of the consummation, the great judgment in which the *age* shall be consummated, over the Watchers and the godless, yea, shall be wholly consummated.' And now as to the Watchers . . . [say to them]: '*You have been in heaven, but all the mysteries had not yet been revealed to you.* . . .'"[10] This motif of a secret of redemption hidden from the heavenly *archontes* may be alluded to in Col. 1:26—"the mystery hidden *apo tōn aiōnōn kai apo tōn geneōn.* The RSV translates "for ages and generations" but in a note registers the possible reading "hidden from angels and men." More explicit is 1 Tim. 3:16, which speaks liturgically of Christ:

> Who was manifested in flesh
> Vindicated in Spirit
> Seen by angels
> Preached in nations
> Believed in the cosmos
> Taken up in glory.[11]

Why "seen by angels"? Are they cited merely as witnesses (e.g., Mark 16:5 par.)? Or is this an allusion to the angels of the nations, who must first "see" the risen Christ before their nations can be evangelized? In any case, the text does appear to assume the ignorance of the angels and their need for revelation.

We do know that other writers in the same period were developing the same thought. *Ass. Mos.* 1:12–13 mentions God's keeping the election of Israel hidden from the nations in order that the Gentiles might be convicted. But it is in the *Ascension of Isaiah* that the notion is most fully elaborated. The relevant material is from the Vision section, a Christian writing dated by Charles at the end of the first century.[12] From

---

10. *Jub.* 1:25 also reflects the idea: In the future, "every angel and every spirit shall know . . . that these [Israel] are My children." Apparently they do not know yet! *2 Enoch* 24:3 reads: "For not to My angels have I told my secret, and I have not told them their rise, nor my endless realm, nor have they understood my creating, which I tell thee to-day" (version A).

11. Author's translation.

12. R. H. Charles, trans., *Ascension of Isaiah* (1900). Ignatius, *Eph.* 19, is dependent on *Asc. Isa.* 11:16–17 and clearly not the other way around, since the theme of hiddenness is integral to the whole of chaps. 9–11 of *Asc. Isa.*, whereas it is introduced abruptly in *Eph.*, clearly as a piece of well-known tradition. Hence this date seems reasonable. But

Asc. Isa. 8:7 we learn that the name of the Elect One "has not been
made known, and none of the heavens can learn His name" prior to his
incarnation. Christ will be "made in your form," the angel prophesies
to Isaiah, "And the god of that world will stretch forth his hand against
the Son, and they will crucify Him on a tree, and will slay Him not
knowing who He is. And thus his descent will be hidden even from the
heavens, so that it will not be known who He is" (9:13–15; so also
10:10–12). When he reaches "the firmament where dwelleth the ruler
of this world," all the angels "were envying one another and fighting"
and failed to notice his passage (10:29–31). He was to be born of the
Virgin Mary and "escaped all the heavens and all the princes (*archontes*)
and all the gods of this world" (11:14, 16). "And after this the adversary
envied Him and roused the children of Israel against Him, not knowing
who He was, and they delivered Him to the king, and crucified Him,
and He descended to the angel [of Sheol]" (11:19). When he would be
raised from the dead in his glorious body and ascend again through the
heavens, "all the angels of the firmament and the Satans saw Him and
they worshipped. And there was much sorrow there, while they said:
'How did our Lord descend in our midst, and we perceived not the
glory . . . ?'" (11:24).

This kind of speculation teased the imagination of later writers, Christian and gnostic alike.[13] The very fact that Ignatius is dependent on the
tradition preserved in the *Ascension of Isaiah* indicates that 1 Cor. 2:6–
8 was already being interpreted by Christians prior to the end of the first
century as referring to demonic powers.

So what are we to do? Both the argument that the *archontes* in 1 Cor.
2:6–8 are human and the argument that they are divine are plausible. On
the basis of our previous word studies and the criterion drawn from Col.
1:16, the solution that virtually forces itself on us is that both views are
correct. Both human and demonic powers are meant. Every *archon* involved in Jesus' death is intended. This, in fact, is actually what the

allowance must also be made for later Christian editing. The so-called "gnosticizing"
tendencies are vastly overrated. The true home of the work is Jewish-Christian merkabah
mysticism (see Rev. 4–5).

13. Origen, *Hom. on Ezek.*, 13, § 1; *Comm. on St. Mt.*, § 125; Justin, *Dial.* 36; 49;
Acts Thom. 32; 45; 143; *Epist. Apost.* 13–14; Legends from the Pistis Sophia (*NT Apoc.*
1:402); *History of John the Son of Zebedee* 49 (*AAA*, p. 45); and from the *NHL: Pr.
Paul* 25–29; *Gos. Phil.* 55:14–16; *Great Pow.* 41:15—42:31; *2 Apoc. Jas.* 56:17–24;
Tri. Trac. 64:28–39; *Paraph. Shem* 36:14–15; *Treat. Seth* 60:1, 15; *Zost.* 128:15–18;
Melch. 6:20ff.; *Trim. Prot.* 43:27—44:49; 47:24–25. See, in addition, the texts assembled
by Michael Stone and John Strugnell, *The Books of Elijah Parts 1 and 2* (Missoula,
Mont.: Scholars Press, 1979), 41–73.

Ascension of Isaiah itself says; "the *adversary* envied Him and roused *the children of Israel* against Him, not knowing who He was, and *they delivered Him to the king,* and crucified Him" (11:19; also 9:13–15). Demonic and human agents are also involved in *Acts Thom.* 32: The serpent boasts, "'I am he who inflamed Herod and kindled Caiaphas to the false accusation of the lie before Pilate. . . . I am he who kindled Judas and bribed him to betray Christ to death. . . . But the Son of God did me wrong against my will.'"[14] Ignatius, who considered that "the death of the Lord" was "hidden from the archon of this world" (*Eph.* 19), nevertheless spoke elsewhere of the crucifixion as taking place "under Pontius Pilate and Herod the Tetrarch" (*Smyr.* 1) or "at the time of the procuratorship (*hēgemonias*) of Pontius Pilate" (*Mag.* 11). Jesus died, he says, "in the sight of those in heaven and on earth and under the earth" (*Trall.* 9:1). Surely then Günther Dehn is right when he says that 1 Cor. 2:6–8 actually represents in itself an immediate coincidence of heavenly and earthly activity, in which Pilate, the high priests, and the rest brought Jesus to death at the instigation of the higher Powers.[15] Just how this heavenly and earthly activity are connected will be the subject of Part Three.

If in 1 Cor. 2:6–8 Paul believes that Jesus was crucified by both earthly and heavenly Powers, are we then to conclude that whenever he uses the language of power he means both heavenly and earthly aspects? Not necessarily, as we shall see when we turn to his famous statement about obedience to the state.

Romans 13:1–3

Let every person be subject to the governing authorities (*exousiais hyperechousais*). For there is no authority (*exousia*) except from God, and those that exist have been instituted by God. Therefore [one] who resists authority (*exousia*) resists what God has appointed, and those who resist will incur judgment. For rulers (*archontes*) are not a terror to good conduct, but to bad. Would you have no fear of [one] who is in authority (*tēn exousian*)? Then do what is good. . . .

We will leave aside all other problems in this fertile passage and focus only on the identity of the *archontes* and *exousiai* in the first three verses.[16]

---

14. So also the *NHL Tri. Trac.* 121:1–22, where "men and angels" kill Jesus, desiring to be "rulers (*archontes*?)" of the universe."

15. Günther Dehn, "Engel und Obrigkeit: Ein Beitrag zum Verständnis von Römer 13, 1–7," in *Theologische Aufsätze: Karl Barth zum 50 Geburtstag* (Munich: Chr. Kaiser, 1936), 104

16. Even that severe a limitation leaves us faced with a formidable bibliography. The

It is agreed by all interpreters that the "rulers" (*archontes*) of verse 3 are human, since they wield the sword (v. 4) and collect taxes (v. 6). In all this they are "servants" and "ministers" of God (vv. 4, 6), deserving of honor and respect (v. 7). By analogy one would expect that the *exousiai* in v. 1 are also human authorities, especially in the light of the high degree of interchangeability that we have discovered between *exousia* and *archē/archōn*. Paul would then be issuing advice exactly parallel to that in 1 Pet. 2:13–17—"Be subject for the Lord's sake to every human institution (*anthrōpinē ktisei*) whether it be to the emperor as supreme, or to governors (*hēgemosin*) as sent by him to punish those who do wrong and to praise those who do right. . . . Honor the emperor." The similarities are so great, in fact, that one suspects that the passage in 1 Peter is the earliest commentary on Romans 13. If so, the author clearly interprets *hyperechousais* as referring to higher human authorities, not to authorities higher than humans. On analogy with Philo (*De agr.* 121) we could translate Rom. 13:1 as "preeminent authorities." The case for their being angelic powers seems weak indeed.

However, that way of bifurcating the question is, as we have seen, itself problematic. If a connection exists between authorities and angelic powers, then we must at least consider the possibility that when Paul speaks of authorities the thought of the angels who stand behind the authorities is mingled with it. As Günther Dehn persuasively argued, no modern or "secular" view of the state was possible for Paul. If elsewhere he can use *exousiai* to refer to angelic beings, he must regard authority as a single whole, including earthly and heavenly powers, with no clear line of demarcation between them.[17]

Oscar Cullmann has argued for this position most vigorously, but without grounding his case adequately in data from the period,[18] a task undertaken with admirable objectivity by Clinton Morrison in *The Powers That Be.* As we saw in Part One, if Paul presupposes the Jewish notion of angelic representatives for each nation in the heavenly council, he

---

most thorough treatment is Clinton Morrison's *The Powers That Be* (London: SCM Press, 1960), an entire book focused solely on identifying the Powers in Rom. 13. See his bibliographies, pp. 11, 17–18, 40, 63–64, 137. For more recent contributions to the debate, see Ernst Käsemann, *Commentary on Romans* (Grand Rapids: Wm. B. Eerdmans, 1980), 350 (bibliography); and J. Friedrich, W. Pöhlmann, and P. Stuhlmacher, "Zur historische Situation und Intention von Röm 13, 1–7," *ZThK* 73 (1976): 131–66.

17. Dehn, "Engel und Obrigkeit," 90–109.

18. *Christ and Time* (Philadelphia: Westminster Press, 1950), 185–210; *The State in the New Testament* (New York: Charles Scribner's Sons, 1956), 50–70, 93–114 (in the second German edition he states his case more tentatively [pp. 68ff.]).

never feels compelled to make this conception explicit. But he certainly does subscribe to the broader Greco-Roman conception of spiritual forces behind all earthly institutions, of which the Jewish notion of angels of the nations was a special adaptation.[19] No one could reasonably deny that Paul held such a worldview. The only question is, does *exousia* in Rom. 13:1–3 refer to such spiritual powers? There can be no question that Paul at least has earthly *exousiai* in mind here, for *exousia* in v. 3 is used in apposition to *archontes* in the same verse, and everyone agrees that humans are intended by the latter. The only question is whether Paul *also* means to refer to spiritual powers "behind the throne." If pressed, Paul would probably have readily acknowledged that such powers exist. In this paragraph, however, they are not his primary concern. He is attempting to spell out in completely practical terms the way Christians should behave toward magistrates and tax collectors in the interim before the end.[20]

Perhaps the most we can say, then, is that while Paul would have certainly affirmed the existence of higher spiritual powers behind all the physical expressions of government, he is simply not concerned with that dimension of power here. He is preoccupied instead with the very mundane and practical issue of the church's behavior toward bureaucratic officials (*exousiai*) in the brief dark interval before the Light dawns (vv. 11–12).

Thus the context is all-important in determining the identity of the Powers. If in the first text (1 Cor. 2:6–8) they appeared to be both human and divine, and in Romans 13 they seemed to be primarily human, in the next text to be considered they have the look of spiritual forces.

Romans 8:38–39

For I am sure that neither death, nor life, nor angels, nor principalities,[21] nor things present, nor things to come, nor powers, nor height, nor depth, nor any other creature, will be able to separate us from the love of God in Christ Jesus our Lord.[22]

19. Even Celsus in his attempt to refute Christianity argued that it is advisable to worship daemons, precisely because those in authority on earth hold power only by the daemons' help (Origen, *Against Celsus* 8.63).
20. There is a similar concern in Matt. 17:24–27, where the disciples are declared free from the tax but advised to pay it from sheer expediency.
21. Codex Bezae (D) adds *exousia* before *archai*; Codex Ephraemi (C) 81. 104 *al* sy^h** bo^mss add it in the plural after *archai*. The evidence is too weak to consider adopting the fuller reading.
22. Author's translation.

This concluding doxology to the central theological section of Romans begins to gain momentum in 8:31 with the rhetorical flourish "If God is for us, who is against us?" The rest of the paragraph is a rising crescendo of phrases that thunder louder and louder, No one! No one! No one at all! Is God against us? Absurd; God gave Christ in order that we might be reconciled (v. 32). Can anyone bring a charge then? To what effect could they? God alone is our judge, and he has justified us (v. 33). Might Christ condemn us? How could he; he died for us and is right now at God's side interceding for us (v. 34). Can anyone separate us from Christ's love? No, nothing that the evil will of human beings can concoct—neither oppression (*thlipsis*) nor distress nor persecution nor starvation (*limos*)[23] nor destitution (*gymnotēs*)[24] nor peril nor sword (v. 35). In short, every sanction that the state, religion, the economic system, the courts, police, the army, public opinion, mob action, or peer pressure can bring to bear to enforce our complicity in the great defection from God has been robbed of its power. They can kill us all day long, as Ps. 44:22 says, but they cannot separate us from Christ, and so they can no longer compel us to comply (v. 36). That is our victory in Christ (v. 37). Regardless of what they do to us, they cannot turn the clock back to the hour before they were unmasked in the cross. Now their idolatry can no longer be hidden.

With this buildup, the final exultant acclamation breaks forth. Verse 35, as we saw, listed the sanctions of primarily human powers, a fact that is usually overlooked in this paragraph, where all the attention tends to gravitate toward the cosmic powers in vv. 38–39. The latter verses now broaden the canvas to take in even cosmic or astronomical dimensions, so that every lingering doubt in the believer's mind is swept away. These cosmic forces are a series of mostly paired opposites:

neither death	nor life
nor angels	nor *archai*
nor things present	nor things to come
nor *dynameis*[25]	
nor height	nor depth
nor any other creature	

23. So BAG, 476. The sentence refers not simply to hardships, such as "famine" (RSV) but to things done to us by "someone" (*tis*) who wants to "separate us from the love of Christ." See Luke 15:17—the Prodigal is "dying of hunger" (*limō*), that is, starving to death.

24. So again BAG, 167. The Christian does not walk around naked; he or she is prevented by economic sanctions or persecution from being able to buy adequate clothing.

25. *Dynameis* is found in some manuscripts after *archai*, but this is not well attested

The fact that every other pair is made up of opposites has led some scholars to suggest that "angels and *archai*" are opposites as well; if so, the *archai* could represent either evil spirits or human governors. But as I have already noted, the human agents were dealt with in vv. 31–37. It would appear likely, then, that the *archai* here are evil spiritual powers.

But perhaps we should not try to overspecify. The fact that *dynameis* and "any other creature" violate the series of pairs may mean that Paul is not all that conscious of the poetic structure and is intent not on contrasting the items in his list but on creating the cumulative impression that nothing at any of life's extremities, not even the cosmic powers themselves, whether good or evil, can separate us from the love of God in Christ Jesus.[26] Paul's readers would probably assume that he is referring primarily to evil powers, since only such would be likely to try to separate them from Christ. But even the good, made absolute, becomes evil. Even the best can be perverted by idolatry (the Law, the Temple, religion itself). None is immune to apostasy. None is able, however apostate, to negate the work of Christ.[27]

"Things to come" probably refers not to the new age but to events in the immediate future prior to the *parousia*.[28] "Height" and "depth" (*hypsōma* and *bathos*) are technical terms in later astrological writings but not in the New Testament period.[29] They are, however, astronomical. A clue to their background is provided by *1 Enoch* 18:3, 11:

> And I saw how the winds stretch out the vaults of heaven, and have their station between heaven and earth: these are the pillars of the heaven. . . . And I saw a deep abyss, with columns of heavenly fire, and among them I saw columns of fire fall, which were beyond measure alike *towards the height and towards the depth.*

This abyss is where the disobedient stars are punished "because they did not come forth at their appointed times" (v. 15; 21:6–7). "Height" and

---

and is clearly the work of copyists who wished to improve the sequence (Metzger, *Textual Commentary*). Phillips suggestively translates *dynameis* as modified by the two following nouns: "neither a power from on high nor a power from below."

26. So rightly *A&P*, 112. Carr concludes, however, that only good angelic powers could be involved.

27. *1 Enoch* 41:9 has this obscure statement: "For no angel hinders and no power is able to hinder." This seems to be a denial that angels or powers can be blamed for human sin; each person is accountable before the Messiah at the Last Day (41:9b). The passage provides a striking parallel, though perhaps later than Romans.

28. Dibelius, *Die Geisterwelt*, 112.

29. Ibid.; *A&P*, 113.

"depth" apparently refer, then, to the top and bottom of the pillars that support the firmament of heaven. For Paul they merely provide, with "things present and things to come," an exhaustive sweep of all the spatio-temporal dimensions, after the fashion of Ps. 139:8–9, where spatial imagery is used to express the impossibility of escaping the presence of God.[30] In short, neither human (vv. 31–37) nor cosmic (vv. 38–39) powers, nor time and space itself, can undermine the victory the believer shares in Christ. The "et cetera" Paul adds at the end ("nor any other creature") shows how much in agreement with Col. 1:16 he really is: all these Powers—human, structural, or divine—are "creatures" of the good God. "Any other creature" indicates that creaturehood is the generic category from which the whole preceding series is derived. Every Power is a "creature." The Powers are not mere accidents of history or human fabrications. They have their place in the created order. They suffer all the consequences of the fall. Yet even when they attempt to obstruct the salvation of the elect, they are not able for one instant to separate themselves from the love of God in Christ Jesus. They cannot separate believers from the love of God because they cannot even separate themselves!

In the three previous passages the emphasis fell on establishing whether the Powers involved were heavenly or earthly and good or evil. That quest continues in the next three, but with a specific focus on eschatology: when and how we are to conceive of Christ being victorious over the Powers.

1 Corinthians 15:24–27a

Then comes the end, when he [Christ] delivers the kingdom to God the Father after neutralizing every rule and every authority and power. For he must reign until he has put all his enemies under his feet. The last enemy to be neutralized is death. "For God has put all things in subjection under his feet."[31]

The reiterated use of "every" and "all" here really tells us all we need to know to identify these Powers: without exception, every structure of authority, role, office, incumbent, institution, system, nation, ruler, angel, in heaven and earth and under the earth—all will be brought into

30. *A&P*, 112–13; see also Eph. 3:18.
31. Author's translation.

subjection under his feet. Only that which has been in revolt needs to be subjected. They are "enemies" (v. 25). Hence these must be rebellious powers.[32]

The translation of *katargeō* in 1 Cor. 15:24 and 26, however, poses a problem. The RSV reads "destroy."[33] This would preclude any possibility of reconciliation, putting the passage at odds not only with Col. 1:20 (which may not be Pauline anyway) but also with other statements of Paul himself (2 Cor. 5:19; Phil. 3:21). The word is used 27 times in the New Testament, 23 times by Paul, sometimes with meanings as mild as "make void," "give up," "fading," "remove," and "nullify." The latter is suggestive of a translation for 1 Cor. 15:24—"after *neutralizing* [or *depotentiating*] every rule and every authority and power." For if they are *destroyed*, what will there be left to be in subjection to him? Paul is playing here with Ps. 110:1 and 8:6,[34] spinning off from *hypotassō* ("to subject," used 6 times in only 3 verses) a commentary on the lordship of Christ. Whatever happens to the Powers in v. 24, they cannot be "destroyed," because they are presupposed again in 1 Cor. 15:27–28. However we decide to translate v. 26, then, v. 24 should indicate the *subjection* of the Powers, not their annihilation.[35]

At first, v. 26 seems to require something final, like "abolished" or "destroyed," for this is the end of death. Other passages certainly seem

32. Carr's attempts (*A&P*, 90–92) to interpret the power terms here as solely human is necessitated by his thesis, namely, that the Powers in the New Testament are angels and wholly good. Since this passage speaks in a negative way about the Powers, Carr must reduce them to human beings in order to dispose of the passage. His attempts to dissociate these powers from their serial linkage with death utterly ignores the catchword connection between "enemies" (v. 25) and "enemy" (v. 26). They are all a single phalanx of opposition to God's will for the world.

33. For v. 24 other versions read "put down" (KJV), "abolishing" (NEB, Phillips), "done away with" (JB); for v. 26, "destroyed" (KJV, Phillips, JB), "abolished" (NEB).

34. Ps. 8:6 (8:7, LXX) alone contains *hypotassō*, but Ps. 110:1 has the reference to "enemies" and to two "Lords," developed in 1 Cor. 15:27–28.

35. H. Berkhof (*Christ and the Powers* [Scottdale, Pa.: Herald Press, 1962], 32–35) brings to the question of the final disposition of the Powers the reasoning of a systematician: (1) In the kingdom that comes, life would still require definite powers and orders to hold it together in harmony. (2) If the Powers were originally created good and are not intrinsically evil, their loss or annihilation in the consummation of all things would mark not a victory for God but a defeat. (3) Col. 1:19–20 speaks of a cosmic reconciliation of these very Powers, when they will return to their original function as instruments of God's fellowship with the creation (so also Eph. 1:10). "The Powers, which now seek headship for themselves, will be subjected to the true Head, Christ" (ibid., 33). (4) Eph. 1:21–22 says that Christ is exalted above every Name, even in the age to come. This implies continuance of the Powers in the kingdom.

to require such a translation, such as 2 Thess. 2:8 and 1 Cor. 6:13. Elsewhere, however, Gerhard Delling suggests such translations as "robbed of its power" (Rom. 6:6; 2 Tim. 1:10) or "condemn to inactivity or ineffectiveness" (Heb. 2:14) or "make to fade away, put out of action, or deprive of power" (2 Cor. 3:11).[36] Perhaps Rom. 6:9 is just the clue we need, since it too deals with Christ's power over death: "Christ being raised from the dead will never die again; death no longer has dominion (*kyrieuei*) over him." Along the same lines, but on a cosmic scale, Paul in 1 Cor. 15:26 is describing a final victory in which death no longer has dominion over *anyone*. In the new age to come, those who are raised will live by the life of God. Death will have no more victims: it will no longer have dominion, as Rom. 6:9 says. Dominion is the opposite of subjection. Paul chooses *katargeō* in 1 Cor. 15:26 as a virtual synonym of *hypotassō*; he is saying, in effect, that the last enemy to be subjected is death. It is rendered null and void. It is neutralized, depotentiated.[37]

If the Powers, in being subjugated to Christ, will have thus been neutralized, then 1 Cor. 15:20–28 anticipates a cosmic restitution of all things at the end. This cosmic restitution will even include the physical universe.[38] This motif continues the vision already shared by both the Old Testament and the apocalyptic literature of Judaism. "And the first heaven shall depart and pass away and a new heaven shall appear, and all the powers of the heavens shall give sevenfold light" (*1 Enoch* 91:16).

36. Delling, "Argos," *TDNT* 1 (1964): 452–54.
37. The same observations help clarify two non-Pauline uses of *katargeō* as well. When in 2 Tim. 1:10 *katargēsantos* describes Christ's victory over death, "abolished" (RSV) is certainly not an adequate translation, since Christians continue to die. Rather, Christ has abolished the sting of death (1 Cor. 15:55–56), that is, he has nullified, neutralized, depotentiated it.
A similar case could be argued for Heb. 2:14—"that through death he might *katargēsē* him who has the power of death, that is, the devil." The RSV renders *katargēsē* by "destroy," but the NEB uses "break the power of," and the JB uses "take away all the power of." The latter are correct, for Christ's death is a *past* event whose efficacy is already manifest. Its benefits do not await the eschaton, but are already in effect. Satan surely has not been *destroyed*—that much is clear just four verses later (2:18). He has only been depotentiated. In Heinrich Schlier's fine phrase, "Christ has left the devil only whatever power unbelief allows him" (*Principalities and Powers in the New Testament* [New York: Herder & Herder, 1961], 58).
38. Rom. 8:18–25; see Rev. 21:1, 5, 23; 22:5; Mark 13:24–25 par. According to *Pirke R. El.* 74 B ii., in the end time "every field and vineyard which did not yield fruit, people water them with those waters [from under the throne] and they yield fruit . . . '*that all things may be healed and live.*' Then [the waters] enter the Salt Sea and they heal it. And the waters 'shall go towards the sea   . *and the waters shall be healed.*' And there they generate all kinds [of fish]."

Not only will the stars be regenerated in power but the Powers themselves will be redeemed "when heaven and earth and all their creatures will be renewed [to new life] like the powers of heaven and all the creatures of earth" (*Jub.* 1:29). Not just earth but heaven will be shaken (Heb. 12:26) and made new: "Then I saw a new heaven and a new earth; for the first heaven and the first earth had passed away" (Rev. 21:1).[39] This is almost poignantly expressed in the later *NHL Tripartite Tractate*: "Not only do humans need redemption but also the angels, too, need redemption" (124:25–28). And though it is but a mutilated fragment, the ending of the same document is profound: "with [the sound] of a trumpet he will proclaim the great, complete amnesty from the beauteous east, in the bridal chamber which is the love of God the Father . . ." (138:6–12).

This theme of total and harmonious restitution at the end is discordant even within the New Testament itself with strains that announce the condemnation of the devil and all his angels and their torture in the lake of fire for ever and ever (Rev. 20:10; Matt. 25:41). Does this not simply reflect the tension between the Christian ideal of love for the enemy and the unredeemed "shadow" side which thirsts for revenge? Is the vision of eternal hell not a secondary projection, in which fear and hatred are satisfied by deferred gratification at the prospect of the enemy's sufferings in an eternal hell, the hater all the while being freed from guilt by assigning the dirty work to God?

Traces of this dynamic of revenge no doubt have found their way into the New Testament, although one will look in vain to find it in Paul. But even in Revelation, one of the most vindictive works ever penned, something more than revenge is at work. Picking up the narrative at Rev. 19:15, we see Christ with a sharp sword issuing from his mouth, "with which to smite the nations." Spoken truth, not cold steel, is what in fact destroys them. In the great scene of carnage that follows, vultures gather "to eat the flesh of kings, the flesh of captains, the flesh of mighty men" (19:18). All these opponents are slain (19:21). The messianic kingdom is inaugurated; then after a thousand years the devil is unchained and "will come out to deceive the nations" (20:8). They too are then destroyed by fire from heaven. One would think that this was the final solution to the problem of the Powers. Yet when the holy city comes down from heaven to earth, after all its perfect wonders have been described, here come the nations, led by their kings! We would have thought they were all dead, but they come, bringing "the glory and the honor of the nations"

39. See *1 Enoch* 45:4–5: "And I will transform the heaven and make it an eternal blessing and light; and I will transform the earth and make it a blessing."

(21:24, 26), and the leaves of the tree of life will be "for the healing of the nations" (22:2).

The fact that John depicts (destroyed) kings and nations entering the New Jerusalem indicates that they have not been completely demonized. Something redeemed survives: their "glory and honor" (21:24, 26). Perhaps we are to think of the distinctive contribution made by each nation to language, to culture, to art, to wisdom and truth and science.[40] In any case, as deeply as he loathes them, he cannot let them go.[41] There is a place even for the pagan nations in the heavenly city that comes from God.

Paul only hints at the final restitution of evil. The Powers, and death itself, are only depotentiated. There is no positive statement of their reconciliation, as in Revelation 21 and 22. Here Paul is concerned only with their negation. He does not go beyond that, as John does, to a vision of resolution in a new and final synthesis. Is this then Paul's last word on the subject?

Col. 1:20 is, I believe, that last word, either written by Paul himself or rightly divined as the necessary logic of his own position by his disciples.[42] This verse looks to God's reconciliation of "all things, whether on earth or in heaven, making peace by the blood of his cross." The phrase "whether on earth or in heaven" is a reprise of v. 16 and un-

40. The contradictory images we find in Revelation are not simply the product of an inconsistent mind, but are characteristic of thought itself when it attempts to leap the bounds of what is, in order to posit something new. There is an illuminating parallel from the prison notebooks of Antonio Gramsci, who reflected that the antithesis, as a new idea, must be posited as the radical antagonist of the thesis. It cannot simply "evolve" from the thesis, but must rather attempt the *complete destruction* of the thesis in order to make its own space. The synthesis that emerges overcomes or resolves this conflict eventually, but no one can say in advance what of the original thesis will be conserved in the synthesis (Guiseppe Fiori, *Antonio Gramsci: Life of a Revolutionary* [New York: E. P. Dutton, 1971], 240). In terms of John's image, we might say that the nations only appear to be destroyed; what is in fact destroyed is their idolatry, their alienation from God, their rapacity. The destruction of all of that leaves them free to be what they were intended by God to be in their creation.

41. So also Rev. 15:2–4. The same symbolic structure is reflected in *Asc. Isa.* 10:12 and 15. Christ's coming to earth is to "judge and destroy the princes and angels and gods of that world"; yet on his ascension to God's right hand, "thereupon the princes and powers of that world will worship Thee." Charles (*Ascension of Isaiah*) would emend "princes" in v. 12 to "prince," following two of his texts (SL[2]) and John 16:11. But the harder reading is to be preferred, on the assumption that SL[2] are conforming the text to John and to Christian theology generally. This is confirmed by the plural *principes* in v. 15.

42. I tend to favor the notion that Paul wrote Colossians but not Ephesians. Powerful arguments have been advanced from either side regarding Colossians; see, e.g., Eduard Lohse, "Pauline Theology in the Letter to the Colossians," *NTS* 15 (1969): 211–20;

mistakably points to the Powers. The very structures of reality themselves will be made right, when God at last (to advert again to 1 Cor. 15:28) becomes "all in all."

Even if Paul does look toward a cosmic restitution of all things, including the Powers, he seems to see it in the future. Col. 2:15 and Eph. 1:20ff., on the other hand, seem to declare that this subjection of the Powers to Christ has already taken place, an assertion which is not only contrary to Paul's view in 1 Corinthians 15 but seems to fly in the face of everyday experience. We must examine each of these passages in turn.

Colossians 2:13–15

And you, who were dead in trespasses and the uncircumcision of your flesh, God made alive together with him, having forgiven us all our trespasses, having canceled the bond (*cheirographon*) which stood against us with its legal demands; this he set aside, nailing it to the cross. He disarmed (*apekdysamenos*) the principalities and powers and made a public example (*edeigmatisen*) of them, triumphing (*thriambeusas*) over them in him [or "it"].

Not one line of this passage is simple to interpret. The most tortured questions are the meaning of the *cheirographon*, the use of the image of the Triumph, and the translation of *apekdysamenos*.

Cheirographon

Carr has ingeniously suggested that the term *cheirographon* refers to the "handwritten" confessional steles discovered in Asia Minor which were set up by penitent offenders of a holy cult as a public record of misdeeds. Christ, Carr suggests, has obliterated this (metaphorical) public self-accusation. If after being freed from the charge the Colossians bind themselves with their own rules and regulations all over again, they would once more be writing their *cheirographon tois dogmasin* for all to see (cf. Col. 2:20).[43]

The idea that Paul used a vivid local custom as a point of contact with the Colossians' own Gentile traditions as a way of helping them understand the meaning of freedom from pagan obligations is appealing. But the metaphor self-destructs visually, despite Carr's warning not to press it too far. Indeed, Carr himself has pressed too far: the image of a stone stele nailed to the cross is simply more weight than the metaphor can

---

Eduard Schweizer, *The Letter to the Colossians* (Minneapolis: Augsburg Publishing House, 1982), 15–24. We cannot speak with much assurance either way. I will call the author "Paul," and the reader who disagrees can feel free to read "Paul's disciples."
43. "Two Notes on Colossians," *JTS*, n.s. 24 (1973): 492–500; *A&P*, 52–58.

bear![44] More satisfying is the older view that the *cheirograph* is an IOU and that the image is a wordplay on the crossing out of a debt in writing. Adolf Deissmann describes the originals of papyri that have been "crossed out" with the Greek cross-letter *X* (*chi*) and cites one Florentine papyrus of 85 C.E. in which the governor of Egypt gives this order in the course of a trial: "Let the handwriting (*cheirographon*) be crossed out."[45] The *cheirograph* would then be not the Law as such but the record of our infractions of it, possibly that record which is written in the heavenly books (Rev. 20:12; *Apoc. Zeph.* 7:1–11). The page is torn out and nailed to the cross, a public record of our forgiveness by God (2:13) through the death of Christ, appropriated through baptism (2:12). Just how the cross cancels the debt is not elaborated.

The Triumph

The meaning of *thriambeusas* is not "to gain a triumph" but "to celebrate a triumph," "to enjoy a triumphal procession,"[46] and could be referring to (a) the Powers as captives, (b) the convert as freed, or (c) Christians as Christ's soldiers. The last image seems to be used in 2 Cor. 2:14— "But thanks be to God, who in Christ always leads us in triumph, and through us spreads the fragrance of the knowledge of him everywhere." But that sense is excluded here by the reference to principalities and powers.

Lamar Williamson comments that when *thriambeuō* is followed by a

---

44. The earliest extant example of these steles dates from 126 C.E.; most come from the late second or third century. In light of Carr's own criteria, he should have rejected this interpretation, since he insists that the kind of religious fervor these monuments witness to appeared in the revival of paganism that only began in the second century of our era (*A&P*, Part I).

45. Adolf Deissmann, *Light from the Ancient East*, rev. ed. (London: Hodder & Stoughton, 1927), 332–38.

46. The Roman triumph unfolded before bystanders' eyes in this order: (a) Captured arms and spoils of war, pictures of battle scenes and of towns conquered, boards with names of peoples subjugated; (b) gifts of honor presented by conquered peoples; (c) white oxen to be sacrificed to Jupiter; (d) chained prisoners; (e) lictors in red war dress with laureate *fasces*; (f) magistrates and senate; (g) *triumphator* in a chariot with his smaller children (his older sons accompany him on horseback, along with his officers); (h) Romans liberated from slavery; (i) soldiers wearing laurel-wreaths on their heads and singing ribald songs deriding their commander (H. S. Versnel, *Triumphus: An Inquiry into the Origin, Development, and Meaning of the Roman Triumph* [Leiden: E. J. Brill, 1970], 95). The fact that the image of a triumphal procession is used at Qumran, however, may indicate that Col. 2:15 draws on a much broader and less specific tradition of triumphs celebrated by all victorious armies in the Hellenistic Near East. See 1QM 19:2—"Rise up, O Hero! Lead off Thy captives, O Glorious One! Gather up Thy spoils, O Author of mighty deeds!" This figure is apparently not God but an angelic deliverer, probably Michael (see 1QM 17), functioning here as the angel of the nation Israel.

direct object (here *autous*) it means "to lead [them] as a conquered enemy in a victory parade." Since the most exciting part of the parade was dragging the defeated enemies through the streets and exposing them to public ridicule, they appear frequently as the direct object of the verb "to triumph someone," that is, to lead someone captive in a victory parade. By extension, then, it later comes to mean "to expose to ridicule."[47]

"Exposure," however, is a theme that runs through the entire sentence. It is inevitably the sense of *apekdysamenos*, however it is translated, and it is central to the meaning of *deigmatizō*, the only finite verb in the sentence. Carr dismisses the latter as "a neutral, an otherwise colourless word."[48] But this "colourless" word is regularly used for the public disgracing of an adulteress by exposure.[49] Matt. 1:19 uses it of Mary's seeming adultery: Joseph did not wish "to expose her to public shame." The public shaming of an adulterer in Judaism involved stripping a woman of her garments so that her breasts were laid bare (M. *Sota* 1:5). From all this we can deduce a fairly consistent translation: "to shame by public exposure." The additional phrase *en parrēsia* ("in boldness," Col. 2:15) emphasized the public nature of this humiliation.

Apekdysamenos

We have been edging up to *apekdysamenos* from behind, hoping to surprise a solution from it, the most difficult of all the terms in this passage. Our effort so far has yielded the phrase "he shamed them by public exposure, displaying them [the principalities and powers] in his triumphal

47. Lamar Williamson, Jr., "Led in Triumph," *Int.* 22 (1968): 317ff. In support of his translation, Williamson cites Plutarch's *Coriolanus* 35.3—"For it does not behove me to await that day on which I shall behold my son either led in triumph (*thriambeuomenon*) by his fellow-citizens or triumphing (*thriambeuonta*) over his country." (The phrase "to lead in triumph" is used of captives even though they precede the *triumphator* [Plutarch, *Aemilius Paulus* 32–34].)

48. *A&P*, 63.

49. References in BAG. *Protevang. Jacobi* 14:1 specifically mentions the possibility of Mary's being "exposed" for her apparent adultery. In *Asc. Isa.* 3:13[G2], in a passage with striking affinities to Col. 2:15, Beliar is thrown into great wrath against Isaiah "because of the exposure (*deigmatismou*) wherewith he had exposed (*edeigmatisen*) Sammael," a figure identified later in the book as Satan himself (11:41). In the *Acts of Peter and Paul* 33, the apostle "spoke to the people in order that . . . they might expose" Simon Magus as a fraud and loathe him. Athanasius uses the term with the same brutality, pairing it with a variant form of *apekdyō:* "But since they themselves conceal it [this heresy] and are afraid to speak, it is necessary for me to strip off (*apodysai*) the veil from their impiety, and to expose their heresy to public view (*deigmatisai*)" (*Letter to the Bishops of Egypt and Libya*, 11, cited by Heirich Schlier, "Deigmatizō," *TDNT* 2 (1964): 31–32.

procession through him (or "it," the cross)." The common theme, we have found, is exposure. That also is the sense of *apekdyō*, "to undress, to strip off." The problem lies in the middle voice used here. In Col. 3:9 the same word in the middle carries the usual reflexive sense: "to put off (of oneself) the old nature," the old nature being the object of the reflexive act.[50] If *apekdysamenos* in 2:15 is read as reflexive, then it must have the sense "having stripped off for himself." But having stripped off what? J. A. T. Robinson suggests we supply, as if assumed, "the flesh,"[51] a suggestion that Carr develops along the lines of the Roman triumph. The central event of the triumph, he argues, was the act of putting off the old clothes of the victor and putting on the ceremonial dress of a *triumphator*. By analogy, Christ put aside his battle dress, his flesh. Carr is certain that the principalities and powers cannot be evil; hence they must be accompanying him in celebration of his victory. There on the cross he led them rejoicing in his triumphal procession.[52]

The text, however, says nothing at all about Christ's having been further clothed in the dress of the victor; in Carr's image he must parade in the nude![53] What Paul thinks about public nudity is made clear enough in 2 Cor. 5:3. This is not a matter of carping at metaphors, for there was one group who were stripped of their armaments and publicly disgraced in the Triumph—the vanquished.[54] If we take the principalities and powers as the natural object of *apekdysamenos* (as the word order suggests), they would be the ones who have been stripped, disarmed, exposed, unmasked by the crucifixion of Jesus. Then the whole phrase makes plain sense

50. So, similarly, *Odes of Sol.* 11:9—"I forsook the folly which is diffused over the earth; and I stripped it off and cast it from me."
51. *The Body: A Study in Pauline Theology* (London: SCM Press, 1952), 41 n. 3. The gnostics tended to read the passage as a stripping off of Christ's flesh: *NHL 2 Apoc. Jas.* 46:14–16—"[he who] stripped [himself and] went about naked"; *NHL Gos. Truth* 20:24–33—"he put on that book; he was nailed to a tree; he published the edict of the Father on the cross. . . . Having stripped himself of the perishable rags, he put on imperishability. . . ." Chrysostom, for his part, translates in the middle but makes the Powers the object of the reflexive act (*Hom. on Col.*, 6).
52. *A&P*, 52–68.
53. One spoke of being "garbed as triumphator"; the emphasis was wholly on his dress, not his being undressed (J. Rufus Fears, "The Cult of Jupiter and Roman Imperial Ideology," in *ANRW* 2.17.1 [1981]: 44).
54. In Plutarch's *Triumph of Aemilius Paulus*, the arms of the conquered army are hauled through the streets on wagons, "carefully and artfully arranged to look exactly as though they had been piled together in heaps and at random, helmets lying upon shields and breast-plates upon greaves" (32–34). The next day the defeated house of Perseus was marched before the *triumphator* on foot, clad only in robes, stripped of all armor and insignia. The humiliation was so great that Perseus pleaded that he be excused.

without having to change the subject from God to Christ in the middle of the sentence or supply any additional words: "unmasking the principalities and powers, he [God] publicly shamed them, exposing them in his triumphal procession through him (or 'it,' the cross)." This is precisely how Athanasius read it: In the cross, "the Saviour stripped them [the demons] and made an example of them" (*Life of St. Anthony*, 35).[55]

Some of the confusion in the passage may derive from the image of the Triumph itself. If God is viewed as the *imperator mundi* who has bestowed on Christ this the highest of honors (for the Triumph was considered the greatest distinction Rome could confer[56]) and Christ is conceived of as the *triumphator*, then the cross may be pictured as being carried before the entire procession as the trophy of victory, the paradoxical spoils of war by which the Powers were themselves despoiled. Hence the ambiguous *en autō*, which refers apparently simultaneously to Christ as the victor and to the cross as the means of victory. Once more, when something is ambiguous, that is what it means; *autō* should continue to vacillate between "him" and "it," or better, refer to both: "in his cross."

If indeed the Powers have been "stripped" or "unmasked" in the cross of Christ, and so decisively that they can be described as already chained and captive in God's triumphal victory celebration for him, we do seem to have a case of genuine contradiction with 1 Cor. 15:20-28.

55. BDF 316.1 cites *apekdysamenos* as an instance where the middle is used in an active sense. James H. Moulton and Nigel Turner (*A Grammar of New Testament Greek* [Edinburgh: T. & T. Clark, 1963]) agree, rendering it "strip" or "spoil." They note the considerable confusion in the use of middle and active in the New Testament. Not only is the middle often used where we expect the active, but we even find active and middle forms of the same verb used together in the same phrase. If any distinction is intended, none is apparent. They cite as an example the use, in the very same epistle, of the middle *karpophoroumenon* in Col. 1:6 and the active *karpophorountes* in 1:10, with no discernible difference between them. "In our period there is not always any significance in the writer's choice of middle or active, and the reflexive middle in the NT is relatively rare" (ibid., 54). The participle paired with *apekdysamenos* in our very sentence, *thriambeusas*, is itself an original intransitive used in an active sense (BDF 148.1). In addition to other witnesses already cited, the *NHL Gos. Eg.* 64:3-7 and 65:18 interpret *apekdysamenos* as active.

The reflexive sense is possible, taking the Powers as the object: "He stripped off of himself the principalities and powers," that is, he got them "off his back." But the context requires more than his winning freedom *from* them; he wins a victory *over* them. "If it was only by putting off His human body on the Cross that He could put off from Himself the powers of evil that beset His humanity, this would not be victory, but retreat." T. K. Abbott, *The Epistles to the Ephesians and to the Colossians*, 6th ed., ICC (Edinburgh: T. & T. Clark, 1953), 259.

56. Versnel, *Triumphus*, 304.

Both look to a cosmic reconciliation in which all the Powers are subdued, but Colossians seems to locate that event in the past, while 1 Corinthians fixes its hope on the future. Common experience would certainly seem to side with 1 Corinthians; the Powers most certainly have not been defeated. They were as strong the day after the resurrection as ever before. The cross of Christ may have mitigated the evil of the world; it would be unfair to slight the sincere attempts of politicians and kings, sales clerks and businesspeople, preachers and popes, to create a world of justice and morality, to abolish inhuman practices, even to give correct change. But they have had to struggle to do so against almost insuperable odds. The fact is that the Powers are as powerful as ever, as no people should know better than we who have survived into the grim twilight of the twentieth century since the crucifixion. This problem is only compounded by Eph. 1:20–23, which depicts as already accomplished the subjection of the Powers which 1 Cor. 15:24–26 saw only in the future.

Ephesians 1:20–23

. . . which he [God] accomplished in Christ when he raised him from the dead and made him sit at his right hand in the heavenly places, far above all rule and authority and power and dominion, and above every name that is named, not only in this age but also in that which is to come; and he has put all things under his feet and has made him head over all things for the church, which is his body, the fulness of him who fills all in all.

It would be tempting to take these Powers as heavenly only and interpret the text as proclaiming that in Christ the affairs of heaven have been set straight, even if nothing has changed on earth. But that would be nonsensical in terms of the first-century worldview. Nothing in heaven can happen without profound repercussions on earth; indeed, that is the way true change on earth is brought about. Nor would the message of peace in heaven constitute much "good news" for those seeking salvation on earth. No, the use of "all" . . . "every" . . . "all" here is uncompromising in its breadth; no power or name in this world or the world to come is exempted. Otherwise Christ's present lordship would be incomplete. In Ephesians, Christ already has established sovereignty over those Powers which, according to 1 Cor. 15:24–26, he will only subject at the end.

Perhaps the tension between these two texts is only a result of their emphasizing different poles of the "already/not yet" notion of eschatology which characterized most early Christian thought. Christ is Lord/

will be Lord; believers already experience liberation from the Powers in the present but will continue until the end to be assaulted by them. The difference between 1 Corinthians and Ephesians is then not fundamental but a matter of emphasis, accelerated by the delay of the end and the need to identify grounds for hope in present existence as well as future promises.

The image of Christ at God's right hand with all authority is not limited to Ephesians. We find it in Jesus' statement "From now on the Son of man shall be seated at the right hand of the Power (*dynameōs*) of God" (Luke 22:69; see also Mark 14:62; Matt. 26:64). It appears in the charge of the risen Christ in Matthew: "All authority (*exousia*) in heaven and on earth has been given to me" (Matt. 28:18). This power is not confined to the risen Christ; the disciples themselves are given authority over evil spirits by Jesus ("Behold, I have given you authority [*exousian*] to tread upon serpents and scorpions, and over all the power [*dynamin*] of the enemy; and nothing shall hurt you" (Luke 10:19; see also Mark 16:17–18).[57]

John's Gospel also sees the cross as the moment in which Satan's power is broken: "Now is the judgment of this world, now shall the ruler (*archōn*) of this world be cast out" (12:31). The eschatological judgment of the fallen angels (see above, pp. 25, 33) takes place when Jesus is crucified: "the prince (*archōn*) of this world is judged" (16:11).

I am not of the view that Paul wrote Ephesians, but the Paul who could write 1 Cor. 15:24–28 also speaks in a vein surprisingly similar to that of Eph. 1:20–23 and to the other texts just quoted. The way in which he does so shows that he has already moved a considerable distance toward demythologizing the language of power. Paul's use of traditional apocalyptic terminology in reference to the Powers is restricted to 1 Cor. 15:24–28, Rom. 8:38–39, and 1 Cor. 2:6–8, unless Colossians be regarded as Pauline (1:15–20; 2:8–10, 15, 20). He prefers elsewhere to speak of those ontological powers that determine the human situation

---

57. *Test. Levi* 18:12, possibly a Christian interpolation, shows that at least some would have interpreted Luke 10:19 in a metaphorical rather than a literal way: "And Beliar shall be bound by him, and he shall give power to his children to tread upon the evil spirits." Justin also understood Christian existence as a radical freedom from the Powers: "Thank God for having created the world, with all things therein, for the sake of humanity, and for delivering us from the evil in which we were, and for utterly overthrowing [literally, "overthrowing with a perfect overthrow"] principalities and powers by Him who suffered according to His will" (*Dial.* 41). So also Chrysostom, *Hom. on Eph.*, 3.

within the context of God's created order and comprise the "field" of death, sin, the law, and the flesh.[58] This field, says J. Christiaan Beker, is an alliance of powers under the sovereign rule of death.

> All the powers of the field have their specific reign or dominion: persons are "under the power of sin" (*hamartia*, Rom. 3:9) or "under the power of law" (*nomos*, Rom. 6:15); sin "reigns" (Rom. 5:21) and death (*thanatos*) "reigns" (Rom. 6:9; cf. 5:17); the flesh (*sarx*) has a "mindset" of its own (Rom. 8:5–7) or "desires" (Gal. 5:17). The field operates as an interrelated whole; its forces cannot be genetically delineated, and no power can be viewed in isolation from the others.[59]

Within this field of interlocking forces, death is the primal power, "the last enemy" (1 Cor. 15:26). "And death remains in some way the signature of this world, even after its allies—the law, the flesh, and sin— have been defeated in the death and resurrection of Christ. . . . The death of Christ now marks the defeat of the apocalyptic power alliance and signals the imminent defeat of death."[60] Beker therefore concludes that the author of Colossians (whom he believes was *not* Paul) interprets Paul correctly on this point in Col. 2:15—the Powers have already been dethroned.

Paul is thus able to mark the death and resurrection of Christ as the watershed between the two ages. In Christ's death God's judgment on the Powers has already been rendered. This is a cosmic victory over death and its allies—sin, the law, and the flesh.[61]

When I spoke of "demythologizing," I meant simply the withdrawal of the mythic projection of the real determinants of human existence out onto the cosmos and their identification as actual physical, psychic, and social forces at work in us, in society, and in the universe. The length to which Paul has already carried this process of demythologizing is visible especially in his treatment of wisdom and law. As the structures of value and normative behavior in this age, wisdom and law are the

---

58. J. Christiaan Beker, *Paul the Apostle: The Triumph of God in Life and Thought* (Philadelphia: Fortress Press, 1980), 189. I will be following Beker throughout this discussion of Paul.

59. Ibid., 189–90.

60. Ibid., 190.

61. See Gal. 3:13; 4:4–5; Rom. 6:1–10; 8:3; 2 Cor. 5:21. See Beker: "The death of Christ addresses itself to sin as a cosmic power and slavemaster, that is, to the human condition 'under the power of sin.' It announces the negation of the power of sin that controls the world, and thus it has not only a moral but also an ontological meaning" (ibid., 191).

powers that regulate existence for Gentile and Jew respectively. They are symbolic abbreviations of what the civilized and religious world considers its highest values. But neither can withstand the cross, which unmasks the folly of wisdom and the lawlessness of law. "The cross negates and judges the worlds of religion and culture: it contradicts wisdom (1 Cor. 1:18); it crucifies the law and the world (Gal. 2:20; 6:14); it invites public hostility (Phil. 3:18); it is foolishness (1 Cor. 1:14); a scandal to Jews and folly to Gentiles (1 Cor. 1:23; see Gal. 5:11); and truly a manifestation of weakness. . . ."[62] By radically overturning the standards of the world—its investment in glory, achievement, wisdom, and religiosity—the cross becomes the apocalyptic turning point of history, the transvaluator of values, the beginning of the ontological renewal of creation that will come to completion in God's new age.[63]

This understanding of Paul provides the clue we need to interpret Eph. 1:20ff. (whoever its author), and indeed any assertion (such as Phil. 2:5–11 or Col. 2:10) that Christ is already Lord of all. If we ask what meaning is operative in the symbol of Christ at God's right hand, with all the Powers already under his feet, we might see here an expression of the everyday experience of the early Christians that demons could be and were being cast out, the sick healed, compulsive and obsessive behavior changed, harmful and violent ways of living rectified, new meaning and joy being poured into life. In retrospect, they could see that they had been living in the shackles of inauthentic behavior not even entirely of their own choosing; that they had indeed "known better" and had struggled to conceal from themselves this knowledge; that they had willfully disobeyed their own best inner promptings in order to satisfy egocentric desires. They had, in short, been captives, and now were to an astonishing measure free. Death remained, but not its fear. Sin could still be committed, but not of necessity. The victory over death and sin could already be celebrated in anticipation of its completion at the end (1 Cor. 15:55–57). The world has already become the possession of believers (1 Cor. 3:21–23). The "new creation" is already in process of being established; "the old has passed away, behold, the new has come" (2 Cor. 5:17; see Gal. 6:15).

The assertion in Ephesians that Christ is already "Lord of the Powers" is not then at odds with Paul's own understanding of the victory of Christ in the cross. Both Paul and the disciple of Paul who most likely penned

62. Ibid., 205.
63. Ibid., 206, 209.

Ephesians claim that a new existence has become possible within the old reality. Not fantasy but actual experience is what has minted these audacious claims.

Colossians 1:16

. . . For in him all things were created, in heaven and on earth, visible and invisible, whether thrones or dominions or principalities or authorities—all things were created through him and for him.

Nor does this audacity cease with claims for the cross of Christ as the pivot of history. Col. 1:15–20 presses the meaning of that event (1:20) and that person (1:15) all the way back to the origin of the universe. What came to light in the cross was what had been true of reality from the very beginning.

What Rom. 8:38–39 had only hinted at is here made explicit: the Powers, despite their idolatry, rebellion, and hostility to God, were created in, through, and for Christ. The functions of Wisdom in Proverbs 8 and Wisdom of Solomon 7 are here ascribed to the preexistent Christ, but in an unexpected way, for it is not just the physical universe that was created with Christ as its means, medium, and goal, but quite specifically the Powers. They only have their being because of him; they are upheld, even in their defections, by him. They exist to serve the purpose of the whole creation as it comes to its focus in him.

But if the Powers have been created by God in and through and for Christ, then they cannot be wholly demonized. No matter how evil the empire or a monarch or the priesthood or the local magistrate or Satan himself becomes, none of them can be ascribed Manichean or dualistic status. They are still, despite themselves, inseparably bonded to the principle of rationality and cohesiveness in the universe (Col. 1:17). Like a cancer dependent on the host organism for its very destructive energies, evil remains inescapably parasitic of the whole. Try as they will to become autonomous and set up their own interests as the highest good, the Powers must inevitably come to terms with the Power of the Powers.

Throughout Christian history the claim that the Powers have been created in and through and for Christ has all too easily been perverted into a justification of the status quo, a rationalization of every current evil, a legitimation of corrupt regimes. Perhaps we could avoid such travesties if we conceived the Powers to be related to Christ the way humanity is related to the physical ecology. We can plunder, ravage, poison, and imbalance the ecology all we want, yet in the very act of spoiling our own nest we are at every moment sustained by means of the life-giving nutrients and energies the ecosystem is still able to provide. But the ecology is not mocked. There comes a point of irreversibility when the poisons we dump become our own drink, and we come under the "judgment" of the ecosystem.

This text then also becomes the basis for prophetic judgment of the Powers. Their purpose in creation is to be "for" Christ, to serve that end in and through and for which they were created. Any deviation from that goal violates their created purpose, and it becomes the task of the church to call them back to their origins (Col. 1:18; Eph. 3:10). That task is made immeasurably easier, however, by the knowledge that, in their essence, the Powers, like humans, are the good creations of a good God.

Can we specify which Powers are intended here, or are we dealing with a "string" or series whose meaning is simply *all* the Powers? The latter is undeniably the case, as the repetition of "all" and "whether" in this paragraph indicates. But within that universality, can we distinguish specific functions? Our earlier findings on the casual interchangeability of these terms forewarns us against overspecification. The attempt is worth the effort, however, because the writer seems to intend to speak of the universality of the Powers in structural terms. Thus "thrones," as we have seen already, refers less to the inhabitant than to the location of power in a symbolic "place" that outlasts its incumbents. We speak of the county *seat,* the judge's *bench,* the *chair*person, the *oval office*, meaning in each case the authority invested in an office regardless of its current occupant. When the pope wishes to speak infallibly, therefore, he cannot do so in his own name, but only *ex cathedra*—from the chair. That alone endows his words with authority for believers. "Thrones" thus clearly indicate the institutionalization of power in a set of symbols that guarantee its continuity over time.

Kyriotētes, by the same logic, would refer to those "dominions" over which "thrones" preside or hold sway. Until recently Canadians spoke of the "Dominion of Canada," referring to that territory which fell under Canadian sovereignty. *Kyriotēs,* in short, appears to be that over which a *kyrios* exercises lordship. It is the "sphere of influence" which the "throne" possesses, whether visible (the actual land or area ruled) or invisible (its capacity to influence other Powers by threat or persuasion).

Archē might then specify the incumbent in office, the occupant of the chair, the temporary but fully authorized agent of all the power invested in the office. The *archē* is not the person as such but the person-in-office, the agent-in-role. It represents the confluence of symbolic authority and human actor, the investiture of power in a person. No matter how "charismatic" a leader may be, he or she is nothing without the authorization or permission to act, represented by office. It is the fortuitous conjunction of a powerful personality in a powerful office that makes a powerful leader.

And finally, *exousiai* might refer to the legitimations and sanctions by which authority is maintained. These are the invisible and visible authorizations and enforcements that undergird the chair. Legitimations would include the laws, rules, taboos, mores, codes, and constitutions by which power is licensed, and all the customs, traditions, rituals, manners, etiquette, and ideologies by which it is rationalized, justified, and made habitual. Sanctions would include the forces, visible and invisible, by which compliance to these legitimations is enforced: public opinion, peer pressure, ostracism, the ban, shunning, blacklisting, boycott, gossip, propaganda, the police, the army, the courts, punishments, torture, imprisonment, death.

That all these terms were in fact used of social structures in the New Testament is beyond question, as our earlier survey shows.[64] Whether the author intended such an analysis of social structures here is an open question. Looking back on the series of terms from our modern vantage point, however, we can at least appreciate what a neat sociological instrument lay at hand had the ancients chosen to use it. For with these four terms one could in principle analyze any conceivable institution or system of power "on earth or in heaven."

Paraphrased, Col. 1:16 might then be rendered thus: For within his [the Cosmic Christ's] wisdom every power in the universe has been created, those in heaven and those on earth, those visible and those invisible—whether seats of power or spheres of influence, whether incumbents-in-office or the legitimations and sanctions that keep them there—all these social and spiritual structures of reality are stamped with his imprint and exist solely to serve his purposes.

If Christ is lord not only of persons but also of the Powers, if his sovereignty extends beyond the individual to the social structures and spiritual influences that organize the world, does it extend beyond even that to the very constituent properties of the physical universe? Does it

---

64. See above, pp. 7–12. Key passages are Luke 20:20, "the authority (*archē*) and jurisdiction (*exousia*) of the governor" (Pilate); Jude 6, the "position" (*archēn*) of angels; Luke 23:7, "Herod's jurisdiction" (*exousias*); Rev. 16:9, God's jurisdiction (*exousian*). And "throne" is almost always used as a symbol for all the power resident in the "chair" of office.

encompass the laws of nature? Is Christ lord even of the elements of the universe?

The Elements of the
Universe

To this point we have been examining individual texts. Now we must take on as a group the seven references to the *stoicheia* ("elements") in the New Testament, since no single usage can be deciphered in isolation from the rest. The term *stoicheia* has puzzled interpreters for centuries and has been the occasion of a massive etymological excavation. While more bits and shards may yet emerge, enough is now known to consider at least the broad outlines of its meaning settled once for all.[65]

The irony is that this has been primarily a modern debate. No such controversy seems to have involved its use by the Greek-speaking early Christian theologians. Various modern scholars have proposed translations ranging all the way from the four physical elements (earth, air, fire, water), to the rudiments or first principles of philosophy, to the basics of religious rituals, rules, and beliefs, to the precepts of the Jewish law, to the stars conceived as demonic powers. For reasons not altogether clear, the notion of demonic astral spirits seems to have gained the most adherents, so much so that the RSV (and many other versions as well) usually translates the term "elemental spirits."[66]

The fact is that there is simply no evidence that the "elements of the universe" were regarded as astral spirits until the third century C.E.[67] But the problem is by no means to be solved merely by excluding that solution and turning to one of the others, for the mischief all along has lain in the attempt to reduce the term to a single meaning and impose that meaning on every occurrence of the term. Aristotle himself had already

65. This section is an extensively recast version of an earlier discussion that appeared in *Zygon* 13 (1978): 225–48, under the title "The 'Elements of the Universe' in Biblical and Scientific Perspective." I will not repeat here the history of the debate or much of the documentation; for that, the reader is referred to the earlier work; cf. Appendix 4.

66. This is the case in Gal. 4:3, 9 and Col. 2:8, 20. Yet in Heb. 5:12 and 2 Pet. 3:10, 12 the RSV uses "first principles" and the physical "elements," respectively. Ironically, the worst paraphrase of Scripture, *The Living Bible*, is consistently correct in its versatile treatment of *stoicheia* as context-dependent for its meaning, because the author, not competent in Greek, had to take all his clues from the context and therefore stumbled on the right solution. The Jerusalem Bible and Phillips versions are also excellent in their treatment of *stoicheia*. The NEB follows the RSV's "elemental spirits" in the text but acknowledges in footnotes that other translations are possible, such as "the elements of the natural world" or "elementary ideas belonging to this world."

67. *Test. Sol.* 8:1–4; 18:1 are the earliest known instances.

long before made clear that the idea common and basic to all meanings of *stoicheion* is the primary component immanent in a thing that is indivisible into kinds different from itself.[68] It is the most basic constituent of any substance or entity. By extension the term came to stand for anything that is small, simple, and indivisible: a genus (because it has only one definition—Aristotle); a premise or fundamental proposition (Aristotle); a simple or elementary principle of knowledge or instruction (Heb. 5:12).[69]

In Greek usage the letters of the alphabet were the *stoicheia* or irreducible constituents of words, as were phonemes for syllables, numbers for arithmetic, theorems for geometry, notes for the musical scale, or the basic physical elements for matter. All these had long been dubbed *stoicheia* before the first century lumbered onto the scene, and apparently everybody knew it.[70] Scarcely a single ancient writer who uses the term feels any urge to define it or even to indicate the particular nuance with which it is being applied. It is, as Bandstra rightly concludes, a generic term or a "formal word," which of itself has no specific content. It denotes merely an irreducible component; what it is an irreducible component of must be supplied by the context in which it is used.[71]

That conclusion should occasion no surprise, for we use the English word "element" in precisely the same way. We speak of physical elements, the "elements" of the Lord's Supper, the elements of a problem, the raging elements of a storm, in each case understanding immediately from the context whether the table of chemical elements is meant, or bread and wine, or the fundamental issues of a given problem, or the howling wind and driving rain. So also the context prevents our confusing an elementary school with the elementary particles of physics.

68. Aristotle *Metaphysics* 1014a 26–1014b 15 (A. J. Bandstra, *The Law and the Elements of the World* [Kampen, Netherlands: J. H. Kok, 1964], 32). Plato defines *stoicheion* as an "original constituent," and Empedocles is cited by Hesychius as speaking of *stoicheia* as "all that which is indivisible and without parts" (Gerhard Delling, "Stoicheō-stoicheion," *TDNT* 7 (1971): 666–87).

69. Ernest DeWitt Burton, *The Epistle to the Galatians*, ICC (Edinburgh: T. & T. Clark, 1921), 510–18.

70. Thus Isocrates spoke about "the elements of a good commonwealth" (*Ad Nicodem* 55), Plutarch of the "prime elements of virtue" (*De Liberis Educ.*, sec. 16). Galen wrote a medical book "concerning the Hippocratic elements (principles)"; Euclid did the same on the elements (theorums) of geometry.

71. Bandstra, *Law and Elements*. See also the superb work of Gerhard Delling, "Stoicheion." A. W. Cramer (*Stoicheia tou kosmou: Interpretatie van een nieuwtestamentische term* [Nieuwkoop, Netherlands: De Graf, 1961]) successfully refuted the interpretation of the *stoicheia* as demonic or astral spirits. All three books provide extensive bibliographies on the theme, which I will not reproduce here.

This solution makes it possible to abandon the myriad attempts at a single, specific definition of *stoicheia* and to treat each occurrence of the term as the context determines. We can with profit test this thesis by Philo's works, since his more frequent use of *stoicheia* provides a broader range of nuances than the New Testament

	Frequency	*Meaning*
Nature:	54	The four elements: earth, air, fire, water
	3	That which has been created
	3	Forces of nature
Grammar:	13	Letters of the alphabet
	1	The basic sounds of speech
	1	The vowels
	1	The alphabet itself
Number:	1	The source of number
Other:	2	A constituent part of something
	1	Elementary (opposite of "completed")
	1	Elemental (having a state of existence)
	4	(Idiomatic expressions)
	85	

Most significantly, Philo uses *stoicheia* with different meanings not only in the same book but even within the same passage, trusting the immediate context to determine its precise meaning, just as the proposed solution would have led us to predict.[72] And nowhere do we find him using *stoicheia* to denote spirits, stars, or demons.

The term *stoicheion* apparently had no Hebrew antecedent, but was current in Greek from the time of Plato. The use of the term in Hebrews and 2 Peter is unexceptional; that in Galatians and Colossians is uniquely

---

72. In *Quis her.* Philo uses *stoicheia* for the four physical elements (secs. 134, 140, 152, 197, 226 [3 times], 227), of the letters (sec. 282), the vowels (sec. 210), the source of number (sec. 190), and the sense "elementary" (sec. 209). In *De aet.* 111 he uses it of the four elements and two sections later (sec. 113) of letters. In *Quod det.* 8, *stoicheia* represents the four elements and in the very same paragraph a constitutive part of something (2 times). In *Mos.* I,155 and 216 it means the elements of nature, in 156 the four elements; examples could be multiplied. Three times we find a phrase strikingly similar to Paul's: *ta stoicheia tou pantos*—"the elements of the universe" (*Mos.* I,96; *De spec. leg.* II,255; *Flacc.* 125). Yet in the first two cases it refers to the four elements, in the latter, to that which has been created generally.

Archē, as usual, shoulders its way onto *stoicheia*'s turf, once in a phrase also similar to Paul's: *tōn holōn archas*—"the elementary principles of the universe" (*De fuga* 148). See also *Mos.* I,22; II,285; *De dec.* 53. *Dynamis* also is used in a parallel way: "forces of the universe" (*De post. Caini* 5; *De mig. Ab.* 181).

Pauline. In Heb. 5:12 the *stoicheia* are the "elementary" or "first principles" of God's word. Since *stoicheion* often refers to the alphabet, Phillips and the NEB render a nice pun when they translate it as "the ABCs," as if to say, "You need someone to teach you the ABCs of God's oracles all over again—proof that you are still children, needing milk, not solid food."

In 2 Pet. 3:10 and 12 the context again is a clear guide. When the author writes that "the day of the Lord will come like a thief, and then the heavens will pass away with a loud noise, and the elements will be dissolved with fire, and the earth and the works that are upon it will be burned up," he clearly does not mean angels or astral spirits, who have very little substance to ignite or melt, but simply the constituent elements of the physical universe—a theme well-rehearsed in Stoicism as well.[73]

The Pauline usage is not so easy to decipher. The reference to *stoicheia tou kosmou* in Gal. 4:3 falls in the epicenter of a convulsive struggle with Judaizers who insist that full Christian belief requires taking on circumcision and other legal and ritual requirements of the Law. Paul has just been speaking about the Law as a custodian or guardian until Christ came. "Now before we came of age we were as good as slaves to the *stoicheia tou kosmou*" (Gal. 4:3). He continues with a statement about Christ's being "born a subject of the Law, to redeem the subjects of the Law" (4:4–5, JB). To what were they enslaved? Clearly the Law lies at the center of focus; if believers are "redeemed" from the Law, then it must be by the Law that they were "enslaved." But why refer to the Law as the "elements of the world"? Some commentators have suggested that Paul is alluding back to the angelic mediators who delivered the Law (3:19), whose subjects those subjected to Law allegedly became. But even if he did regard angelic ordination of the Law as a sign of its inferiority to Christ, that is a far cry from thinking of these angels as evil spirits.[74] His sole preoccupation is with the danger that the Galatians are

---

73. This use of elements as the physical stuff of the universe was already routine in the LXX (Wisd. Sol. 7:17; 19:18; 4 Macc. 12:13). In Wis. Sol. 7:17 the physical elements are expressly distinguished from "the powers of spirits" (v. 20b). The usage in 2 Peter is similar to that of the early apologetic writings, where the term *stoicheia*, while including the heavenly bodies, also encompasses fire and earth. And even where the stars or sun are called *stoicheia*, they are not conceived as astral spirits, but simply as part of the physical creation. See Justin, *Dial.* 23.3; *Apol.* II,5.2; *Ep. to Diog.* 7:2; Theophilus, *Autol.* 1:4; Theodoret, *Comm. on Gal. & Col.*; Aristides, *Apol.*, chaps. 3–5 (Burton, *Galatians*, 513).

74. Josephus speaks of the law as mediated through angels (*Ant.* 15.136). Human "messengers" cannot be intended, since these heralds "can bring God's presence to

attempting to establish their own righteousness by means of the Jewish Law. The confusion here is caused by the fact that those whom he addresses were in the main not former Jews and had not been, as Paul, under the Law, but under the gods of paganism. Paul wants them to realize that submitting to Jewish religious practices would be, in principle, no different from their former life under the religious practices of polytheism. Both are established on elements fundamental to human life. Both involve special celebrations, sacred calendars, feast days, and even whole years set apart as holy (Gal. 4:10).[75] People cannot live without such rites, but such rites cannot give life (3:21–22). They can only celebrate its having been given as a gift (2:20–21).

In Gal. 4:8–11 Paul directly addresses the Galatians' pagan past. "Formerly, when you did not acknowledge God, you were slaves to 'gods' which in reality do not exist" (4:8, NEB note). Having once known the living God, however, he is incredulous that they desire to revert "back to elemental things like these, that can do nothing and give nothing, and be their slaves" (4:9, JB). Their defection, however, would not be to paganism as such but to something equally futile: a Judaizing Christianity, with its requirements of circumcision and observances and laws (4:10).

Perhaps, given the metaphor of childhood in 3:23–4:7, *stoicheia* should even be translated "childish superstitions." Belief in gods was among the "elementary things" allowed in their time of minority (Deut. 4:19), but to turn back to such infantilisms in the time of their seniority would be to relapse into just another form of slavery. This reading would be similar, then, to Heb. 5:12 ("the ABCs"). The "elementary things"

---

men," which is precisely the function of angels. In Acts 7:53 the point seems to be that the Jews refused to keep the law even though it was delivered by angels, just as they rejected Moses who had received visions of an angel (7:30, 35) and received the law from an angel (7:38). The view of angelic mediation here is wholly positive. So also in Heb. 2:2; *Jub.* 1:29.

75. We are perhaps more familiar with Judaism's "days" (sabbath), "months" (its calendrical systems), "seasons" (passover, tabernacles), and "years" (the sabbatical and jubilee years). But paganism had comparable celebrations, going further, however, in ascribing divinity to the occasion itself. "Zeus," wrote Cicero, "attributed a divine power (*vis divina*) to the stars, but also to the years, the months, and the seasons." "General opinion," said Proclus, "makes the Hours goddesses and the Month a god, and their worship has been handed on to us: we say also that the Day and the Night are deities, and the gods themselves have taught us how to call upon them. Does it not follow that Time also should be a god, seeing that it includes at once months and hours, days and nights?" (as quoted by Franz Cumont, *Astrology and Religion among the Greeks and Romans* [New York: G. P. Putman's Sons, 1912], 109).

would then be the basic constituents of Gentile and Jewish cultus and ceremonial, belief and behavior, that acted like manacles to check their worst passions prior to the revelation of faith. These religious practices may have been unavoidable, but to return to them after having experienced the incomparable freedom of faith would be a catastrophe.

Stoicheia in Galatians thus would appear to refer to those basic practices, beliefs, rituals, and celebrations which are fundamental to the religious existence of all peoples, Jew and Gentile alike. In 4:3 the term is used to sweep Gentiles into a discussion of Judaism which would otherwise appear to leave them out. They too, like the Jews, formerly were held captive under the guardianship of religious notions that in fact had prevented their knowing—or being known by—the living God. Galatians 4:9 develops the same thought, but in reverse: having been in bondage during the time of their minority to such elementary beliefs and doctrines and practices, they are in danger of selling themselves back into slavery by taking on the Jewish Law, which is no different in kind from what formerly enslaved them. If they have once tasted life in the Spirit, freed from law, living from a heart indwelt by the risen Christ, how could they ever desire to turn back to a life of being dictated to by heteronomous rules and regulations? *Stoicheia* here thus points to those religious practices basic and common to pagan and Jewish observance alike, all equally inadequate.

The last two references to *stoicheia* fall in Col. 2:8 and 20. Since the correct interpretation of *stoicheia* is so context-dependent, we must first be clear about the occasion of Paul's writing. M. D. Hooker has recently argued that the famous "Colossian error" is an invention of scholars.[76] Paul (or one of his disciples) does not upbraid the Colossians for holding heretical views. He praises them for their love, obedience, and harmony (1:4; 4:12). He rejoices "to see your good order and the firmness of your faith in Christ" (2:5). The cautionary notes are all warnings to avoid certain beliefs and behaviors, not to repent of them (with the possible exception of 2:20, but see below). No one in Colossae is singled out as an opponent, nor are there any signs of parties or factions dividing the church.

Instead, Paul is intent on preparing the Colossians in advance for a

76. "Were There False Teachers in Colossae?" in B. Lindars and S. S. Smalley, eds., *Christ and the Spirit in the New Testament* (New York and Cambridge: Cambridge University Press, 1973), 315–31. Similarly *A&P*, 77–85. I agree that there were no false teachers *in* Colossae, but part company with these authors in believing that there was a real and present danger of their *arriving* in Colossae

possible incursion of Judaizers of the sort we found in Galatians. They are characterized as skilled in rhetoric: *pithanalogia* in 2:4 is a technical term from rhetoric, referring to skill in using probable arguments, making demonstrations, speaking persuasively. In rhetoric this became a game, however; the verb form *pithanopoieō* meant merely "to sharpen the wits." The Greek historian Arrian (second century C.E) reflects the general repugnance at the degeneration of rhetoric to mere show when he, like the author of Colossians, uses a form of the term to mean "specious arguments" (*Epict.* I,8.7). Paul felt particularly disadvantaged by writers and speakers trained formally in rhetoric, not knowing he was creating a wholly new style of direct, unadorned, honest speech and writing that would irreversibly alter the history of letters.[77]

Note that these orators have not yet arrived on the scene; Paul's warning is made so that no one *might* delude them with beguiling speech (Col. 2:4). The epistle is a vaccination against heresy, not an antibiotic for those already afflicted. Likewise in 2:8—one of the verses where our term *stoicheia* appears—his injunction is a warning, not a rebuke: "Make sure that no one traps you and deprives you of your freedom by some secondhand, empty, rational philosophy based on the principles of this world (*stoicheia tou kosmou*) instead of on Christ" (JB). What kind of philosophy is this? Everything has been proposed from popular neo-Pythagoreanism[78] to mystery religions[79] to that syncretistic meld of mysticism and speculation that burst full-blown on the second century as gnosticism.[80] That it was syncretistic is probable; that it involved ascetic practices and a rigorously Judaizing Christianity is beyond question.

Apparently there were some Jewish-Christian evangelists working the area whose message was characterized by an unusually philosophical bent

77. 1 Cor. 1:17–25; 2:1–13; 3:18–20; 2 Cor. 10:5; 11:6; and esp. 2 Cor. 10:10—Paul's opponents claim that "his bodily presence is weak, and his speech is contemptible" (translation mine). See the comments of the classicist W. R. Halliday on the impact of the Pauline epistolary style (*The Pagan Background of Early Christianity* [Liverpool: Liverpool University Press, 1925], 194–202), and Edwyn Bevan, *Hellenism and Christianity* (London: George Allen & Unwin, 1921), 70ff.

78. Eduard Schweizer, "Die 'Elemente der Welt' in Gal. 4,3.9; Kol. 2,8.20," in *Verborum Veritas: Festschrift für Gustav Stählin zum 70. Geburtstag*, ed. Otto Böcher and Klaus Haacher (Wuppertal: Theologischer Verlag Rolf Brockhaus, 1970), 245–59.

79. *A&P*, 82, referring to worship of Sabazius, Attis, or Dionysus.

80. H.-M. Schenke, "Der Widerstreit gnostischer und kirchlicher Christologie im Spiegel des Kol," *ZThK* 61 (1964): 391ff. Since Paul does not specify any particular philosophical school, it is more likely that he is referring to philosophy in general, the task of which, according to Varro, was to concern itself with the physical gods, or first principles of nature (cited by Augustine *City of God* 4.27; 6.5).

and who were skilled in the arts of rhetoric. Alexandrine Christianity is reported to have made inroads in the near vicinity, and Apollos, its spokesman, was gifted rhetorically (Acts 18:24—19:7). Perhaps the preaching that Paul is attempting to ward off in Colossae is related to the kind of philosophical speculation so common in Alexandria, wedded to a peculiarly mystical and ascetic brand of Jewish Christianity.

In that context, how is *stoicheia* used? In Col. 2:8 it seems to refer to the philosophical search for the first elements or founding principles of the physical universe. *Stoicheion* had long since become synonymous with *archē* in the sense of "first principle,"[81] and the Colossians hymn stresses that Christ is not only prior to all the *archai* but is himself the firstborn of all creation (1:15–16). All the *archai* exist in and through and for him (1:16). He is before all things, the head of the body (the church), the firstborn from the dead (1:18), preeminent in everything. In short, Christ is the *archē* of the whole creation. Against those who might be inclined to set Christ alongside other basic elements or principles, Paul repeats in 2:10—"[Christ] is the head of every *archēs* and *exousias.*" Christ alone is the first principle of the universe. Thus *stoicheia* here seems to refer to the basic principles or constituent elements of reality, to which some people (at least according to the reports that have reached Paul's ears) are apparently granting an ultimacy that threatens the sole sufficiency of Christ.

As early as the fifth century B.C.E., Empedocles had argued that those elements which are original and constitutive of reality deserve the name "gods," since everything is made from them. He called the fire Zeus, the air Hera, and so forth. There was no unanimity as to which god represented which element. Others identified not Zeus but Hestia or Hephaestos with fire. The elements are more like attributes or characteristics of the gods as such. The divinization of the elements was a commonplace in the whole Greco-Roman period. Philo is witness to its currency in the first century C.E.: "For some have deified the four elements (*archas*), earth, water, air, and fire" (*De dec.* 53),[82] and Clement of Alexandria

81. Delling, "Stoicheion," 672; Arnold Ehrhardt, *The Beginning: A Philosophical Approach to the Concept of Creation from Anaximander to St. John* (Manchester: Manchester University Press, 1968). Various philosophical solutions had been offered concerning the first principles of the universe. Plato, the Stoics, the LXX, the New Testament, and the rabbis all considered the basic building blocks of the universe to be earth, air, fire, and water. Aristotle, however, proposed two sets of polarities as more fundamental still: hot and cold, dryness and moisture. Democritus, for his part, reduced everything that exists to atoms. The idea of basic elements is not offensive to Paul, of course. The problem is their idolization as ultimate.

82. Wis. Sol. 13:2 reflects on the failure of humanity to discern God in the unques-

mounts a major assault on the notion in his remarkable commentary on Col. 2:8:

Let us now, if you like, run through the opinions which the philosophers, on their part, assert confidently about the gods. Perchance we may find philosophy herself, through vanity, forming her conceptions of the godhead out of matter; or else we may be able to show in passing that when deifying certain divine powers, she sees the truth in a dream. Some philosophers, then, left us the elements (*stoicheia*) as first principles (*archas*) of all things. Water was selected for praise by Thales of Miletus; air by Anaximenes of the same city, who was followed afterwards by Diogenes of Apollonia. Fire and earth were introduced as gods by Parmenides of Elea; but only one of this pair, namely fire, is god according to the supposition of both Hippasus of Metapontum and Heracleitus of Ephesus. As to Empedocles of Acragas, he chooses plurality, and reckons "love" and "strife" in his list of gods, in addition to these four elements (*stoicheia*).

These men also were really atheists, since with a foolish show of wisdom they worshipped matter. They did not, it is true, honour stocks or stones, but they made a god out of earth, which is the mother of these. They do not fashion a Poseidon, but they adore water itself. For what in the world is Poseidon, except a kind of liquid substance named from *posis*, drink? . . . Let the philosophers therefore confess that Persians, Sauromatians, and Magi are their teachers, from whom they have learnt the atheistic doctrine of their venerated "first principles" (*archōn*). The great original, the maker of all things, and creator of the "first principles" themselves, God without beginning, they know not, but offer adoration to these "weak and beggarly elements," as the apostle calls them, made for the service of men.[83]

Modern Christians, for most of whom religion is tantamount to a personal relationship with a personal God, have had difficulty appreciating the impersonality of such divinized elements. Translators and commentators insist on treating as animate personal beings what for the ancients were inanimate principles. For them, divinity implied not personality but primacy, not an indwelling presence but ultimacy. That which is "first"

---

tionable beauty of creation: "But either fire, or wind, or swift air, or circling stars, or raging water, or luminaries of heaven, they thought to be gods that rule the world." Of the four elements, only earth is omitted here.

83. *Exhort. to the Greeks* 5 (trans. G. W. Butterworth, LCL 92 [Cambridge, Mass.: Harvard University Press, 1960]). It is not surprising that the gnostics, with their hatred of matter, virtually ignored the elements and certainly refused them veneration. In the *NHL* I have found only one reference, *Trim. Prot.* 43:8, where the elements of the physical universe tremble at the birth of the Redeemer, which heralds their destruction. It is significant that they are not personified; they are evil simply by virtue of their material existence.

(*archē*) is deserving of worship.[84] That is why Col. 1:15–20 stresses Christ's primacy over the entire created order.

In Col. 2:20, on the other hand, *stoicheia* has a quite different sense. The intervening verses have dealt with the teaching of the roving Judaizers. In 2:20 Paul addresses the Colossians with the hypothetical question "If with Christ you died to the elements of the universe, why do you live in the world as if you were still being dictated to by rules and regulations?"[85] Here alone in the epistle his anxiety that they will succumb to the traveling evangelists clouds the picture; he reproves them for an act which elsewhere in the letter they are warned to avoid![86] He does not want them to turn back. Since they were previously pagans, *stoicheia* can only refer to the rites and practices of paganism, to which they died in baptism, and to which they will in fact revert if they accept the program of the Judaizers. So here *stoicheia* means the same as it meant in Galatians: the elements common to religion, pagan and Jewish alike.

The word "religion" is itself anachronistic here, however. Paul means something far more fundamental than voluntary beliefs and practices; he means the inescapably necessary way we identify and relate to what we conceive to be most fundamental in existence. No one can avoid such an orientation. But if one is oriented to a subsystem rather than the whole, the result is a kind of slavery and the forfeiture of life. As partial truths the "elements" of philosophy or piety contain a "shadow" (2:17) of reality, but they all end in the attempt to lay claim on God by reason (2:8), ritual (2:11, 16), or self-mortification (2:20–23). Paul wants the Colossians to stay "dead" to such human strivings and not shed the chains of paganism only to stumble headlong into slavery to precepts taken from the Jewish Law.

Stoicheia in Col. 2:20 is thus given fairly precise definition by its context. It is the whole bundle of practices and beliefs that provide one's basic orientation to life. It is those rudimentary notions and ritualized acts and socially required behaviors that characterize all human life, in

84. Tertullian comments in exasperation on "the demons and the spirits of angelic apostates," who "would turn into idolatry all the elements (*elementa*), all the garniture of the universe, all things contained in the heaven, in the sea, in the earth, that they might be consecrated as God, in opposition to God" (*De Idol.* 4, ostensibly quoting *1 Enoch*).

85. Author's translation.

86. Hooker attempts to circumvent this problem by reading *dogmatizesthe* as "Why subject yourselves?" or "Why submit?"—i.e., to any attempt which might be made to impose such regulations—rather than "Why *do* you subject yourselves?" ("False Teachers in Colossae?" 317). But the latter is the more natural reading.

whatever society. Whereas in Col. 2:8 *stoicheia* seems to focus more on the specific threat of a Judaizing form of Christianity which is making the rounds and includes a syncretistic and speculative emphasis on the elements as first principles of reality, in 2:20 it is extended to encompass both paganism and the new threat. In each case the meaning is specified only by the context.

Looking back over our survey, we see *stoicheia* used in the following ways:

- The ABCs, the elementary or first principles of faith—Heb. 5:12, and Gal. 4:9 in part
- The constituent elements of the physical universe—2 Pet. 3:10, 12
- The basic constituents of religious existence common to Jews and Gentiles alike (rituals, festivals, laws, beliefs)—Gal. 4:3, 9; Col. 2:20
- The first elements or founding principles of the physical universe—Col. 2:8

The first-century reader was apparently expected to grasp each of these meanings immediately, on the basis of clues given by the authors in each context. We have labored to conclude where they began: with the understanding of *stoicheia* as a formal category for whatever is most fundamentally constitutive of a thing.

The theological issue, as it emerges in Paul's use of the term, focuses on the problem of idolatry. What is most basic to existence begins to be worshiped, either overtly or, as more often happens, unconsciously, as people abandon themselves to religious practices or philosophical ideals or ideological principles. When that happens, the *stoicheia* become functional gods, and their devotees are alienated from the One in and through and for whom even these most basic things in existence were created. (The practical implications of the worship of *stoicheia* will be explored in volume 2, *Unmasking the Powers*.)

Colossians 2:9–10

For in him the whole fulness of deity dwells bodily, and you have come to fulness of life in him, who is the head of all rule (*archēs*) and authority (*exousias*).

If *stoicheia tou kosmou* in Col. 2:8 refers to the first principles or constituent elements of the world and is synonymous with the philosophical use of *archē,* and if the stress on Christ as the *archē* of all things in the Christ hymn of 1:15–20 is meant to scotch any attempt to posit some other first principles as ultimate, then *archē* in 2:10 must also refer to the search for the first principles of creation. Its pairing with *exousia*, however, can only be an allusion back to the Powers listed in the hymn (1:16). Christ is the head, not only of every first principle but also of every authority; in conjunction with "human tradition" and "philosophy" in 2:8 one thinks of the authority ascribed to or claimed for the various philosophical teachings passed down along a chain of teachers. But since the term "philosophy" had in the context of Hellenistic syncretism been extended to include virtually every tradition of teaching (including the various parties within Judaism[87] and even Judaism itself,[88] to say nothing of mystery cults and magical groups[89]), "authority" would signify any rival teaching that lays claim to ultimacy. This would include even those who might lay claim to be the authentic transmitters of the teachings of Jesus of Nazareth (see Gal. 1:6–9; 2 Cor. 11:1–6). That the teaching Paul has in mind here is a kind of Judaizing Christianity can be seen at a glance from the sets of items he singles out for censure in Colossians 2:

Religious Ritual

Circumcision (v. 11)
Festivals, new moon,
    sabbath (v. 16)
Self-abasement (vv. 18, 21–23)
Worship of or with angels
    (v. 18)
Dependence on visions (v. 18)

Religious Rules

Legal demands (v. 14)
Jewish food laws (v. 16)
Regulations (v. 20)
Prohibitions (v. 21)

Belief Systems

Philosophy (v. 8)
Human tradition (v. 8)
Human precepts and
    doctrines (v.22)

Powers

Elements of the world
    (vv. 8, 20)
All rule and authority (v. 10)
Principalities and powers
    (v. 15)
Angels (v. 18)
Flesh (v. 23)

Against all these Paul places Christ; he is "the head of all rule and

87. Jos., *Ant.* 18.11–25.
88. 4 Macc. 5:11; Philo, *De leg.* 245.
89. Eduard Lohse, *Die Briefe an die Kolosser und an Philemon* (Göttingen: Vandenhoeck & Ruprecht, 1968), 144.

authority'' (v. 10). "Rule" here seems to mean rules, rituals, and belief systems, and "authority" seems to mean the spiritual power that adheres to them, investing them with transcendent status and the capacity to impose themselves as normative for life. We seem to be dealing not so much with spiritual beings as with the spiritual power exerted by religious traditions and teachings. "The Law says," "Moses says," "God has commanded that"—these are the kinds of constraints these evangelists would lay on their hearers.

Suppose we try to imagine the inner debate Paul is carrying on with these Judaizing Christians as he formulates his argument, not just in Col. 2:10, but from 2:8 right through 3:11, for we cannot understand Paul's attitude toward the Powers here in isolation from the larger context in which they appear. If we can grasp the inner dynamic of the author's treatment of the Powers in this section, perhaps we will be better able to interpret—and engage—the Powers when they manifest themselves elsewhere.

Paul must know the ideas of these opponents fairly well, if only from Galatia. This is the kind of thing they are apparently going around saying:

"But the Law requires circumcision!"

To which Paul responds, "No! You were circumcized with a circumcision made without hands [v. 11].''

"But the Law is one of the *archai,* created before the world itself was made, by means of which and for which the world itself was fashioned.[90] It cannot be abridged, it must be obeyed!"

"No! Christ is the *archē,* the world was created in and through and for him [1:15–16]. And if we have died and been buried with Christ in baptism, we have been freed from our sins through faith in Christ, not through Law. The IOU signed in self-incrimination by our own guilty consciences has been canceled and nailed to the cross. The chief priests, the elders and scribes, all the religious leaders who put him to death are now unmasked, shown to love religion more than truth. Pilate, the soldiers, and Rome itself are all unmasked for worshiping power instead of God. Behind them, the Law, the Temple, the State, all the legitimations of the status quo, are unmasked, revealed as resisting the truly legitimate reign of God. All these Powers are now stripped naked by the cross for

---

90. In Jewish thought the Law was identified with Wisdom (*Sifre Deut.* 11:10) and thus seen as the agent of creation (*Pirqe Avoth* 3:19) and that for which the world was created (*Gen. Rab.* 12:2). The parallels with Col. 1:15–16 are striking. See W. D. Davies, *Paul and Rabbinic Judaism,* 4th ed. (Philadelphia: Fortress Press, 1980), 147–76. Davies gives the evidence for his assertion that this identification was already commonplace in first-century Palestine.

all humanity to see. Therefore we do not concede them final status any more [2:12–15]."

"But the law enjoins Jewish food regulations[91] and the organization of all of life by means of a (perhaps special) Jewish calendar. Faith in Christ is not enough by itself; it must be integrated into a system of religious practices that touches every aspect of life. There must be annual festivals, observances around the new moon, the keeping of the sabbath. The church cannot avoid this if it is to reach into the whole of a people's life."

"Yes, but these rituals and practices are not the reality but only a shadow, and where they are stressed they invariably are made the reality itself. Hold fast to Christ [vv. 17, 19]."

"But we are not so foolish as to substitute ritual for the divine reality. Worship is a means, not an end. Our goal is the attainment of a vision of the divine throne-chariot that Ezekiel, Daniel, Enoch, and the other great worthies saw. We mortify the flesh by fasting;[92] we silence the cries of the body; we starve the carnal appetite in order to whet it for heavenly food. Our sole desire is to join the angelic chorus in the high heavens in singing the Thrice-Holy before the throne."[93]

"No! Those of you who have been graced with such visions are treating

---

91. There may be a hint of Essene influence on Paul's opponents, since their concern for normal Jewish requirements extends to drink as well. The Essenes regarded drink as even more susceptible to contamination than food. See Geza Vermes, *The Dead Sea Scrolls* (Philadelphia: Fortress Press, 1981), 96; and on Essene influence on the opponents headed for Colossae, see Herbert Braun, "Qumran und das Neue Testament: Eine Bericht über 10 Jahre Forschung (1950–1959)," *ThR* 29 (1963): 245–53; E. Yamauchi, "Qumran and Colossae," *Bib Sac* 121 (1964): 141–52; E. W. Saunders, "The Colossian Heresy and Qumran Theology," in *Studies in the History and Text of the New Testament* (Salt Lake City: University of Utah Press, 1967), 133–45. However, the Essenes and sectarian Jewish groups generally followed a solar calendar, whereas the people Paul is attacking apparently subscribe to a lunar calendar ("new moons," 2:16) such as that of establishment Judaism.

92. *Tapeinophrosynē* (2:18) is a technical term for fasting in Hermas, *Vis.* 3.10.6; *Sim.* 5.3.7, according to C. F. D. Moule (*The Epistles of Paul the Apostle to the Colossians and to Philemon*, CGTC [Cambridge: Cambridge University Press, 1962], 104). Fasting is used to induce visions in many religious traditions.

93. F. O. Francis has offered this appealing interpretation of the phrase "worship of angels," reading it not as an objective genitive (with the angels the object of worship) but as a subjective genitive (the worship the angels offer). The aim of the visionary or ecstatic is to share in the heavenly liturgy "of the angels," as Isaiah (Isaiah 6) and the Seer of the Apocalypse (Revelation 4–5) and apparently Paul himself (2 Cor. 12:1–10) had done. The case is not conclusive. Hebrews 1–2, Rev. 22:8–9, *Asc. Isa.* 7:21, and the *Kerygma Petrou* (in Clement of Alexandria, *Strom.* VI.5.39–41) certainly suggest that the possibility of angel worship was real, so that could possibly be the problem alluded to in Colossians. (See F. O. Francis, "Humility and Angelic Worship in Col. 2:18," *ST* 16 [1962]: 109–34; and A. T. Lincoln, *Paradise Now and Not Yet*, SNTSMS 43 [Cambridge and New York: Cambridge University Press, 1981], 112.)

them as personal achievements gained by your own piety and heroic self-denial. You flaunt your experiences before the church, boasting in what should have leveled your pride once and for all. You judge others to be unworthy, inferior, deficient in their Christian experience if they have not attained to your vision. You threaten to split the church into first- and second-class members. You make an experience the criterion of salvation rather than faith. You have turned the religious life into a work of mystical ascent. You no longer hold to the Head, who is Christ, whose descent alone matters for salvation and whose will is that the church be a single healthy organism in which every part nourishes and upbuilds the other parts. Your spiritualism does not build up the Body, but tears it apart; it is merely a disguised form of egocentric one-upsmanship [vv. 18–19]."

"But you are only objecting to the misuse of valid experiences and indispensable practices. All religions have taught the value of self-discipline, mortification of the flesh, the silencing of the ego. You have relaxed the demands of true religion by making faith easily available to all. You jettison the Law only to open wide the door for Gentile converts, who have not even taken on themselves the minimum standards of decency. They must take on the yoke of the Law in order to conform their whole lives to the will of God revealed in Christ Jesus."

"No! You have confused the struggle against the 'flesh' with the struggle against pleasure and the body. The arrogance with which you bandy your piety about shows that your very asceticism is an exercise in boasting. You are not giving up your 'I' but merely affirming its power over the natural instincts. The 'flesh,' however, is that whole way of living which sets the 'I' at the center. Your prohibitions 'Do not eat, do not enjoy, do not consume' do nothing to break the dominance of the 'I'; rather they confirm it, under a show of devotion and rigor and self-abasement. You have substituted ego-conquest for ego-surrender. You are no different from a hedonist, or those Gentiles you despise as lacking minimum standards of decency [vv. 20–23]."

"But," our imagined Paul continues, "let a person die with Christ to all these basic principles and rules of behavior ['elements of the world,' v. 20] and that person will know from the heart what it means to love God and the neighbor. You seek visions? Then focus on Christ, seated at the right hand of God [3:1]. You do not need to try to ascend to that throne, however; you have been established there already. If the old ego has died, your life is hid with Christ in God [3:3; see 1:27; 2:6]. Your instincts are right: put to death what is earthly in you, and you will not be tempted to play the spiritual virtuoso [3:5]. Not visions, but actual new behavior is the sign that you have put off the old ego with its practices and have put on the new humanity, which grows in stature not by personal achievement but by the inner work of God [3:6–10]. Before God there can be no longer Greek or Jew, nor does it matter whether we circumcise or not. All that matters is that Christ be all and in all [3:11]."

In the light of this extended "archaeology of the opposition" and paraphrase of our author's response, the Powers from which Paul would protect his Colossian correspondents are not evil spirits in the sky, but philosophy, tradition, rules and rituals, food laws and ascetic practices, the basic elements of religion, and even the good angels. None of these Powers is evil in itself. All can even be useful aids. The author himself counsels self-mortification (3:5), religious rituals (baptism, 2:12; singing psalms and hymns and spiritual songs, 3:16; acts of prayer and thanksgiving, 1:12; 4:2–3), and makes rules (3:18—4:1). They become dangerous only when they become ends in themselves, or divisive, or egocentric, or divert the believer from union with Christ—as they of course were to do in Christianity every bit as much as in Judaism.

Earlier we listed as one of our criteria the fact that the terms for power in the New Testament are interchangeable to a degree, and that one or a pair or a series can be made to represent them all. This is clearly the case with *stoicheia tou kosmou* in Col. 2:20 and *archai kai exousiai* in 2:15. Yet in each case these terms are also given specific focus by their context. It would appear then that the Powers are understood to operate as a single front of opposition to God but that in any given moment they are discernible only in a particular historical manifestation. The New Testament is not fond of the spiritualistic reductionism of later Christendom, which limited the Powers to hostile spirits in the air. The New Testament prefers to speak of the Powers only in their concretions, their structural inertia, their physical embodiments in history. The Powers that Paul was most concerned with did not fly; they were carved in stone.

Ephesians 2:1–2

And you he made alive, when you were dead through the trespasses and sins in which you once walked,
  following the course (*aiōna*)
    of this world,
  following the prince (*archonta*)
    of the power (*exousias*) of the air (*aeros*),
    of the spirit that is now at work in the sons of disobedience.[94]

94. Author's translation. "Sons of disobedience" is a Semitism meaning the whole class of those thus described.

I have translated literally and graphically in order to indicate the parallelism of subordinate clauses. "World," "power," and "spirit" are thus clearly seen to be in parallel genitive clauses[95] and refer not to personified beings but to a world-atmosphere presided over by Satan.

Many exegetes, and with them the NEB, take *exousia* here as a collective expression, equivalent to "the spiritual powers whose dwelling is the air." But the author is perfectly capable of producing the plural of *exousia* (3:10; 6:12); apparently the singular carries the intended meaning. It cannot then refer to hosts of demons in the sky; it refers instead to an atmosphere that envelops people and seals their fate. In parallelism with "world" and "spirit" it seems to mean the quality of alienated existence, the general spiritual climate that influences humanity, in which we live, and move, and lose our beings. We breathe it, absorb it, and drink it in as the normative definition of our possibilities. *Exousia* here is not personified but abstract. It represents the subjectivity of a world epoch (*aion*), the spirituality of the age, the permissions, license, restrictions, advices, and restraints imposed by the times we live in.

And imposed also by their prince (*archōn*). For Satan is here made master of this age. To follow nothing more malignant than the mere course of this world thus is deadly. We "were dead," because the total world-system is a conspiracy against God, a lie perpetuated by people and presided over by Satan. We "were dead" because we were born into such a world and never had any other options. "Dead," because having taken in its deadly vapors, we breathe them out on others; we become its carriers, passing it into our institutions, structures, and systems even as these have reciprocally passed on the same deadly fumes to us.

This sense of evil as a cultural and spiritual legacy which is contagious marks a radical step away from the mythicization of evil in personified demonic spirits. To some degree the language of power here has been demythologized, although it remains highly metaphorical. It is not at all clear whether the idea that demons reside in the air was even current in the New Testament period. None of our sources gives evidence for the idea of *evil* spirits in the air prior to the time of Paul.[96] Whether the image

95. The NEB and JB incorrectly read "spirit" as synonymous with "prince."
96. Hesiod reflected popular belief when he wrote, "Three times ten thousand immortal watchers does Zeus possess on the all-nourishing earth for men, who observe decisions of law and unwholesome deeds and go about the whole earth clothed in air" (*Works and Days* 252–253). Likewise Posidonius and Xenocrates. (Cited by Martin Hengel, *Judaism and Hellenism* [Philadelphia: Fortress Press, 1974], 233.) But none of these are evil. Philo refers to spirits in the air, but his too are wholly good (*De gig.* 6–7; *De somn.* I.135; *De spec. leg.* II.45; *De conf.* 174; *De plant.* 14). Rev. 12:3 speaks of the Dragon "in heaven"; this would be better translated, "in the sky," that is, the firmament, the

was current or not, however, the author of Ephesians does not go down that road. He uses the figure of the "power of the air" to specify not the locale of demons but the world-atmosphere, which Satan exploits for our destruction. The *exousia* of the air is not then to be classed with personified spiritual powers, such as the *archōn* who rules over it. It is rather the invisible dominion or realm created by the sum total of choices for evil. It is the spiritual matrix of inauthentic living. It is the "surround" constellated by fields of forces in rebellion against God. It is nothing other than what Paul called "the spirit of the cosmos" (1 Cor. 2:12), a pseudo-environment that ascribes to itself absoluteness and permanence and thus, *by simply appearing to be*, wins from all who submit to it their total and unwitting obedience. It is, in short, what we mean today by such terms as ideologies, the *Zeitgeist*, customs, public opinion, peer pressure, institutional expectations, mob psychology, jingoistic patriotism, and negative vibes. These constitute "the power of the air," the invisible but palpable environment of opinions, beliefs, propaganda, convictions, prejudices, hatreds, racial and class biases, taboos, and loyalties that condition our perception of the world long before we reach the age of choice, often before we reach the age of speech. It "kills" us precisely because we "breathe" it in before we even realize it is noxious. Like fish in water, we are not even aware that it exists, much less that it determines the way we think, speak, and act. To seem not to appear is part of its essence, as Schlier put it.[97] So invisible are its assaults, in fact, that only a special coat of invisible arms can protect even those who have been made aware of and delivered from it. I refer, of course, to the "panoply of God's armor" spoken of in Eph. 6:10–20.

Ephesians 6:12

For we are not contending against flesh and blood, but against the principalities (*archas*), against the powers (*exousias*), against the world rulers (*kosmokratoras*) of this present darkness, against the spiritual hosts (*pneumatika*) of wickedness in the heavenly places.

---

lower heaven of the "fixed stars" (G. Quispel, *The Secret Book of Revelation* [New York: McGraw-Hill, 1979], 77). That is the extent of our first-century witnesses, only one of which refers to evil spirits in the air, and it is from around 95 C.E. The other references are all second century or later: *Asc. Isa.* 10:30; 7:9–12; Origen, *Exhortatio ad martyr.*, 45; *2 Enoch* 29:5 (A only); *Test. Benj.* 3:4 (S¹ only), *Mag. Pap.* V,2698ff.; IV,1135; IV,1115; V,164ff. (*PGM* 1:158, 110; *PGM* 1 = Papyrus-Berlin 5025); *Test. Sol.* 20: 12; Athenagoras, *Suppl.* 25:1; *NHL Asclepius 21–29* (73:18 and 76:22–29). Carr is thus correct when he says that the idea of the lower air being peopled with hostile forces is one that postdates the thought of Paul (*A&P*, 64, 146).

97. *Principalities and Powers*, 29.

This text is the *locus classicus* for the demonic interpretation of the powers; indeed, no other interpretation except the demonic is possible.[98] *Kosmokratores* is used for the first time here, so far as we know, and clearly refers to demonic beings. Parallels are all quite late and on the whole derive from this text. Its meaning here is to be sought in its parallelism with *archai, exousiai,* and *pneumatika.* Here once again we have what is essentially a series, a heaping up of terms to describe the ineffable, invisible world-enveloping reach of a spiritual network of powers inimical to life. The very intention of series such as this, as we have seen repeatedly, is to be comprehensive. We must include here, then, all the *archai* and *exousiai* we have encountered, not only divine but human, not only personified but structural, not only demons and kings but the world atmosphere and power invested in institutions, laws, traditions and rituals as well, for it is the cumulative, totalizing effect of all these taken together that creates the sense of bondage to a "dominion of darkness" (see Col. 1:13) presided over by higher powers. *Kosmokratores* would be similarly those who have mastery over the world, both those humans who by all the marks of aristocracy, education, political skill, and wealth seem to be of a higher order than ourselves, and those other powers, both above and below the range of visibility, from the world elements which determine its physical composition to those higher instructions which regulate the growth of plants or the revolution of the heavens. We must not neglect to mention here the spirit of empire, which perpetuates itself through a succession of rulers and which was so powerful, in the case of Rome, that it was able to sustain the madness of three emperors in one century (Caligula, Nero, Domitian). Nor can we leave aside all forms of institutional idolatry, whereby religion, commerce, education, and state make their own well-being and survival the final criteria of morality, and by which they justify the liquidation of prophets, the persecution of deviants, and the ostracism of opponents.

So formidable a phalanx of hostility demands spiritual weaponry, for it is clear that we contend not against human beings as such ("blood and flesh") but against the legitimations, seats of authority, hierarchical systems, ideological justifications, and punitive sanctions which their human incumbents exercise and which transcend these incumbents in both time and power. It is the suprahuman dimension of power in institutions and

98. Even Carr acknowledges this and excises the verse from the text in order to get around its devastating effect on his thesis that all the Powers are good angels. This desperate expedient is taken without any support in the manuscript tradition and with only a string of pseudo-problems fabricated as an excuse for surgery (*A&P*, 104–10).

the cosmos which must be fought, not the mere human agent. For the institution will guarantee the replacement of *this* person with another virtually the same, who despite personal preferences will replicate decisions made by a whole string of predecessors because that is what the institution requires for its survival. It is this suprahuman quality which accounts for the apparent "heavenly," bigger than life, quasi-eternal character of the Powers.

Against such we are advised to put on the whole armor of God.[99] It is humorous to watch the statement bob from scholar to scholar that the weapons listed here are all "defensive." The Pentagon says the same about nuclear missiles. The terms employed are taken straight from the legionnaire's equipment, and the metaphor is of the church like the Roman wedge, the most efficient and terrifying military formation known up to that time and for some thousand years after.

Armaments were both offensive and defensive.[100] The shield, helmet, breastplate, and greaves (for girding the loins) were for protection against blows. For attacking, the legionnaire had two seven-foot javelins (the *pilum*), which he threw at the beginning of the charge. These had soft metal points that bent and stuck in opponents' shields, rendering them too heavy to wield. Then when the lines closed the legionnaire used the short two-edged *gladius* (Gk., *machaira*[101]) to thrust up under the enemy's shield and disembowel him. In such close quarters the long swords used by most of Rome's enemies were rendered ineffective.

In addition the legionnaire carried a knife in his girdle. He did not carry the *hasta*, or thrusting spear;[102] that and the longer sword (the *spatha*) were carried by the auxiliaries for mopping-up operations. The round shield of the early legionnaires had long since been elongated (the *scutum*);

99. A first sketch of this metaphor appears as early as 1 Thess. 5:8—"Put on the breastplate of faith and love, and for a helmet the hope of salvation." See also Rom. 13:12—"Put on the armor of light."

100. Harold Mattingly calls the sword and dagger "offensive armour" (*Roman Imperial Civilization* [New York: St. Martin's Press, 1957], 144). Dionysius of Halicarnassus (XIV,9[13]) says of the Roman outfittings: "Some of them being protective armour, such as not to yield readily to blows, and others offensive, of a sort to pierce through any defense."

101. The Vulgate renders *machairos* here by *gladius*, indicating that the legionnaire's sword was specifically in mind.

102. As Carr alleges, *A&P*, 105 n. 38. The general's select bodyguard carried the *hasta*, as well as the round shield, a sign that they were outfitted in the traditional, earlier weaponry of the Republic (see Josephus, *War* 3.94–96). But regular soldiers no longer used them.

two-thirds covered his body and one-third covered his comrade to the left. This brilliant innovation encouraged tight ranks, since each fighter was in part dependent on his neighbor for protection.[103]

The author of Ephesians omits the *pilum* (javelin) and *pugio* (dagger), but the dagger may be implied by "girding up the loins," and the *pilum* was more for disarming than killing the enemy.[104] Their absence does nothing to turn the *gladius* into a "defensive" weapon. It was the centerpiece of the Roman army's devastating military efficiency.[105]

The repeated use of "stand" has perhaps contributed to the idea that the Christian is not on the attack so much as trying to keep from being overwhelmed. Chrysostom, who was familiar with legionary ways, clarifies the sense of this.

> The very first feature in tactics is, to know how to stand well, and many things will depend upon that. . . . Doubtless then he [Paul] does not mean merely any way of standing, but a correct way, and as many as have had experience in wars know how to stand. For if in the case of boxers and wrestlers, the trainer recommends this before anything else, namely, to stand firm, much more will it be the first thing in warfare, and military matters.[106]

"Stand" in vv. 11 and 14 has the sense of the "drawing up a military formation for combat"; in v. 13 it refers to the triumphant stance of the victor.[107] In the latter verse it is linked with *katergasamenoi;* Bauer translates, "after *proving victorious* over everything, to stand your

---

103. Aelius Aristides, *Roman Oration* 84, trans. J. H. Oliver, *The Ruling Power* (Philadelphia: American Philological Society, 1953), 904. See also H. M. D. Parker, *The Roman Legions* (Oxford: Clarendon Press, 1928), 250ff.; Graham Webster, *The Roman Imperial Army* (London: A. & C. Black, 1969), 24ff., 123–30, 222; Lynn Montross, *War through the Ages* (New York: Harper & Brothers, 1944), 45, 73; James L. Jones, "The Roman Army," in Stephen Benko and John J. O'Rourke, *Early Church History* (London: Oliphant, 1972), 187–217.

104. In Ignatius's use of the military metaphor, he significantly does not include the spear *(doru)* among the arms *(hopla)* *(To Polycarp* 6.2).

105. Conceivably the description is that of a gladiator, who fought without the *pilum*, but were gladiators that well known in the East? Had the author been forewarned about the "incompleteness" of his metaphor, I suspect he would have hastened to add, "Oh, yes, and take the javelin of hope and the dagger of commitment . . . ," or something of the sort.

106. *Hom. on Eph.*, 23. See LSJ, p. 1634: *Stasis* ("a stand") was used technically of a military formation (Ascl. *Tact.* 5.1). It could also designate a revolt (Mark 15:7; Luke 23:19, 25).

107. Erich Haupt, *Die Gefangenschaftsbriefe* (KEK) (Göttingen: Vandenhoeck & Ruprecht, 1897).

ground.''[108] The writer has no notion here of Christian life as a last-ditch, rear-guard, defensive operation; this is war with the powers of evil. He depicts the church taking the fight to the enemy, and *he expects the church to win.* It was precisely its sovereign freedom from terror before the Powers, its success in exorcisms and healings, its transcendence of conditioning and its indifference even before death that won the church awe and admiration from the pagans and released a flood of converts. The early Christian *Odes of Solomon* are continuous then with the sentiments expressed in Ephesians when the believer sings that the Lord "gave me the rod of His power, that I might subdue the imaginations of the peoples; and the power of the men of might to bring them low: to make war by His word, and to take victory by His power" (29:7–9).

But for all that, this armor turns out to be strange armor indeed. Faith, the gospel of peace, the word of God, truth, salvation, and righteousness— these are not "weapons" in any usual sense of the word. It is a warfare to be waged with an enormous concentration of prayer (6:18–20, continuous with the weaponry metaphor). What good is truth—unless it is the way the Powers are finally unmasked? What use righteousness— unless it reveals God's true will for the world? What value salvation— unless the certainty of it is needed for reassurance in the moments of despair or darkness when the gathered might of the Powers makes doubt seem only sensible? What can the shield of faith do—unless we have learned to discern when flaming darts are aimed at our hearts, with their insinuations of inadequacy and guilt or their appeals to egotism and the worship of the golden calf? What good is a sword made only of words, in the face of such monolithic evil—unless evil is not nearly so much a physical phenomenon as a spiritual construct, itself born of words, and capable of destruction by the word of God? And why pray—unless that is the only way we can consolidate, by continual affirmation, the divine counterreality which alone is real, and freight it into being?

Against such evil the church is well advised to stand shoulder to shoulder, shields overlapping. Hence this instruction in armaments is issued in the plural throughout the paragraph. Not individuals but the whole people of God is addressed. Solitary efforts may at times be necessary, but far better when many, each individually equipped thus, can struggle (*palē,* 6:12) together and perhaps even "prove victorious over every-

---

108. Bauer cites as possible meanings of *katergazomai* "accomplish, bring about, produce, create, overpower, subdue, conquer" (BAG, pp. 422–423).

thing," whether dead or alive. All this, then, figures in the church's task vis-à-vis the Powers, a task which the next passage makes explicit.

Ephesians 3:10

. . . That through the church the manifold wisdom of God might now be made known to the principalities (*archais*) and powers (*exousiais*) in the heavenly places (*tois epouraniois*).

The church's task is articulated here as preaching to the Powers. It is engaged in a kind of spiritual warfare, but it also has a mission that carries the truth of the gospel into the very heart of power and expects some result. Are we then to envisage the *conversion* of the Powers? What is the church to tell them? Where are "the heavenly places," and how is the church to have access to Powers there?

None of these questions is easily answered. We will begin with the last. It is difficult to construct a consistent interpretation of all five of the uses of *ta epourania* in Ephesians. In Eph. 1:3 Christians are described as already blessed "in Christ with every spiritual blessing in the heavenly places"; in 2:6 they are described as already raised up with him and made to "sit with him in the heavenly places in Christ Jesus." Christ by his exaltation has been made to sit at God's right hand "in the heavenly places" (1:20). These all suggest that "the heavenlies" is that sphere where Christians, with one foot in each of two worlds, already experience the risen life in Christ.[109] That much, at least, seems undeniable. How then are we to relate to that meaning the other two: 3:10, where the church must preach to the Powers in the heavenlies, and 6:12, where the "spiritual hosts of wickedness" are located "in the heavenly places"? Its formulary repetition suggests that the phrase should probably mean the same thing each time it is used.[110] If that is the case, we must think of "the heavenlies" as a dimension of reality into which believers have already while on earth been admitted yet in which unredeemed Powers still exercise dominion and must be fought with, preached to, and made to know the manifold wisdom of God.

109. Carr, *A&P*, 98; see also Hugo Odeberg, *The View of the Universe in the Epistle to the Ephesians* (Lund: C. W. K. Gleerup, 1934).

110. A. T. Lincoln, "A Re-examination of 'the Heavenlies' in Ephesians," *NTS* 19 (1973): 468–83. See also R. M. Pope, "Studies in Pauline Vocabulary: Of the Heavenly Places," *ExpTim* 23 (1912): 365–68; E. Percy, *Die Problem der Kolosser- und Ephes-erbriefe* (Lund: C. W. K. Gleerup, 1946), 81ff.; F. Mussner, *Christus das All und die Kirche* (Trier: Paulinus Verlag, 1955), 9–12.

The Jewish heaven was not the perfect heaven of later Christian cosmology, but there was no unanimity on how far up the levels of heaven evil powers were allowed to reach. *Asc. Isa.* 4:2 admits them to a plane no higher than the firmament which lies under the first heaven. Ephesians seems to place no limit on them, unless we are to take "air" in 2:2 as synonymous with "the heavenlies"; but that would seem to be excluded by the use of the latter in 1:3, 20, and 2:6. It is the presence of evil, ignorant, or shortsighted Powers in heaven that accounts for so much of what is evil on earth.[111] Hence in the new age God will create a *new heaven* and a new earth (Rev. 21:1).[112] Ephesians seems to be continuous with the view that heaven is integrally implicated in this present evil age and that war in heaven and war on earth will continue until the final victory of God brings in the new heaven and new earth.[113] In the meantime, Christians already experience the powers of the new age now, in union with Christ, and use them to wage war on evil in both the earthly and the heavenly spheres. The author of Ephesians sees Christian existence as encompassing two times and two realms, all of them coextensive with the present world (see Figure 1). The two times are the old age and the new (the horizontal axis), the two realms are the earthly and the heavenly (the vertical axis). The times, as he conceived them, virtually overlapped, since the last things had already begun to happen. The realms, too, largely interpenetrated one another. In the diagram (Figure 1), the "heavenlies" would be everything above the horizontal axis. To be seated with Christ in the heavenly places (Eph. 1:3, 20; 2:6) would then refer primarily to the upper right-hand quadrant. The "war in heaven" would be with Powers ranged in the upper left-hand quadrant.

Contrary to much modern prejudice, "heaven" as used in Ephesians was already metaphorical, not spatio-literal. The physical image of heaven as "up" was a symbol, even for those times, of transcendence. But the

111. The demon in *Test. Sol.* 2:3 dwells in the "heavenly regions" (*epi tous ouranious topous*).

112. So also *Apoc. Elijah* (P. Chester Beatty 2018) 18:1; 43:13–14; Syriac *Test. Adam* 3:3 (Recensions 1, 3); and *Pirke R. El.* 73 Bi–Bii—all the host of heaven in the future are "destined to pass away and to be renewed." See, generally, Bietenhard, *Die himmlische Welt im Urchristentum und Spätjudentum*, WUNT (Tübingen: J. C. B. Mohr [Paul Siebeck], 1951), 205ff. The motif is already developed in the Old Testament (Amos 8:9; Hag. 2:6) and, most pertinent, in the judgment of the angels in the older sections of *1 Enoch* (16:1–4; 21:1–6; 91:16).

113. The eschatological future hope is still vibrantly alive in Ephesians, however much the language may be shifting toward a more realized eschatology. See Eph. 1:4, 18, 21; 2:7; 4:30; 5:16, 27; 6:8.

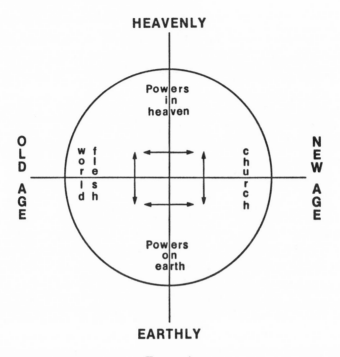

FIGURE 1

literal pole of the metaphor had an effect on them quite different from the effect it has on us. We think of "the heavens" as vast intergalactic reaches of empty space, peppered with solar systems infinite light-years apart. As an image of transcendence it fails for us, because we take it too literally/scientifically and because it serves only to make God more remote. Their heaven, by contrast, was a local affair. The sun and the moon were very close and far smaller than we have now calculated them to be. The "air" was not emptiness, but "stuff," one of four elements out of which all things are fabricated. The firmament was a relatively narrow channel separating heaven and earth, and the contemplative or mystic could hope to bridge it. Philo describes this "flight" of the spirit: "while their bodies are firmly planted on the land they provide their souls with wings, so that they may traverse the upper air and gain full contemplation of the powers (*dynameis*) which dwell there" (*De spec. leg.* II.45). Paul himself had traveled in ecstasy to the third heaven, although he himself is not at all clear how (2 Cor. 12:2–3). The author of the Apocalypse made a similar trip (Rev. 4:1ff.).

Nor was heaven itself all that fixed; the LXX of Jer. 49:38 (25:17, LXX) says that God will destroy Elam by bringing upon them wind and sword, "and I will set my throne (*thronon*) in Elam, and destroy their kings and princes, says the Lord."[114] Just as God's "throne" is where God is effectively acting, so "the heavenlies" are where Christ is already effectively lord, with all Powers under his sovereignty (Eph. 1:22) even though not yet under his control (6:12).

This seeming contradiction between sovereignty and control is the consequence of the struggle at the juncture between two ages. To use a modern analogy, Christ's provisional revolutionary government has already been formed in exile, and parts of the country are already effectively under its sovereignty. The old regime, however, still holds the capital and the loyalty of the army and practices brutal and indiscriminate warfare against its own people in a desperate attempt to preserve its privilege and wealth. But the outcome, however long in coming, is assured.

"The heavenlies," in short, is that dimension of reality of which the believer becomes aware as a result of being "raised up" by God with Christ. It is a heightened awareness, the consciousness of a noumenal realm in which the final contest for the lordship of all reality is being waged. The "sons of disobedience" are "dead" to this reality.[115] It is known only by revelation.[116] It is a gift that cannot be achieved,[117] a mystery that cannot be plumbed apart from divine illumination,[118] a knowledge that cannot simply be added to existing knowledge but that requires an altogether new mind, indeed, a new humanity.[119]

But it is not simply a state of rapture. It is an actual, new, epistemic standpoint which surpasses *gnosis* (Eph. 3:19), and the believer's comprehension pertains not just to the things of God, but also to the reality, deceptions, and delusionary snares of evil. Against this they must be armed (6:10–20); thus armed, they are able to "expose" the "unfruitful works of darkness" (5:11) and make them become "visible" (5:13).

This is of utmost importance. The true dimensions of evil, according to the writer, are known only through revelation, however bad life may have seemed before. And the consequence of revelation, conversely, is

114. Similarly, in the *Enuma Elish* the assembly of the gods convenes not in the high heaven but in Babylon, and prior to its founding, in Ubshukkinna, the court of assembly in Nippur (II.126; III.61, 131, etc.; cited by E. Theodore Mullen, Jr., *The Assembly of the Gods: The Divine Council in Canaanite and Early Hebrew Literature,* HSM 24 [Chico, Calif.: Scholars Press, 1980], 166–67).

115. Eph. 2:1–3; 4:17–19; 5:8.

116. Eph. 1:9–10, 13, 17–19; 2:8, 17; 3:3–6, 8–10, 18–19; 4:13, 17–18, 20–21, 23; 5:8, 10, 11–14, 15–17; 6:19.

117. Eph. 2:4–10; 1:17ff.

118. Eph. 3:3–6, 8–10, 18–19; 6:19.

119. Eph. 4:22–24.

not to rescue the believers from a world of evil but to open their eyes, to bring them "light" (Eph. 5:14), and thereby to enlist them in the struggle for liberation. Just as peasants liberated from the control of a military dictatorship are not freed from conflict but freed *for* conflict, the Christian is recruited into the ranks of God in the grace-ful struggle to bring the world to the truth (1:13) that the crucified and risen Christ is its principle of harmony and power (1:20–23). "The heavenlies" where the believer has already been established is thus a kind of "liberated zone," in John Pairman Brown's phrase,[120] although with this caveat: those who are in this "liberated zone" are not at all free from the possibility of collusion with the old Powers or even of apostasy. But they are provided a space of relative freedom from determination by the Powers. *Ta epourania* is thus very similar to the phrase "the kingdom of God" as used in the Gospels, and subject to the same ambiguities.

What does it mean, then, that the church is now to make the manifold wisdom of God known to those principalities and powers which the Christian, from this new vantage point, can now see to be the chief impediments to authentic human life? We can approach this question best through a consideration of the immediate context. Why are the Powers mentioned at all in a discussion of the opening up of salvation to the *ethnē* (Gentiles/nations)? Indeed, to the reader who begins at Eph. 2:11 and reads straight through, the reference to the Powers in 3:10 comes as a total surprise. One would have expected "that through the church the manifold wisdom of God might now be made known to" the Gentiles/ nations! That in fact *is* what v. 8 says. Why "principalities and powers in the heavenlies"? Nothing prepares us for their mention, not even 1:20ff.—*especially* not 1:20ff., for there the "powers problem" would seem to have been solved: They are under Christ's feet.

The only sense I can make of this apparent non sequitur is to see the reference to the conversion of the *ethnē* as demanding revelation to the *angels* of the *ethnē*. Some manuscripts omit *pantas* in Eph. 3:9, suggesting that the Gentile nations are to be included among those who will "see what is the plan of the mystery hidden for ages." The nations would then be among the Powers mentioned in v. 10. *Patria* in 3:15 may also continue the allusion to the angels of the nations, for *patria* can also be translated "nation," which meaning may echo in the phrase "from whom every *family* in heaven and on earth is named."[121]

120. *The Liberated Zone* (Richmond: John Knox Press, 1969).
121. The pre-Christian Hebrew *Test. Napht.* 8 uses "families" in just this way, to refer to the nations presided over by their angels.

In any case, the writer intends here to speak of the cosmic reconciliation wrought by Christ in God's "plan for the fulness of time, to unite all things in him, things in heaven and things on earth" (Eph. 1:10). When the saints are enjoined in 3:18 to comprehend "what is the breadth and length and height and depth," both sets of polarities are captured geometrically and fused in the *axis mundi,* the cross (2:16)[122] and comprehended in "the church, which is his body, the fullness of him who fills all in all" (1:22–23). By encompassing these polarities, Christ creates the union which, according to the author, is the whole goal of redemption (1:10).

This is why the author can describe salvation as being raised up with Christ and made to sit with him in the heavenlies (Eph. 2:6). Christians, that is to say, already celebrate the marriage of heaven and earth (5:21–33) proleptically, through the actual reconciliation of Jew and Gentile in the body of Christ. But the heathen who have been received into the church were formerly under the dominion of the *archai* and *exousiai.* If in Christ they are now free it is because these Powers have been placed under Christ's feet (1:21–23). Now the claim of these powers to dominion is effectively broken. It remains the church's task not only to proclaim to people that they have been redeemed from the darkness that once held them in bondage (5:8–14), but also to proclaim to the Powers that they are not supreme. That Christ is their sovereign. That those human beings under their dominion (here the concept of national angels comes immediately to mind) belong to Christ.[123]

The church does not exercise the power of the Powers, however. It has no hope of success in a frontal encounter. That is why the writer ends this paragraph celebrating the "boldness and confidence of access through our faith in him" (Eph. 3:12). This can only mean access to the heavenly presence, the divine throne, the heavenly council (see 2:6, "made us sit . . . in the heavenlies"). Full admittance to that distin-

---

122. The *axis mundi* theme is developed quite remarkably in the second-century *Acts of Andrew* (Martyrdom, reconstructed in *NT Apoc.* 2:418–19). Andrew, faced with crucifixion, "went to the cross and with a strong voice addressed it as if it were a living creature: Hail, O Cross . . . you are set up in the cosmos to establish the unstable. And one part of you stretches up to heaven so that you may point out the heavenly Logos, the head of all things. Another part of you is stretched out to right and left that you may put to flight the fearful and inimical power and draw the cosmos into unity. And another part of you is set on the earth, rooted in the depths, that you may bring what is on earth and under the earth into contact with what is in heaven. . . . Well done, O Cross, that you have bound the circumference of the world!"

123. Mussner, *Christus,* 21.

guished circle awaits the future ages (2:7; see also Rev. 3:12, 21; 7:9–17; 14:1–5). But even now, through intercessory prayer, the church is confident that it has access to God's presence and power in the struggle with the Powers. It is this very confidence that causes the writer to launch immediately into prayer for his readers ("For this reason," 3:14–19).

But why must the church proclaim God's manifold wisdom to the Powers? Why not Christ or an angel? The writer clearly assumes that God had kept secret the means of salvation from the beginning of creation (3:3–11). Not even angels knew it. For angels are not omniscient; they are told only what they have to know to perform their mission.[124] "St. Paul speaks here of a mystery," wrote Chrysostom of Eph. 3:10, "because not even the angels knew" that the *nations* would be saved. "God had said He would save His people Israel, but had said nothing about the nations. The angels knew that the nations were called, but could not imagine that they would be called to the same end and would be seated upon the throne of God!"[125] Because the spiritual rulers of the world, in charge of nations, institutions (see the "angels of the churches," Rev. 2–3), individuals (guardian angels, Matt. 18:10; Acts 12:15), and nature (Rev. 7:1; 16:5), operate with a license from God but without reference to God's secret plan hidden from the ages, they apparently behave without a view to the total purposes of creation (see 1 Pet. 1:12—"things into which angels long to look"). Each is responsible for the interests of its own charge; if these interests are pursued without knowledge of God's will for the whole of history, conflict becomes inevitable. Competing interests clash. When the angel of Persia withstood Michael and the other angel in Daniel 10, it was from ignorance, wrote Chrysostom, not evil.[126] As a result the Powers become agents of fate, of necessity, of an inexorability that determines lives without reference to the will of God; in short, of a nonprovidential governance of human life. To these Powers, then, the church is to proclaim the divine plan made known only now in the fullness of time in Christ Jesus, that the God who is above all and through all and in all is uniting all things in Christ, things in heaven and things on earth (Eph. 4:6; 1:10).

The most puzzling aspect of Eph. 3:10, however, is why—and how—the church is to preach to the Powers in the heavenlies. The image is

---

124. George M. Landes, "Shall We Neglect the Angels?" *USQR* 14 (1959): 19–25
125. *Hom. on Eph.*, 7. The translation is Jean Daniélou's, *The Angels and Their Mission* (Westminster, Md.: Newman Press, 1957), 33. The ignorance of the *archontes* is treated above on 1 Cor. 2:6–8, pp. 40–45.
126. *Hom. on Eph.*, 7.

similar to Revelation 1–3, where the one like a son of man commands John to tell the angels of the churches what needs to be done in their churches. We are not told why this communication is not made directly by Christ to the angels. Apparently humans are necessary as intermediaries to the angels: angels' angels! But how this message is to be communicated to the Powers is not said, nor do any commentators remark on it.[127] Rev. 12:11 speaks of Satan being conquered by the faith and testimony of the martyrs, but not of their addressing Satan. The same is true of the passage in Ignatius which speaks of "the powers (*dynameis*) of Satan" being destroyed by the frequent gatherings of the church to give thanks and glory to God; "his mischief is brought to nothing, by the concord of your faith. There is nothing better than peace, by which every war in heaven and on earth is abolished" (*Eph.* 13). In both cases the Powers are *affected* by what the church does on earth, but in neither case does the church *address* them.

How is the church supposed to make known the manifold wisdom of God in the present time to the principalities and powers in the heavenlies? This question cannot be answered short of a thoroughgoing attempt to translate the entire mythic conception that finds expression in the New Testament language of power. Try as we may to place ourselves within the thought-world of the first century, the idea of the church preaching to heavenly powers is simply not intelligible. Somehow the interpretive key, known and assumed by the authors, has been omitted. In its absence, interpretation inevitably takes on itself considerable risk and can at best only hope to provide helpful approximations. But that very risk is the glory and joy of interpretation as well. To that attempt, as a conclusion to the entire study, we now turn.

127. I have found only two instances where the church teaches angels. In *Gos. Thom.* 88—"Jesus said, 'The angels and the prophets will come to you and give to you those things you (already) have. And you too, give them those things which you have, and say to yourselves, "When will they come and take what is theirs?" ' " (*NHL*, p. 127). But "angels" here could simply mean human messengers. Chrysostom remarks that the church does indeed preach to angels, but does not say how (*Hom. on Eph.*, 7).

3

INTERPRETING THE POWERS

4. Toward an Interpretation

Before turning to the interpretive task, we need to look back over the ground we have covered and try to sense the overall pattern in the language of power. We began with a set of preliminary observations that functioned at the outset as hypotheses justified by an initial listing of data. These have now been massively and cumulatively confirmed:

1. *The language of power pervades the whole New Testament.* Surveying all the data covered, it is amazing that this has been so consistently overlooked. On every page of the New Testament one finds the terminology of power: those incumbents, offices, structures, roles, institutions, ideologies, rituals, rules, agents, and spiritual influences by which power is established and exercised. The language and reality of power pervade the New Testament because power is one of the primary ways the world is organized and run. No human activity can be described without recourse to this language.

Earlier scholarly preoccupation with personified aspects of power has diverted attention from the pervasiveness of this use of the language of power. Since the Book of Revelation fails to use the stereotypical phrases of the Pauline and Paulinist literature, some scholars have declared that it lacks interest in such matters altogether—a staggering claim, since no other writing in the New Testament burns with such intense political fury. When we broaden the issue to the language of power generally, however, quite a different picture of Revelation emerges. John the Seer uses *thronos* 45 times, *onoma* 36 times, *exousia* 20 times, *dynamis* 2 times, and *archōn* 1 time, a veritable thesaurus of power terms. But with the sole exception of the latter (used of Christ in 1:5), John uses these terms not as names of spiritual powers (for which he prefers more surrealistic images, such as Dragon, Beast, frogs, locusts, etc.), but as names of political rulership (2:26; 17:12–13), the dominion of angels (14:18), delegated authority (9:3; 13:4, 5, 7, 12), and so forth. The fact is that no book in the whole Bible is so thoroughly preoccupied with evil powers and their defeat.

Another surprising finding of our study is that the synoptic Gospels use the terminology of power almost as frequently as does Paul, whose name is most often associated with the Powers. This fact has been overlooked simply because the Gospels tend to use the language of power of human or structural, rather than spiritual, entities. Paul for his part developed a quite unique manner of dealing with the determinants of human existence, substituting such quasi-hypostatized words as sin, law, flesh, and death for the terms more frequently encountered in Jewish apocalyptic: Satan, Azazel, Beliar, evil spirits, demons. In short, when we attend not merely to the terminology but the meaning field which is being denoted, Paul's letters, like the rest of the New Testament, can be described as a theology of power.[1]

2. *The language of power in the New Testament is extremely imprecise, liquid, interchangeable, and unsystematic,* yet

3. *Despite all this imprecision and interchangeability, certain clear patterns of usage emerge.* We found ourselves to be dealing not with analytically precise categories used consistently from one passage to another but with terms that cluster and swarm around the reality they describe, as if by heaping up synonymous phrases and parallel constructions an intuitive sense of the reality described might emerge. So we discovered series, strings, and pairs of terms used with a kind of consistent indiscriminateness, and within this field of language, a genuine power-reality that comes to expression. However, this very promiscuity of language meant that

4. *Because these terms are to a degree interchangeable, one or a pair or a series can be made to represent them all.* Furthermore, an initial sifting of data suggested that

5. *These Powers are both heavenly and earthly, divine and human, spiritual and political, invisible and structural,* and that

6. *These Powers are also both good and evil.* Evidence for these two observations should have by now proven cumulatively overwhelming and needs no further elaboration.

7. *Unless the context further specifies, we are to take the terms for power in their most comprehensive sense,* understanding them to mean both heavenly *and* earthly, divine *and* human, good *and* evil powers (see beginning of Part Two, p. 39).

1. Bengt Holmberg's *Paul and Power: The Structure of Authority in the Primitive Church as Reflected in the Pauline Epistles* (Philadelphia: Fortress Press, 1980) makes critical use of Weber's sociological categories in analyzing Paul's use of power, but his study is limited to the structure of the church.

Aided by these observations, we discovered in the history of the usage of terms for power a rich and subtle awareness by the ancients of the various forms power takes. The most frequent usage was for human incumbents-in-office, but there was also a pervasive awareness of the ways power is organized, which required a more abstract or structural usage of the terms. Thus *archai* could represent, like *archontes*, persons-in-roles, magistrates, governors, elders, and kings-in-office. But it could also denote the office itself, or the power the office represents. *Thronos* too seemed to emphasize not the occupant of the "seat" of power but the "seat" itself as the symbol of continuity, perpetuity, legitimacy, and popular consent. *Kyriotēs*, if we may speak with any assurance at all about it, seemed to point more to the sphere of influence or territory ruled by a *kyrios* than to the ruler as such. *Exousia* blurred easily on the edges, but it most frequently denoted the legitimations, sanctions, and permissions that undergird or authorize the use of power, while *dynameis* pointed more specifically to the sanctions or forces by which power is imposed. But all these could also be applied as need arose to spiritual powers, good and evil. The latter, however, have been overemphasized; the vast preponderance of uses refer to the *human* and *structural* dimensions of power, and only a curious preoccupation by scholars with the spiritual dimension of the word field could have obscured this fact.

However, it is precisely this spiritual aspect, in its very alienness to the modern worldview, that reveals how inadequate our categories are for interpretation. Scholars' instincts were not wrong, then, to focus on the spiritual dimension of the Powers, but they tended to do so on an attenuated base. It is precisely this spiritual element which does not and cannot be made to fit our modern reductionist categories that most cries out for explanation.

Recent studies in the sociology of the New Testament have done much to open the theme of power for fresh examination.[2] The danger to be guarded against in such study is the tendency to make modern sociological theory, and the unconscious ideological assumptions on which it is founded, normative for New Testament reality, imposing on the New Testament data a framework that is foreign to it. Such an interpretive grid may be ill-suited for filtering out and examining the most essential elements in the first-century understanding of power. For example, the "methodo-

2. See the survey by Robin Scroggs, "The Sociological Interpretation of the New Testament: The Present State of Research," *NTS* 26 (1980): 164–79.

logical atheism" of Peter Berger's *The Sacred Canopy*,[3] despite its analytical lucidity, brackets out what is (for New Testament writers at least)
the most central aspect of reality: belief in the existence of God. "Meth-
odological *atheism*" is itself methodologically indefensible: "agnosti-
cism" would have been more appropriate, since sociology is incompetent
to judge the question of God's reality one way or the other. The fact that
atheism is chosen instead is evidence of an ideological preference that is
fundamentally antitheological. Such sociology is thus inevitably an apologetic and defense for a counterevangel, in this case the enlightenment
belief that humanity creates its gods. While much can be learned from
such approaches, they must not be permitted to guide the development
of hypotheses. Instead we must return to the text and first try to discern
the New Testament's own categories for speaking of social reality.

These categories are mythic. Consequently, our approach to interpretation must avoid all attempts to "modernize" insofar as this means
ignoring the mythic dimension of the text and transferring it in an unmediated way into modern (mythic) categories. It may be that the principalities and powers have been neglected as much as they have since
the Enlightenment precisely because they were *not* easily reducible to
modern themes. For this reason, then, I have attempted in Parts One and
Two to treat the data in all their alienness and, as far as I was capable,
to let the categories and concerns implicit in the language arise out of its
own matrix of meanings.

On the strength of that analysis, we are now ready to engage the ancient
and modern worldviews in dialogue. Now, one hopes, the modern mentality will not overwhelm or violate the ancient, but listen respectfully,
honoring it and learning from it where it can, enriching it and elaborating
where it is able. We will listen, not in order to impose on the past our
own "normative" understanding, but in order to learn from the past
precisely that which we may have lost sight of and need to recover.

---

3 Peter Berger, *The Sacred Canopy: Elements of a Sociological Theory of Religion*
(Garden City, N.Y.: Doubleday & Co., 1967), 100.

5. Interpreting the Myth

We ended Part Two having found ourselves in a cul de sac of interpretation. Eph. 3:10 spoke of the church's task as proclaiming now the manifold wisdom of God to the principalities and powers in the *heavenly* places. We were unable to find anything in the first-century background capable of making that intelligible within the limits of the modern worldview. But perhaps that point of unintelligibility was reached for some readers even earlier, when, for example, Christ was declared to have already put the Powers under his feet, or when God was said to have led them captive in Christ's triumphal procession, or when the Powers were affirmed as having been created in and through and for Christ. For the mythic dimension—the atemporal, cosmic, supernatural aspect of the story—was not inserted in the final text we dealt with, as if we had held back the worst for last. It has accompanied us from the outset, permeating every statement made about the Powers. We found, in short, that the mythic is not the residue left over and discardable after everything meaningful has been explained. It is the very framework of the entire notion of the Powers, the means by which they have been brought to language. For that reason a simply reductionistic explanation of the Powers is closed to us. They cannot be treated as "nothing but" the personification of human institutional and cultural arrangements, since these institutions and cultural arrangements are just as much the creation of the Powers as their creators. Reductionistic explanations are inadequate because they omit the one essential most unique to the New Testament understanding of power: its spiritual dimension.

There is a certain irony in the fact that liberation theologians have, in the main, followed the reductionist path and treated the Powers as *just* institutions and systems, with little attempt to comprehend their spiritual dimension or take seriously their mythic form.

The Powers Are the Inner
Aspect of Material
Reality

What might we learn if we listened to the ancient myth on its own terms and tried to decipher, by an act of interpretive divination, what is moving within it? The ancients regarded the spiritual Powers as non-material, invisible, heavenly entities with specific characteristics or qualities. These Powers are the good creations of a good God, but all of them have "fallen," becoming more or less evil in intent, and may even be set on the destruction of humanity. They were called angels, gods, spirits, demons, devils. This view was carried by the momentum of Jewish apocalyptic thought right into the New Testament, but Paul has already taken key steps toward "demythologizing" or at least depersonalizing it by means of the categories of sin, law, the flesh, and death. I suggest we follow Paul's lead in this, and attempt to reinterpret the mythic language of the Powers. By this I do not mean to abolish the New Testament myth but to transpose it into a new key. Or, put another way, the goal is not "demythologizing" if by that is meant removal of the mythic dimension, but rather juxtaposing the ancient myth with the emerging postmodern (mythic) worldview and asking how they might mutually illuminate each other.[1]

What I propose is viewing the spiritual Powers not as separate heavenly or ethereal entities but as *the inner aspect of material or tangible manifestations of power*. I suggest that the "angels of nature" are the patterning of physical things—rocks, trees, plants, the whole God-glorifying, dancing, visible universe; that the "principalities and powers" are the inner or spiritual essence, or gestalt, of an institution or state or system; that the "demons" are the psychic or spiritual power emanated by organizations or individuals or subaspects of individuals whose energies are bent on overpowering others; that "gods" are the very real archetypal

1. The contours of this "postmodern" worldview, and its value for making sense of the Powers, will be elaborated more fully in subsequent volumes, but I would like to prevent a possible misunderstanding right at the outset. It is not so much the "new physics" itself that is of value here (although it is a great help) as it is the new situation of openness and flux that it makes possible. The worldview fostered by the new physics will eventually calcify and harden; it too will exclude genuine possibilities and will have to be rebelled against and altered. The "new physics" is not, then, a kind of circumcision the Christian is required to undergo as a precondition of faith. It is more akin to the Roman Empire, which provided the earliest church with safe and fast roads, open borders, pirate-free seas, and protection from undue persecution.

or ideological structures that determine or govern reality and its mirror, the human brain; that the mysterious "elements of the universe" (*stoicheia tou kosmou*) are the invariances (formerly called "laws") which, though often idolized by humans, conserve the self-consistency of each level of reality in its harmonious interrelationship with every other level and the Whole; and that "Satan" is the actual power that congeals around collective idolatry, injustice, or inhumanity, a power that increases or decreases according to the degree of collective refusal to choose higher values. The second volume of this work will devote a section to each of these Powers. It is hoped that my cryptic remarks here will carry readers through the remainder of this volume and ready them for the next, where these themes will be given thorough and practical amplification.

These "Powers" do not, then, on this hypothesis, have a separate, spiritual existence. *We encounter them primarily in reference to the material or "earthly" reality of which they are the innermost essence.* The spiritual aspect of the Powers is not simply a "personification" of institutional qualities that would exist whether they were personified or not. On the contrary, the spirituality of an institution exists as a real aspect of the institution even when it is not perceived as such.

Let me illustrate. A "mob spirit" does not hover in the sky waiting to leap down on unruly crowds at a soccer match. It is the actual spirit constellated when the crowd reaches a certain critical flashpoint of excitement and frustration. It comes into existence in that moment, causes people to act in ways of which they would never have dreamed themselves capable, and then ceases to exist the moment the crowd disperses. Or take a high school football team. Its team spirit is high during the season, then cools at the season's close, although it continues to persist to a degree in history (memories) and hope (the coming season). The spirit of a nation endures beyond its actual rule, in the lasting effects of its policies, its contributions to culture, its additions to the sheer weight of human suffering. And the spirits of things that just last and last, like rocks and trees, would appear to be eternal, but they too are inseparable from their material or physical concretions.

None of these "spiritual" realities has an existence independent of its material counterpart. None persists through time without embodiment in cellulose or in a culture or a regime or a corporation or a megalomaniac. An ideology does not just float in the air; it is always the nexus of legitimations and rationales for some actual entity, be it union or management, a social change group or the structure it hopes to change. As the inner aspect of material reality, the spiritual Powers are everywhere around us. Their presence is real and it is inescapable. The issue is not whether we "believe" in them but whether we can learn to identify our actual, everyday encounters with them—what Paul called "discerning the spirits."

If the "spiritual" Powers are the inside or essence of physical or social entities or systems or structures, then the long and inconclusive debate over whether the Powers are human or divine can now be ended. Like most such debates, its very inconclusiveness was evidence that each party held a portion of the truth which it could not in all justice relinquish and that the issue could be resolved only in a higher synthesis encompassing the truth of both. This theory appears to do just that. It understands the spiritual and physical aspects of the Powers to be inseparable but distinguishable components of a single phenomenon—power in its concretions in this world. The writers of the New Testament, as other writers of the period, could thus refer to now the spiritual (or inner) aspect, now the physical (or outer) aspect, depending on which aspect was more apparent or significant in the moment. If pressed, Paul would probably have readily conceded that spiritual forces did lie behind the Roman Empire. But when he wrote Rom. 13:1, he apparently was, *at that moment,* focusing on just those human authorities whom he describes later in the paragraph as wielding the sword and collecting taxes. In 1 Cor. 2:6–8, when Paul mentions the rulers of this age, his language can appear so ambiguous because he is probably thinking simultaneously of both human *and* demonic agents of Jesus' death. No doubt, however, some of his original readers, to say nothing of centuries of interpreters since, would tend to think he meant either human or divine powers, depending on their own bent. Elsewhere Paul could use the very same terms to speak of what seem to be primarily spiritual powers (Rom. 8:38–39), without needing to provide any explanation for the shift. And if in other contexts the writers heap expressions on expressions to indicate the full compass and sweep of power, earthly and heavenly, they use the very same words to accomplish that purpose (see above, pp. 7–12).

The very demons themselves, so long regarded as baleful spirits in the air, are pictured by the Gospels as abhorring decorporealization. When Jesus orders the "Legion" of demons out of the Gerasene demoniac, they plead to be allowed to possess a nearby herd of swine (Mark 5:12). The historicity of the conception is guaranteed regardless of the historicity of the event. The unclean spirit can find no rest without a physical body in which to reside (Luke 11:24–26). The sense is clear: demons can become manifest only through concretion in material reality. They are, in short, the name given that real but invisible spirit of destructiveness and fragmentation that rends persons, communities, and nations.

In light of our analysis, the expression "the Powers" should no longer be reserved for the special category of spiritual forces, but should rather be used generically for all manifestations of power, seen under the dual aspect of their physical or institutional concretion on the one hand, and their inner essence or spirituality on the other. Popular speech, often more accurate in unconscious matters than it is given credit for being, has quite properly referred to the whole range of phenomena as "The Powers That Be."

Even to say, as Cullmann did, that the Powers are *both* earthly *and* heavenly is, on this reading, still too imprecise. "Both" suggests two different sets of agents, some human or institutional, others divine or demonic. What we are arguing is that *the Powers are simultaneously the outer and inner aspects of one and the same indivisible concretion of power.* "Spiritual" here means the inner dimension of the material, the "within" of things, the subjectivity of objective entities in the world.[2] Instead of the old dualism of matter and spirit, we can now regard matter and spirit as united in one indivisible reality, distinguishable in two discrete but interrelated manifestations.[3] Nothing less than insistence on this unity makes sense of the unexplained ambiguity in the usage of the New Testament language of power. Nothing less can account for the authors' apparent expectation that readers will understand exactly what is meant despite the great fluidity and imprecision of usage.

This ambiguity is intrinsic to a degree in every manifestation of power. For example, before us we have the chairperson of a political committee.

---

2. Perhaps Niels Bohr, the father of quantum mechanics, had something like this in mind when he wrote of the "inseparability of materialistic and spiritualistic views," since "materialism and spiritualism, which are defined only by concepts taken from each other, are two aspects of the same thing." Cited by John Honner, "Niels Bohr and the Mysticism of Nature," *Zygon* 17 (1982): 246.

3. The present study is conceived as an attempt to contribute to a unitary worldview in which matter and spirit are seen as indispensable and discrete dimensions of a single reality. At the same time we should avoid philosophical monism. This unitary reality appears to be many-dimensional. Some experiences seem to be less bound to material expression than others; mystical experiences, visions, ESP, near-death experiences, fantasy, and the whole realm of mathematics come to mind. But even imaginal experiences must draw on physical imagery to clothe themselves, and both imaginal and mental experiences can only take place in a body. Even if the content of an experience is not incarnate (such as a mathematical equation or a nightmare), the experience itself is. The angels themselves are not disembodied, but are clad in "garments of the upper world," and God too is clothed in fire and light (*Asc. Isa.* 9:9; *3 Enoch* 12).

Which is really the Power here—the person, or the role? Not the person—she can be replaced with another, and the job will go on being done. Not the role either—for some use it to great benefit and others irresponsibly. Is it then the person-in-the-role? But then what authorizes her to act? Is it then the authority invested in her by the constituting charter of the group? But what gives the charter its binding character? Where is power finally to be located, unless we see it as the total interaction of all these aspects, visible and invisible? And how is power to be brought to heel, unless it is addressed on its own terrain—unless, that is, we address not only the physical manifestations of the group but also its "spirit" or "angel"? This is certainly the way the "one like a son of man" goes about attempting to reform the churches in Revelation 1–3.[4] And to revert to the fundamental question that Eph. 3:10 placed before us at the end of our exegetical survey, *is it not precisely the addressing of this inner reality of power which the author of Eph. 3:10 directs the church to do?*

Franz Hinkelammert has recently formulated a similar analysis in order to clarify theologically the meaning of Marx's theory of "fetishism."[5] He distinguishes between the *material institutions* that organize modern society and the *spirit* of these institutions. Political economics makes manifest the anatomy of the institutions, and the theory of fetishism analyzes the institutionalized spirituality of modern society. The "fetish" is the spirit of the institutions, Hinkelammert writes, and this spirit is every bit as important as the physical aspects of institutions. If someone violates this spirit, though he keeps all the laws and precepts of the system, the system will condemn him to death. Conversely, if someone submits to this spirituality, he will be able to live in spite of violating all its laws and flouting all its institutions.

This makes sense of the way hardened thieves and criminals in communist prisons are made trusties, while decent people being held as political prisoners are subjected to every conceivable indignity.[6] In the logic of Hinkelammert's analysis, the thieves, although they break all the rules, accept the spirit of the system, in some ways actually exemplifying it, whereas the "politicals," though fully law-abiding and in most cases innocent of any real infraction of the law, question the spirit of the system and so are regarded as the worst criminals of all.

4. This image will be elaborated on more fully in Volume Two.
5. Franz Hinkelammert, *Las Armas Ideológicas de la Muerte*, 2d ed. (San José, Costa Rica: Departamento Ecuménico de Investigaciones, Apdo. 339, San Pedro Montes de Oca, 1981). Translation forthcoming from Orbis Books.
6. See, e.g., Aleksandr Solzhenitsyn, *The Gulag Archipelago*, 3 vols. (New York: Harper & Row, 1973–78).

This analysis also explains why it is impossible to discover in the Gospels an "adequate" cause for Jesus' execution. Every such attempt has presupposed that he must have done something punishable by death. But he did not. That is the whole point. He was innocent and yet executed. But the Powers did not err. He had rejected their spirituality; he had shaken the invisible foundations by a series of provocative acts. He was therefore a living terror to the order of things. He *had* to be removed.

The spirituality of institutions does not drop from heaven, however. It only arises, Hinkelammert argues, within a definite social organization. In Marx's view, the single most important determinant of the spirit of institutions is the means of production. The spirit of life or death in a society is not a function, then, of the good will or bad will of individuals, but the consequence of a determinate institutionalized spirituality in a determinate material organization of relations between people. The capitalist system, for example, is able to produce and reproduce not only surplus value and social classes but also its own symbolic universe, its own spirituality, its own religion.

Fetishism, says Hinkelammert, is the personification of capital and the "thingification" of persons. The "invisible hand" is regarded as a benign providence to which people surrender their decisions over their own life or death. An invisible mercantile mechanism thus becomes the arbiter of human destiny, producing results in apparent independence of the human beings who comprise the system it governs. It is the tendency to deify the mechanism and reduce human agents to mere things that creates the peculiar demonism of modern capitalist economics.

It would have been helpful if Hinkelammert had extended his analysis to the peculiar demonism of communist regimes as well. In terms of our hypothesis, perhaps we could say that the dialectic in Marx is between "fetishized" structures and the proletariat, who in becoming aware of their own history and determination by these structures, revolt and establish the dictatorship of the proletariat until all bourgeois tendencies have been overcome. But since in Marx's utopia there will be no institutions, Marxism provides little guidance to a Poland, for example, where the institutional structures of the state are unable to contain the positive spirit of the actual proletariat and hence must crush Solidarity. There are, in effect, no recognized sources of positive authority in institutional structures; hence the sheer need and desire for power becomes a new fetish in the absence of any positive legitimation of present interim institutions.

In the Bible, by contrast, the dialectic is between different possible spiritualities within a given institution (reform) or between different institutions (revolution), and none is granted privileged status. All, even the prophets who oppose the kings, are under the judgment of God. And in the New Jerusalem there will still be a role for institutions ("the nations," Rev. 21:24–26; 22:2).

Hinkelammert's analysis can be broadened to fit every human institution. Every organization is made up of human beings who make its decisions and are responsible for its success or failure, but these institutions tend to have a suprahuman quality. Although created and staffed by humans, decisions are not made so much by people as for them, out of the logic of institutional life itself. And because the institution usually antedates and outlasts its employees, it develops and imposes a set of traditions, expectations, beliefs, and values on everyone in its employ. Usually unspoken, unacknowledged, and even unknown, this invisible, transcendent network of determinants constrains behavior far more rigidly than any printed set of rules could ever do. It governs dress, social class, life-expectations, even choice of marriage partner (or abstention). This institutional momentum through time perpetuates a self-image, a corporate personality, and an institutional spirit which the more discerning are able to grasp as a totality and weigh for its relative sickness or health.

We must learn to break the habit of taking a merely visible part for the whole. No one, comments Hinkelammert, has ever seen a company, a school, a state, or a system of ownership. What they have seen are the physical elements of such institutions, that is to say, the building in which the school or business functions, or the people who are its operatives. The *institution*, however, is the totality of its activities and as such is a mostly invisible object.[7] When we confuse what the eye beholds with the totality, we commit the same reductionist fallacy as those Colossians who mistook the basic elements (*stoicheia*) of things for the ultimate reality (Col. 2:8, 20). The consequence of such confusion is always slavery to the unseen power behind the visible elements: the spirituality of the institution or state or stone.

If, then, the church must now make known the manifold wisdom of God to the principalities and powers in the heavenlies, it cannot be content with addressing the material aspect of an institution alone. It must speak to the spiritual reality of the institution as well.

The early church understood this quite clearly. When the Roman archons (magistrates) ordered the early Christians to worship the imperial spirit or *genius*, they refused, kneeling instead and offering prayers on the emperor's behalf to God. This seemingly innocuous act was far more

7. Hinkelammert, *Las Armas Ideológicas*, 8–9.

exasperating and revolutionary than outright rebellion would have been. Rebellion simply acknowledges the absoluteness and ultimacy of the emperor's power, and attempts to seize it. Prayer denies that ultimacy altogether by acknowledging a higher power. Rebellion would have focused solely on the physical institution and its current incumbents and attempted to displace them by an act of superior force. But prayer challenged the very spirituality of the empire itself and called the empire's "angel," as it were, before the judgment seat of God.

Such sedition could not go unpunished. With rebels the solution was simple. No one challenged the state's right to execute rebels. They had bought into the power-game on the empire's terms and lost, and the rules of the game required their liquidation. The rebels themselves knew this before they started. *But what happens when a state executes those who are praying for it?* When Christians knelt in the Colosseum to pray as lions bore down on them, something sullied the audience's thirst for revenge. Even in death these Christians were not only challenging the ultimacy of the emperor and the "spirit" of empire but also demonstrating the emperor's powerlessness to impose his will even by death. The final sanction had been publicly robbed of its power. Even as the lions lapped the blood of the saints, Caesar was stripped of his arms and led captive in Christ's triumphal procession. His authority was shown to be only penultimate after all. And even those who wished most to deny such a thing were forced, by the very punishment they chose to inflict, to behold its truth. It was a contest of all the brute force of Rome against a small sect that merely prayed. Who could have predicted that the tiny sect would win?

This is not to suggest that in most circumstances prayer is enough, but in that situation it was the most radical response imaginable. Then, "Jesus is Lord" shook the foundations of an empire; in the "free" world today, "Jesus is Lord" bumper stickers mainly occasion yawns. Cars adorned with them are not stopped at police roadblocks or firebombed by paramilitary saboteurs. The only people scandalized by the phrase are those who regard its language as sexist. But there are countries where "Jesus, friend of the poor" can get you killed. Fidelity to the gospel lies not in repeating its slogans but in plunging the prevailing idolatries into its corrosive acids. We must learn to address the spirituality of institutions, as well as their visible manifestations, with the ultimate claim of the Ultimate Human.

The failure of the gnostics to maintain the material pole of this task constituted their great apostasy. As a result of their almost pathological hatred of matter, they spiritualized the Powers altogether. Without a base in materiality, the Powers lost all mooring on the earth. Boundless speculations about heavenly hierarchies replaced careful strategizing about real power in the one and only real world. The Powers vaporized into guardians at the gates of the successive spheres of heaven, whom the soul encountered only after death in its attempt to ascend to God. They no longer represented the inner, spiritual reality of actual earthly entities. Therefore life on earth could, correspondingly, be depoliticized. As Pagels points out, gnostics were notoriously loath to suffer persecution.[8] The created world in its physical and spiritual dimensions was abandoned for a split reality to be experienced serially, the material episode to be despised in order that the later, heavenly episode might be secured.

Here is how the gnostic *Apocalypse of Paul* speaks of divine punishment for sinners: "The soul that had been cast down [went] to"—hell? eternal fires? No!—"[a] body which had been prepared [for it]" (*NHL* 21:19ff.). Reincarnation in a physical body on the earthly plane is hell!

Severed from materiality, the Powers in gnosticism were identified with planetary forces. But the real psychodynamic was one of projection. The gnostics were the earliest psychologists, comments Victor White. They explored the inner world by the indirect means of the language of myth, projecting their interior phantasms out on the screen of the heavens and dressing them out in a pretentious allegorizing philosophy. Their radical introspection led them to reject the material world and to be caught finally in the abyss of the archetypes of the collective unconscious.[9] The gifts they might have brought to the world at large were vitiated by their

8. Elaine Pagels, *The Gnostic Gospels* (New York: Random House, 1979), 84ff. The gnostic "Two Books of Jeu" ascribed this saying to Jesus: "Blessed is he who has crucified the world, and has not allowed the world to crucify him" (*NT Apoc.* 1:261).
9. Victor White, *God and the Unconscious* (Cleveland: World Publishing Co., 1952), 225. The newly published *NHL Discourse on the Eighth and Ninth* provides a striking illustration. The "eighth and ninth" represent the benevolent spheres surrounding the earth, higher than the malevolent first seven spheres, presided over by the sun, moon, and planets. The eighth and ninth spheres thus designate the beginning of the divine realm, the levels beyond control of the lower powers. At death the soul would journey through the seven spheres and after successful passage would reach the eighth and ninth, where it would enjoy heavenly bliss. At the same time, however, the eighth and ninth spheres could also indicate advanced stages of inner or personal spiritual development. (From the introduction by James Brashler, Peter A. Dirkse, and Douglas M. Parrott, *NHL*, 292.) This provides the clue to interpretation: the ascent after death is a projected and postdated cosmological depiction of the stages of spiritual development on earth. But nothing in this text suggests that this clue was lifted up as the conscious basis for interpretation. There may indeed be further developments in an afterlife; but we should be suspicious of any teaching that focuses on it to the neglect of genuinely possible developments in this life.

understandable inability to make this unconscious process conscious. But they were not even drawn to do so, because their ideology had already rejected the structure of this world for a pseudoreality in the beyond.[10]

The orthodox church, for its part, rigidly cleaved to materiality but soon found itself the darling of Constantine. Called on to legitimate the empire, the church abandoned much of its social critique. The Powers were soon divorced from political affairs and made airy spirits who preyed only on individuals. The state was thus freed of one of the most powerful brakes against idolatry, although prophetic voices never ceased to be raised now and again anyway.[11]

These deviations from the New Testament view of the Powers were the result not simply of wrong thinking but of powerful political pressures. Any time the church has chosen to address the spirituality of institutions in their concrete embodiments, persecution has resulted. Far from a show of gratitude at being recalled to the will of God, the Powers explode in a frenzy of rage and retaliation. This brings to focus another curious aspect of the myth.

The Powers Are Ignorant
of God's Plan

None of the archons of this age understands "the *hidden* wisdom of God," "for if they had, they would not have crucified the Lord of glory" (1 Cor. 2:7, 8). Not even angels are omniscient. They are told only what they must know in order to deliver the revelation necessary for a specific moment. They are seldom personified, can be spoken of interchangeably with God, and vanish when the message is received. They are as much "message" as messengers, "informations" as informers.

The hymn that bursts from the lips of the dictating author of 1 Tim.

10. On the positive side, from the point of view of this study, the gnostics did attempt to keep alive a sense of the fallenness of the world order, the reality of intermediate powers and their role in impeding fulfilled life, belief in the value of personal revelations and personal knowledge as opposed to collective dogma, and above all the role of legalism in estrangement.

11. Eusebius of Caesarea, for example, writing to prove that Christians were loyal to the empire, is careful to praise emperors whom the Romans thought good and to damn those the Senate had damned. But the terrible persecution of Christians in Lyons-Vienne in 177 took place during the reign of Marcus Aurelius, a "good" emperor. Eusebius's solution: the church's battle was not against the Roman government but against devils and unseen adversaries (*Eccl. Hist.* V, preface-4). "In shifting the blame from the visible Roman authorities to the invisible demons, Eusebius avoided direct criticism of the government; it was the government's favor he courted. . . . He did not wish to say that the demon wore a toga" (John Helgeland, "Christians and the Roman Army from Marcus Aurelius to Constantine," *ANRW* II.23.1:760–61).

3:16 stresses the revelation that angels themselves received when Christ, after his resurrection, was "seen by angels" and "believed in the cosmos."[12] We saw the same motif of the ignorance of the archons elaborated in the *Ascension of Isaiah*. Apparently it was important that the angels see Christ vindicated. What is the mythic point common to all these texts, with their insistence that Christ was previously unknown to the angels? How is it possible for them to be ignorant of their very own principle of systemicity (Col. 1:17, *synestēken*, the etymological root of our word "system"), the one in whom all things "hold together," "cohere," "find their harmonious unity"? How is it that they are ignorant of that in and through and for which they exist (Col. 1:16)? We must lay aside all systematic and logical objections and simply let the myth speak for itself. What it seems to claim is that the universe itself is blind to its own principle of cohesion. It operates cohesively, but without the parts perceiving that fact. Put in a more modern mode, the universe is late in arriving at awareness of itself as a unity, and this awareness has come into the world for the first time with humanity. We can actually date the moment of its dawning in the axiological period of the great prophets of Israel, the philosophers of Greece, and Buddha and Lao-tzu in the East.[13] It was then that the historically unprecedented sense of the unity of all things first was effectively articulated, although it was probably intuitively sensed far earlier. On the strength of that apprehension, both Israel's conception of Yahweh's universal sovereignty and Greek science and philosophy became possible.

With Christ Jesus a new dimension was added, however. The just man is killed. The embodiment of God's will is executed by God's servants. The incarnation of the orderly principles of the universe is crucified by the guardians of order. The very nucleus of spiritual power in the universe is destroyed by the spiritual powers. The parts do not or cannot know the effect of their acts on the whole, and some, less innocently, by their worship of their own selfish short-term interests, have become detrimental to the good of the whole. The angels did not know the Lord of glory, nor did the captains and jailers and chief priests and governors. The cosmic process of reconciliation could not begin until they "saw" him.

This is why Phil. 2:9–11, Col. 2:15, and Eph. 1:19–23 are so adamant in stressing that Christ is *already* seated at God's right hand, has *already*

---

12. Author's translation.
13. Karl Jaspers, *The Origin and Goal of History* (London: Routledge & Kegan Paul, 1953)

unmasked the Powers, has *already* put these Powers under his feet and has already had bestowed on him the name that is above every name— even though empirical evidence for such claims seems totally nonexistent. For if the crucified Jesus is "Lord"—if the marred and disfigured form of the one truly human being who ever lived has become the criterion and norm of ultimate truth, life, and reality—then we and every power in heaven and on earth and under the earth are forever after utterly without excuse. We can no longer act in ignorance of the Whole or pretend to be oblivious to the value of the Human over every proximate goal. We can no longer act as if the world is not a single system converging on the One in and through and for whom it exists. We are, indeed, free to pretend not to know, and even to deceive ourselves into believing that our own values and goals are ultimate. But it will only be "bad faith," in Sartre's terms, and we will have to learn the truth very precisely in order to conceal it the more carefully. And this suppression will force us to become the more violent and brutal against all we love, in order to mask our remembered deception from ourselves. We can ravage the ecology, suppress the poor, murder protesters, adulterate the gospel, shake our fists defiantly at God, and declare the world a mechanism and human beings machines. But the System of the systems remains the ultimate arbiter, and we can no more secede from its jurisdiction than we can stop breathing air. The judgment comes again, and again, and finally. *For the angels have seen.* And the gospel has been preached to the nations.

The Powers did not know, but they know now. Even many modern secular states bear a legacy of titles that remind them, against even their own dominant ideologies, Whose they are, and why. These states continue to name the various branches of government the civil *service,* the military *service,* the *ministry* of justice, the *ministry* of education, revealing in these very titles the tacit recognition that they exist only on behalf of the Human revealed as the criterion and basis of all governmental action. When such agencies make themselves ends in themselves, or subject human needs to departmental efficiency or budgetary convenience, they do so, consciously or not, in violation of their vocation. "Are they not all ministering spirits sent forth to serve, for the sake of those who are to obtain salvation?" (Heb. 1:14). Did not Paul himself say that the person who is in authority "is God's servant for your good" (Rom. 13:4)?

Even tyrants understand this, perhaps better than most. The adage that runs "Mussolini made the trains run on time" bears witness to the fact that even dictators must manage to win the consent of the governed by providing sufficient services to buy their allegiance. And even the most aggressive nations feel obliged to justify military interventions by placing the loftiest of idealist excuses before the bar of world opinion. One U.S. delegate to the Baptist World Alliance Congress in Berlin in 1934 described his experience of Nazism:

> It was a great relief to be in a country where salacious sex literature cannot be sold; where putrid motion pictures and gangster films cannot be shown. The new Germany has burned great masses of corrupting books and magazines along with its bonfires of Jewish and communistic libraries.

Surely, so the reasoning went, a leader who does not smoke or drink, who wants women to be modest, and who is against pornography cannot be all bad![14] Evil, as always, is parasitic of the good and must masquerade as good in order to remain in office.

The church's task, then, in making known the manifold wisdom of God now to the principalities and powers in the heavenly places, does not involve the arduous and hopeless effort of bringing the Powers to a place they have never been, or to a recognition they have never shared. It involves simply reminding the Powers Whose they are, a knowledge already encoded in their charters, titles, traditions, insignia, and money.

Even in the case of communist regimes, the task is the same: to recall them to the One whose humanity itself is the best promise of a new humanity in the age to come, and to convert them to the humanism which lies at the base of their own ideology.

"The Powers did not know": seen from the perspective provided by our hypothesis, evangelism and social action are the inner and outer approaches to the same phenomenon of power. I have already described the subversive character of the early church's refusal to worship the imperial genius and its recourse instead to prayer. Many modern Christians have unfortunately understood injustice in simply materialistic terms and have not recognized the need to "convert" people from the spirituality that binds them to a particular material expression of power. It is not enough merely to change social structures. People are not simply determined by the material forces that impinge on them. They are also the victims of the very spirituality that the material means of production and

---

14. William Loyd Allen, "How Baptists Assessed Hitler," *Christian Century* 99(September 1–8, 1982):890–91. The quotation is of the Rev. John W. Bradbury in the *Watchman-Examiner*, September 13, 1934.

socialization have fostered, even as these material means are themselves the spin-off of a particular spirituality. In a new structure people will continue to behave on the basis of the old spirituality, as they have to varying degrees in every communist regime, unless not only the structures but also their own psyches are reorganized.

Evangelism is *always* a form of social action. It is an indispensable component of any new "world." Unfortunately, Christian evangelism has all too often been wedded to a politics of the status quo and merely serves to relieve distress by displacing hope to an afterlife and ignoring the causes of oppression. The repugnance with which most liberal Christians regard evangelism betrays their own failure to discern that all liberation involves conversion. Whenever evangelism is carried out in full awareness of the Powers, whether in confronting those in power or liberating those crushed by it, proclaiming the sovereignty of Christ is by that very act a critique of injustice and idolatry. And as the churches of South Korea and Brazil and Chile and around the world have learned, such evangelism will inevitably spark persecution. In sum, structural change is not enough; the heart and soul must also be freed, forgiven, energized, given focus, reunited with their Source.

The converse is equally true: social action is always evangelism, if carried out in full awareness of Christ's sovereignty over the Powers. Jesus did not just forgive sinners, he gave them a new world. And for those who could not go back to what or where they had been, he created a new structure—his vagabond, sexually mixed, scandalous band of followers who shared what they had in common. Too often our social action has been as devoid of spirituality as our evangelism has been politically innocuous. Too often we have told the Powers that they were wrong but not Whose they are. Too much of the time we have drawn on secular models of social change without drawing as well on our own rich fund of symbolism and imagery, liturgy, and story. Many dismissed the hymns and gospel songs, the eucharists and prayers of a Martin Luther King, Jr., or Cesar Chavez as merely shrewd accommodations to the subcultures with which they worked. Such critics did not perceive that these were essential forms of struggle in themselves, that the enemy is not always self-evident, that engaging a Power on its own terms guarantees that the victor, whichever it is, will perpetuate the same terms. They did not address themselves to the transcendent One who alone could work changes which do not themselves bear the seeds of new evils.

How would it change the shape of social struggle if we understood that we wrestle not just against flesh and blood but also against principalities, against powers, against the world rulers of this present darkness, against the spiritual hosts of wickedness in the heavenlies? What are the practical implications of putting on the whole armor of God and praying at all times in the Spirit (Eph. 6:10–20)? How would it change the nature of our wrestling if we did so in the context of continuous Bible study and singing and worship? For those still working their way out from under the weight of an oppressively pious upbringing, that probably does not resound as good news, but it is. It is the way increasing numbers of others have learned they must live, in order to keep on struggling against the Beast without being made bestial.

For the struggle is both physical and spiritual, and for the long haul we need waybread that can replenish hope. We have perhaps forgotten how to use our tradition this way, but our sisters and brothers in the black churches or in the Latin American base communities, and many in the disarmament movement, have known this all along or are relearning it fast. That tradition bears within it, neglected but recoverable, a whole vocabulary about the Powers, and models for their confrontation, and wisdom concerning their stratagems. The myth does not provide final explanations, but it preserves a *structure* by which evil in all its depth can be discerned and held up to consciousness. It mobilizes awareness and catalyzes action. It calls us to a recognition of our own complicity and determination by the Powers and offers us liberation. It is not merely a human creation, but a revelation of the nature of ultimate reality, humanly mediated. Like DNA, the story is a chain of symbols in exquisitely condensed form, providing the culturally encoded information required for social and psychic survival and transformation. Like a holograph, it provides an authentic "picture" of the invisible nature of ultimate reality, discernible even in its most minute parts. There is, put simply, nothing else quite like it, and we neglect it to our peril.

Heaven Is the Transcendent
"Within" of Material
Reality

To this point I have suggested that the Powers can be interpreted as the visible and invisible aspects of real social, structural, and material entities in the world. I suggested further that the writers of the New Testament could refer to either the visible or the invisible aspects of the Powers, or even both together, as the context required. It is most difficult for us, given our modern materialistic worldview, to comprehend the invisible aspect. It was with this very issue that Eph. 3:10 confronted us:

what does it mean to communicate the manifold wisdom of God to the principalities and powers in the *heavenly* places? It is a question children always ask and parents assiduously avoid: what do we mean by "heaven"?

Popular culture has tended to regard heaven (if it has any regard for it at all) as a transcendent, otherworldly sphere qualitatively distinct from human life, to which the dead go if they have been good. What if we were instead to conceive of it as the realm of "withinness," the metaphorical "place" in which the spirituality of everything is "located," as it were. "Heaven," in religions all around the world, is precisely that— the habitat of angels, spirits, cherubim, and seraphim, but also of demons and the devil and all the Powers "in the heavenly places." Heaven is simply where they "reside."

But heaven is a great deal more as well. It is where God is enthroned and thus is the source of the transformative possibilities that God presents to every actual entity. In the language of process theology, God envisions all possibilities and is forever presenting every created thing with the particular relevant possibilities that can maximize the total situation in which it exists, both for itself and for the larger unity of which it is a part. To paraphrase Whitehead, "Heaven" is the "home of the possibles," not simply in the abstract sense that our potentialities have been planted in us like seeds and that it is up to us to make them sprout. Quite the contrary, our own given potentiality, like that of the acorn, is always merely to repeat the past, to go on being and doing what we have always been and done before. The heavenly possibilities are presented to us as a lure challenging us to go beyond our conditioning and habits, our collusion in oppressing or being oppressed, our inertia, fear, and neuroses. God offers the heavenly possibilities for creative novelty, and we can accept wholly, or accept in part, or reject completely and simply go on repeating our past.

When we do realize a transformative possibility, we quite rightly speak of the experience of ecstasy that accompanies that realization as "heavenly." We have a sense of enhanced realness, of becoming more than we knew we could become. There is a rightness about it that resonates throughout the universe and unites us with the larger purposes of God. Thus when Jesus healed or cast out demons or preached to the poor, he could declare that in that instant the "Reign of heaven" had come on them. When justice is done, we experience a sense of heaven. When a person's individual interests coincide with the interest of the Whole, there is an epiphany of heaven. When we die to our egocentricity and abandon ourselves to God, what opens to receive us is heaven. "But God, who is rich in mercy, out of the great love with which he loved us, even when we were dead through our trespasses, made us alive together with Christ . . . and raised us up with him, and made us sit with him in the heavenly places in Christ Jesus" (Eph. 2:4–6).

Heaven is also the negation of possibles. We should conceive possibles no longer as a static set of immutable scenarios drawn up before the world began but as an infinite number of possible worlds dynamically emerging from the internal decisions and interactions of the present world. And because these possibles confront us with an "if . . . then" that is fateful and often irreversible, the possible also confronts us as judgment for lost opportunity, squandered gifts, or rejected love. Hence heaven is where John sees "thrones, and seated on them were those to whom judgment was committed" (Rev. 20:4).

"Heaven" here cannot be conceived of as "up there" in such a way that it is out of relationship with the earth, for believers are already, while alive, established in it. It was precisely this problem that created the impasse in the interpretation of Eph. 3:10. If the church now must make known God's manifold wisdom to the principalities and powers in the heavenlies, the heavenlies must somehow be accessible to the church. Insofar as "heaven" encompasses the entire universe, it is certainly not limited to the earth, but it interpenetrates all things, is present in all things, bearing the secret of the potential and inwardness and unfolding of all things.[15] Thus, according to the *Gospel of Thomas*, when Jesus' disciples ask him when the kingdom will come, he responds, "It will not come by waiting for it. It will not be a matter of saying 'Here it is' or 'There it is.' Rather, the kingdom of the Father is spread out upon the earth, and men do not see it" (*NHL*, sec. 113). It was said just as

15. Angelus Silesius described heaven as I am suggesting.
> Stay! Whither runnest thou?
> God's heaven is in thee.
> If elsewhere thou it seek,
> never shalt thou it see.

> "In a good time we shall see
> God and his light," ye say.
> Fools! Ye shall never see
> what ye see not today.

The Cherubic Wanderer, trans. Willard R. Trask (New York: Pantheon Books, 1953), 53, 60. Emanuel Swedenborg wrote in a similar vein. "The states of the interiors are what make heaven, and . . . heaven is within one, and not outside of him." "For man's interiors are what receive heaven, while his exteriors receive the world." *Heaven and Its Wonders and Hell* (New York: American Swedenborg Printing and Publishing Society, 1758; 1900), 27, 62 (§§ 33, 99).

well by a seventh-grader in a recent confirmation class: "Heaven is wherever God is acknowledged."

The ancients sought to express the ubiquitous quality of heaven by piling up numbers in astronomical proportions to indicate the infinity of the hosts of angels (Rev. 5:11, 13; 19:1, 6). Yahweh was the Lord of the universe, but even more often and specifically, "Lord of hosts," "Lord of Spirits," "Lord of the Powers," as if the real test of lordship is the capacity to control the transcendent realm of determining forces that exercise the real day-to-day governance of every aspect of life on earth. The ancients perceived that there was an angel for everything, down to the last blade of grass. This notion, laughed to scorn for the past few centuries, now appears to have been, symbolically, precisely correct: every blade of grass, every rock crystal, acorn, and ovum has its "messenger" (*angelos*) from God to instruct it in its growth, however we name it (DNA, the "laws" of crystalline formation, etc.).

Such a view of heaven finds it to be "nearer than breathing, closer than hand or foot," yet still transcendent. But its transcendence is not a transcendence of *matter;* that is the bias of the old worldview, infected by Neoplatonic aversion to the material universe. "Heaven" in our hypothesis has a transcendence of an altogether different kind; it is the transcendence of the "worldly" way of viewing reality, of the alienated order of existence, of egocentric ways of living, of idolatry of the part in defiance of the Whole, of the unrealized present by the consummation to come. It is transcendent by virtue of inwardness, invisibility, and futurity, not by remoteness and distance. One must, in traditional terms, be "saved" in order to perceive it, not just be better informed. It cannot just be known about; it must be *known.*

Mystics have traditionally used the language of projection to attempt to describe the ineffable quality of their experience of this dimension of existence. They have spoken of it as "another world," "the beyond," "the spiritual realm," meaning by that a quality of consciousness not reducible to anything perceivable by normal sensory awareness or by thought. In their desperation to awaken those who are content with the world of appearances they sometimes spoke of their being captives held by jailors in the prison of the body. They sometimes (usually under the spell of Neoplatonism) detested the material world, heaping it with derision. They perceived it to be the cause of blindness rather than simply the occasion of it. They blamed the *means* by which people deadened their higher senses rather than the cause, which was a delusion of the spirit.

Recent studies in neurophysiology[16] have reminded us, however, that every human experience is bodily, even so-called "out of body" experiences, insofar as such experiences (quite apart from their interpretation) necessarily involve the brain in order for the subject to be aware of them at all. Thinking and brain activity are simply two sides of a single indivisible process. Neither can be reduced to the other (though some philosophers have fruitlessly treated ideas as the sole reality and some scientists have reduced thought to brain activity). Even archetypes have electromagnetic patterning in the brain. There is, in fact, nothing that affects us psychologically that does not have some corresponding configuration in the brain. Everything spiritual has its concomitant incarnation in the body—even spiritual theories which advocate denial of the body. Kundalini yoga quite rightly insisted that spiritual mastery consists not of transcending the body but of lifting the instinctual energies from "lower" to "higher" centers along the spine (the "chakras"). "Higher" here is used paradoxically, however. It does not mean an increase in instinctual energies but rather their transmutation into more subtle forms, much as an electrical transformer takes the high voltage from the power line and reduces it to an amount usable in the home.[17]

If heaven is not some other reality but the inner essence of present reality in its fullest potentiality, then the mystical "ascent" is not out of the body and into a wholly incorporeal spiritual realm, but *into the body's very own essence as the temple of the Holy Spirit within us*. What seems to be qualitatively different from normal bodily experience is indeed qualitatively different, but not because it escapes the body. On the contrary, it appears to be so different precisely because the inner essence of bodily existence has for once been actually apprehended. The beatific vision does not involve renunciation of the stuff of our humanity, but the recognition that our human stuff can itself become translucent, incandescent with the fire of the divine which indwells us. Perhaps that is why the Sufis called the Holy Spirit the "Angel of Humanity."

It is precisely the Jews' insistence on the inseparability of soul and body that led them to affirm the resurrection of the whole person, spirit,

16. See, e.g., Eugene d'Aquili and Charles Laughlin, Jr., "The Biopsychological Determinants of Religious Ritual Behavior," *Zygon* 10 (1975): 32–58.

17. Ascetic disciplines are a time-honored and helpful means of countering the onesidedness of a life hung up by material reality, as long as the latter is put in its place, not rejected. But the converse is also true: physical joys can be a salutary antidote to a morbidly ascetic nature. And neither is of any use whatever as long as the ego remains in control.

soul, and body. Popular Christianity long since abandoned that for belief in the immortality of the soul, that is, of a bodiless continuation in the pure realm of spirit. Against this view Paul had already coined the notion of a "spiritual body" (1 Cor. 15:35–57). Just what this paradoxical formulation means is not nearly so important as *that* it is asserted. We cannot conceive it, but it serves to hold the myth open into eternity and prevents its collapsing into a dualism of spirit versus matter. However incomprehensible it is in literal terms, it is the necessary symbolic affirmation that life is always life in a body, that spirit cannot exist apart from its concretion in form, that the victory of life over death includes the transformed vehicle by means of which, and solely by means of which, we have known what it means to be alive. All the rest is trust.

So how did Christianity become almost solely preoccupied with getting into heaven after death? One can find very little trace of that concern in the Bible. The Old Testament, for its part, knows almost nothing of eternal life. The idea was late in developing in Judaism. The New Testament itself jostles between the poles of eternity seen as a present experience on the one hand and as a future hope on the other. Ephesians and the Fourth Gospel stress the former, Paul the latter, but all maintain a tension between the "already" and the "not yet" of Christian existence. Paul is far more dubious than they of the adequacy of our foretastes of heaven in this life; he longs to be "at home with the Lord" (2 Cor. 5:8; Phil. 1:23). The Spirit is a down payment, to be sure, but no guarantee against floggings, shipwreck, hunger, or loneliness (2 Cor. 11:23–29). In fact, preoccupation with heavenly existence can become a diversion from the costliness of obedience in the concrete sociopolitical world. The heaven awaited by the faithful is not a "place" in the sky, but a redeemed reality in which even the physical universe will be "freed from the shackles of mortality and enter upon the liberty and splendour of the children of God" (Rom. 8:21, NEB). The soul does not escape the body to return to the ideal realm on high, but is granted a transformed bodily existence when Christ returns to earth at the consummation (Phil. 3:20–21).

Christianity cannot live without the longing for "heaven," for that longing is in part a longing for the realization of the transcendent possibilities of human life *on earth*. It is the sense of these heavenly possibilities that accounts for the restlessness of creation, what Paul called its "eager longing" to be "set free from its bondage to decay" (Rom. 8:19, 21). For heaven is not simply the "within" of all present reality; it is also the womb of the future, that toward which God entices us by offering us in each moment new ways of becoming more real, more vital, more united with that which tends toward the good of the whole. And yet the realization of heavenly possibilities on earth cannot bring complete heavenly peace, since each realization brings with it a new challenge for creative novelty. In that sense, heaven is the negation of all our attempts to build surrogate "heavens" on earth at the expense of the poor and oppressed. It is the sublime subverter of our tendencies to be seduced from further transformations by the pleasure of those already achieved. And finally, heaven is the treasury of every sacrifice and contribution made in time, whereby God receives the world and all our actions in such a way as to try to salvage whatever good can be gained from it, with a tender care "that nothing be lost."[18]

I do not wish to leave the impression, however, that the spiritual is just an epiphenomenon, like Galileo's "secondary qualities," as if the material were primary. The material and spiritual poles of reality are inseparable. They come into existence together and cease to exist together. Neither is the "cause" of the other.[19] Historically, the church has tended to stress the spiritual to the neglect of a genuinely positive respect for the material. In reaction, recent centuries in the West have witnessed a compensatory and equally one-sided emphasis on the material, often in utter disregard for and even denial of the spiritual. Developmentally, in Western societies we tend to lose a sense of the spiritual and be captivated by the material side of reality, and only after often excruciating personal struggle are we "reborn" into the other dimension of the one and only real world.

The New Testament's vision of the Reign of God, however, is of a

18. Alfred North Whitehead, *Process and Reality*, corrected ed. by David R. Griffin and Donald W. Shelburne (New York: Free Press, 1978), p. 346. See also p. 351.

19. If there is no spirit without its concretion and no material entity without a spirit or inwardness or subjectivity, then classical theism is wholly inadequate as a metaphysics, for God could not be conceived of as existing apart from God's concretion in the physical universe. God, on this view, would be something akin to the Soul of the universe, and conversely the universe could be spoken of as the body of God. In a process view, God is conceived of not as standing outside the world as creator but as the creative, artistically ordering, transformative principle within the world. In the Genesis creation stories, there is no hint of creation *ex nihilo;* that is an idea born of Greek emanationist thinking. The "stuff" is already there, and God orders it. In Whitehead's terms,

It is as true to say that the World is immanent in God, as that God is immanent in the World.

It is as true to say that God transcends the World, as that the World transcends God.

It is as true to say that God creates the World, as that the World creates God. (Ibid., 348)

transformed reality that involves both a new heaven (spirituality) and a new earth (materiality). If classical Christianity emphasized the former, Marxism and secular humanism have emphasized the latter. This new metaphor attempts to synthesize the valid elements of both. Marx's real intent, after all, was not to make people materialistic, if by that we mean preoccupied with consumption and themselves. Nor was he set on reducing reality to mere matter and replacing freedom with an iron determinism. His materialism was dialectical; he was attempting to explain how people *are* reduced to mere things and made the slaves of machines and masters, in order to uncover the laws by which they might secure their freedom.[20] If, as proposed here, we join Teilhard de Chardin in locating spirit at the very heart of matter—if we see it as the "within" of actual people, institutions, the state, nature—then the establishment of the material basis for the full and free development of people must be an indispensable aspect of our vision of God's Reign. Acts of justice cannot then simply be an optional movement at the fringe, but the very stuff of existence before God. "Suppose a brother or a sister is in rags with not enough food for the day, and one of you says, 'Good luck to you, keep yourselves warm, and have plenty to eat,' but does nothing to supply their bodily needs, what is the good of that? So with faith. If it does not lead to action, it is in itself a lifeless thing" (James 2:15–17, NEB).

But this formulation leaves me a bit uneasy. I can hear another voice rising up in me, saying: "All this demystifying is just another form of mystification. Here the poor person stands before you in her need and you do not declare immediate solidarity with her and make her cause yours. You want instead to pursue a quixotic and mystical assault on some alleged spiritual Power that 'holds' her in subjection. Anyone with eyes can see that she is held in subjection by the capitalist economic system, and all this talk of 'Powers' merely serves to remove your neighbor from before your eyes and interpose something more 'interesting.' You are still caught in the legacy of idealism. You really believe ideas are more real than bloated bellies. You would rather discuss your thoughts than deal with concrete injustice. So you interpose a realm of Powers that you can go on talking about, maybe even praying about, as a way of avoiding your neighbor."

That cuts straight to the bone. How can I deny the truth of that? And—

20. Nancy Bancroft, "Materialism and the Christian Left: Rethinking Christian Use of Marx," *JES* 20 (1983): 43–66.

suppose a whole new generation of scholars were to become absorbed in exploiting this new field (already dubbed "exousiology" by Berkhof), with no actual opposition to real structures of injustice or contact with those who are most oppressed. If the theology of the future must win its right to speak by being a continual reflection on praxis, on the actual struggle of humanity for authentic being, then we must be careful to keep the ring of that voice clear in our ears.

At the same time, however, one still must ask how the neighbor became oppressed and is kept that way. How has she *internalized* that spirit of oppression and granted legitimacy to the very Powers that oppress her? How can all the "flaming darts of the evil one" that have carried their poisonous secretions into her very bloodstream be pulled out, one by one, and the toxins filtered out? How can she be freed to authentic struggle, unless the very ideas and images that have been planted in her are torn out by the very roots, through the vision of a counterreality capable of improving her lot?

But now I can hear an objection from the other side. Is it *our* responsibility to help her? Isn't it God's task to deliver the captives? Christians all over the globe have raised that very objection, convinced that on biblical and dogmatic grounds the church is *forbidden* to become engaged in struggles against systemic injustice. The issue must be met head-on, because those who argue this way have at least one leg on very firm ground. Just a sample of passages shows that their concern is not simply for proof-texting but for a proper regard for the sovereignty of God. "Stand still and see this great thing, which the Lord will do before your eyes" (1 Sam. 12:16). "A king is not saved by his great army; a warrior is not delivered by his great strength. The war horse is a vain hope for victory, and by its great might it cannot save" (Ps. 33:16). "Power belongs to God" (Ps. 62:11; see also Isa. 30:15; Zech. 4:6). In the face of such texts, quietism and docile trust would seem to be the order of the day.

Yet nowhere in the Bible do we see anyone standing still. All the human agents of God's will are working, not only hard but with almost superhuman effort. Moses' care for his people exhausts him to distraction, and Jesus' movements through Galilee resemble a blitzkrieg. Why then the curious *passivity* that the Bible seems to enjoin in the struggle against the Powers? Perhaps our distinction between outer and inner might cast a feeble light on this baffling paradox of human action and heavenly grace. We are told, on the one hand, "Work out your own salvation with fear and trembling" (Phil. 2:12), because it is our responsibility to change the outer arrangements by which power is structured in the world. We can reform or revamp the organization, elect better leaders, win equal rights for or as the disadvantaged, or even engage in revolution. But we cannot affect the inner, spiritual dimension of institutions directly. Blacks could not simply settle for winning the right to sit at the front of the bus; they needed to lay siege to the very citadel of racism itself, the hearts of members of the white majority. But how were they to *storm* hearts? For we have no unmediated access to the "within" of a system, or institution, or even another person, for their "withins" are a function not of our acts alone but of all the history and traditions, beliefs and experiences that make up their reality at any given moment. That is where faith and prayer come in. We intercede before the Sovereign of the Powers to rectify this institution's or person's balance, to align its spirituality with the good of the whole, to convert it and transform it. That is something we cannot bring about no matter how much outer change we achieve, but it is precisely the outer changes we make that challenge, lure, and goad the oppressor toward inner change. Hence the Philippians passage continues, "for God is at work within you, both to will and to work for his good pleasure" (2:13).

Yes, *stand still*, if you want to carry the battle to the very heart of the matter, if you want fundamental change—still, at the still point of the turning world, where all is action without motion, where God inaugurates the great sea-change that runs deep under countervailing waves to turn the tide.

And yet we are also to struggle, equipped with the whole panoply of God's armor, "and *having done all*, to stand" (Eph. 6:13). We are to work with determined persistence at the outer, and to trust God to change the inner. We may be overfamiliar with this paradox, so frequently stated in Scripture (e.g., Phil. 2:12–13; Gal. 2:20; Mark 8:35); perhaps we can hear it afresh in Henry Corbin's remark on a verse from the Koran: " 'It is not you who cast the dart when you cast it, but Allah casts it' (8:17). And yet, yes, it is you who cast it; and yet, no, it is not you who cast it."[21]

The issue, then, is not social struggle versus inner change, but their orchestration together so that both occur simultaneously. The transformation of society and persons can begin at either end. The early church began from the pole of steadfastness in prayer and the refusal of idolatry,

21. Henry Corbin, *Creative Imagination in the Sūfism of Ibn 'Arabī* (Princeton: Princeton University Press, 1969), 214.

manifesting that *hypomonē* which the Book of Revelation regards as the highest Christian virtue. It is usually somewhat limply rendered "patient endurance," but it is in fact closer to "absolute intransigence," "unbending determination," "an iron will," "the capacity to endure persecution, torture, and death without yielding one's faith."[22] It is one of the fundamental attributes of nonviolent resistance.

But that same transformation can begin at the pole of social struggle and work an inner change along the way. Many people entered the civil rights movement because they were concerned with justice for blacks, and in the course of involvement in nonviolent direct action discovered an even greater change taking place in themselves. When F. D. Dawson III and I drove from Texas to Selma, Alabama, to join the thousands of clergy who had converged to support the black struggle for voting rights there, we were accosted at the edge of town by a man in a pickup who chased us all over town honking his horn and shouting obscenities and threats. His truck was equipped with a gun rack; we were afraid he might be armed. We were terrified. When we finally got away from him, we were as pale as ghosts. We were not ready to die. After two hours of training in nonviolent action the next day, we joined the marchers moving down the main street, fully prepared to die. Perhaps our presence among so many aided their struggle in a minuscule way, but their struggle aided us enormously. We had gone to champion social justice; in the process we were forced to deal with the very personal question of the cost of discipleship. There is no more effective way of undergoing the spiritual discipline of dying to one's ego than to position oneself directly in the path of the possibility of actual death—say, on the tracks of a train loaded with nuclear warheads or before the prow of a Trident sub. Social involvement of that kind can do wonders for the soul—if the leadership understands the essential unity of body and spirit and addresses them both.

This unity must be kept paramount in addressing the Powers. It is easy enough to set oneself against the visible evil of a Power. But we never have control over that inner dimension of reality which we are calling the spiritual dimension of power. The outer signs, symbols, personnel,

---

22. LSJ translates *hypomonē* as "the power to sustain blows," "obstinacy," "endurance." Erich Haupt renders it as "perseverance on the basis of the inner victorious sense that all contrary relationships and hostile forces can be overcome" (*Die Gefangenschaftsbriefe neu bearbeitet* (Göttingen: Vandenhoeck & Ruprecht, 1897), 18. It appears 31 times in the New Testament. See esp. Rev. 1:9; 13:10; 14:12; Luke 21:19; Rom 2:7; 5:3; 8:25; Heb. 10:36; 12:1.

buildings, and structures of a Power can be manipulated, opposed, altered, but we never know if our intervention will in fact affect the essential spirit of the entity and bring genuine change. The students who struck Columbia University in 1968 succeeded in winning significant aspects of their program, but the university's "angel" was not itself changed in any substantial way, and the moment student pressures eased, reaction set in.

Change is possible, but only if the spirit as well as the forms of Power are touched. And that spirit can only be spiritually discerned and spiritually encountered. This is what made Martin Luther King, Jr., a figure of world-historic proportions. With only the powerless at his side, he formulated actions that would provoke and make visible the institutional violence of racism. By absorbing that violence in their own bodies, they exposed the legalized system as immoral, stripped it of legitimacy, and forced unprecedented numbers of people to choose between their racism and their Christianity. He resolutely refused to treat racism as a political issue only; he insisted that it be seen also as a moral and spiritual sickness. He did not attack the soul of America, but appealed to its most profound depths. His confrontational tactics were attempts to address that soul. He called a nation to repent, and significant numbers did. In the process the spirit of the nation itself began to change. His assassination, and the abandonment of the moral basis of the struggle for one of black power versus white power, allowed the worst elements of the ugly racist spirit to reassert themselves, this time with blacks no longer the vanguard of reconciliation and conversion, but openly espousing a counterracism of their own. Those who continued to insist on loving the enemy and working interracially were buried under the flood of poisons now unleashed from both sides. Blacks and whites not only ceased to work together, but even stopped speaking. The adoption of the methods of the oppressor had finally turned all parties into oppressors, and it was now only a matter of finding someone weak enough to oppress. (Black power advocates generally targeted meek white liberals unable to deny their residual racism and unwilling or unable to counter being dumped on.) Once the moral grounds of struggle had been yielded, it was merely a matter of which side had more power. In a contest of that sort, it did not require a Solomon to predict which side would win. The revival and new respectability of the Ku Klux Klan, the collapse of the political coalition of blacks and whites, the abandonment or abatement of efforts for equal rights in employment and housing—all that was predictable the moment the spiritual basis of the struggle shifted from love to resentment, from nonviolence to the rhetoric of violence, from moral force to the force of anger. Impatient with the pace of a struggle that sought not only legal equality but the conversion of the very heart of the nation from racism, black power attempted the quick fix of structural change by a frontal assault on white power. Its epitaph can be formulated as an axiom: the direct use of power against a Power will inevitably be to the advantage of The Powers That Be.

This is a mistake, however, that has been repeated in one struggle after another. The Weather Underground correctly criticized the U.S. government for its barbaric violence in Vietnam and then mirrored the very barbarism it condemned by adopting violence as its means. Whenever we let the terms of struggle be dictated by the Power that we oppose, we are certain to become as evil. Nothing about this insight is new. It is written for anyone to read in Rev. 17:15–18. There the Beast on whom the Harlot (Roma) sits turns against her and shifts his allegiance to the ten enemy kings. These will hate the harlot and burn her up with fire. The Beast can shift loyalties precisely because he knows that the means employed to overthrow the Harlot will make the kings every bit as much the children of hell as she.

That is why we must not engage the Powers without rigorous examination of our own inner evil, which we often project on our opponents. We must ask how we are like the very Power we oppose, and attempt to open these parts of ourselves to divine transformation. We must attempt to stop the spiral of violence both within ourselves and in our tactics vis-à-vis the Powers. We must discern the spirituality that we oppose and be careful not to grant it victory within ourselves. And we must settle it within ourselves, once and for all and then over and over again, that we will not celebrate any victory feast that does not include a setting for our enemy.

In short, we must develop a fine-tuned sensitivity to what the ancients called "the war in heaven."[23] It is the unseen clash of values and ideologies, of the spirituality of institutions and the will of God, of demonic factionalism and heavenly possibilities. The unique calling of the church in social change lies in making clear the dual nature of our task. We wrestle on two planes, the earthly and the heavenly—what I have called the outer and inner aspects of reality. The ancients, in terms far more

23. Rev. 12:7; 2 Macc. 5:1–4; Dan. 10:13, 20–21; Ignatius, *Eph.* 13; *Sib. Or.* 5:512–31; *Apoc. Thom.* (*NT Apoc.* 2:802).

picturesque, spoke of this as the coincidence of what is above with what is below.

What Is Above Is
Also Below

Cultures other than our own have been far more conscious of the existence of these two planes. One way of imaging it goes back to the very beginnings of Near Eastern cosmology. I am referring to the macrocosm/microcosm view of reality—the notion that whatever happens on earth (the "microcosm," or small world) is a mirror image of the activities of Powers in heaven (the "macrocosm," or large world). The idea was already hoary with age when it was chiseled on the buildings erected by the Sidonian kings Bodastart and Esmunazar in the fifth century B.C.E., where the earthly Sidon is depicted as a copy of its heavenly prototype.[24] The idea of heaven as the origination and prototype of all that is can be traced back among the Greeks as early as Pythagoras and finds its most famous advocate in Plato, with his realm of the Ideas or archetypes. Greek Orphism made the unity of heaven and earth the goal of the mystical initiation, in which the quester sought to recapture this deepest and lost unity that characterizes divinization.[25]

Israel, too, held this macrocosm/microcosm view from earliest times,[26] but hedged it carefully to prevent its being used to legitimate tyranny. The prophets especially were on their guard against the divine-kingship ideology, through which the most gross injustices were perpetrated in the

24. Gerhard Von Rad, "Ouranos," *TDNT* 5 (1967): 502–509, esp. 507–508. For other examples, see Mircea Eliade, *Cosmos and History: The Myth of Eternal Return* (New York: Harper & Row, 1959), 6ff. The motif appears to be almost universal; the Sioux medicine man Black Elk spoke of his vision of the transcendent heavenly council, which he called "the nation above" (John G. Neihardt, *Black Elk Speaks* [New York: Pocket Books, (1932) 1972], 33), and the sixteenth-century Chinese novel by Ch'eng-en Wu, *The Journey to the West*, satirizes the heavenly bureaucracy in caricature of the earthly, imperial bureaucracy of the period (trans. and ed. Anthony C. Yu [Chicago: University of Chicago Press, 1982]). Alan F. Segal has recently demonstrated that this above/below conception, featuring either a divine revealer coming down and returning or a human ascending and returning, was "the dominant mythical constellation of late classical antiquity" ("Heavenly Ascent in Hellenistic Judaism, Early Christianity and Their Environment," *ANRW* II.23.2 [1980]: 1333–94).

25. Helmut Traub, "Ouranos," *TDNT* 5 (1967): 497–502, esp. 499.

26. The idea of heavenly/earthly correlation is present in the Old Testament in every reference to the heavenly council. All texts dealing with the angels of the nations also presuppose it (see above, Part One), as do Isa. 24:4–6; Ps. 68:17 (JB); and Judg. 5:20; see also *Jub.* 2:18.

name of heaven. The Jews were able to appropriate the notion of evil spirits, fallen angels, and Satan precisely because they could subsume these Powers within a secure henotheistic[27] framework in which Yahweh was ultimately sovereign. Angelic and demonic activity in heaven was reflected in events on earth but did not serve to justify these events, since God remained judge over all and angels too could err.[28] The freedom of agents human and divine guaranteed their capacity to commit evil, and the same freedom explained the presence of such evils in a world created and governed by a good God.[29] This complex view of the nature of power virtually forced itself on Israel as a consequence of its experience of institutionalized evil.

The motif is frequently employed in the Qumran texts. In the War Scroll (1QM 17) of Qumran, for example, God "will raise up the kingdom of Michael in the midst of the gods [i.e., the heavenly council], and the realm of Israel in the midst of all flesh." Israel's political ascendency on earth will be possible only insofar as it coincides with the ascendency of Michael, Israel's guardian, in heaven. And members of the Essene community who were for any reason unclean were excluded from worship, since the earthly community participated in a conjoint heavenly liturgy, and "holy angels are in the congregation."[30]

Indeed, the idea of heavenly/earthly correspondence crops up in Jewish

27. "Henotheism" refers to the belief that God is the one and only ultimate reality, but that God is surrounded by lesser divinities (gods, angels, powers, cherubim, seraphim) who do the Most High's bidding. "Monolatry" stresses that only God is to be worshiped, and "mono-Yahwism" indicates that Israel was to serve Yahweh alone. All of these terms are more adequate than "monotheism," which has come to mean that only God exists and that the gods have no reality—a conviction that is difficult to document from Scripture. This issue will be treated fully in the chapter on "Gods" in volume 2.

28. See above, p. 29 n. 48: even Gabriel is disobedient at times. And even the four living creatures around the throne vie with one another to serve God best, leading to a certain degree of strain in the heavenly court (*Apoc. Abr.* 18; *Tanhuma* on Gen. 2:4 (ed. Buber, 10). See *I Clem.* 39:4–5—God "hath noted perversity in his angels"; "Yea, the heaven is not pure before him." On this motif in general see Peter Schäfer, *Rivalität zwischen Engeln und Menschen: Untersuchungen zur rabbinischen Engelvorstellung* (New York and Berlin: Walter de Gruyter, 1975).

29. Philo had already thoroughly digested the above/below notion in a manner that provided a neat solution to the problem of how we are able to know reality. God endowed humanity with a nature that corresponds to the constellations, making the human being "in very truth, a miniature heaven," thus capable of fellowship with God and the heavenly powers (*De op.* 82). Using the same Platonic conceptions, the Sufi philosopher-mystic Ibn 'Arabī spoke of his "inner Heaven" as the confirmatory spiritual capacity to know whether a thing is true or not (see Corbin, *Creative Imagination,* 45).

30. 1QSa 2; 1QS 11:17–18; CD 15; 1QH 3:21 (Hymn 5). Thus also God and the holy angels would fight from heaven on the side of the elect (1QM 7; 10:8ff.; 12).

sources of every stripe, sometimes with a droll twist, as when Rabbi Hoshaiah (c. 250) taught:

> When the law courts below reach a decision and declare: Today is the New Year! then the Holy One, Blessed be he, says to the angels who serve: Set up the tribune, appoint the defense attorney, summon the writer of judgments, for the law court below has determined and established: This morning is the New Year!
>
> When all the angels who serve assemble and ask the Holy One, Blessed be he: Lord of the world, when is the New Year? then he answers them, You ask me? You and I, we will ask the law court below.[31]

It would be a mistake of modern rationalism, however, to believe that these mythological accounts of the heavenly council and its sovereignty over affairs on earth were merely the conscious invention of the powerful, or even to suggest that these angels and gods were simply the projection onto the cosmos of the power arrangements of the state. No doubt the heavenly hierarchies were thinly disguised depictions of the structure of human governments transferred to the realm of the gods.[32] But it is inaccurate to speak of all such myths as mystifications of actual power relations aimed at providing divine legitimation for earthly institutions, for Israel's prophets also pictured the divine council thus, even in passages

---

31. *Pesiq. R.*, p. 77 and parallels (cited by Peter Schäfer, *Rivalität zwischen Engeln und Menschen*, 233–34. Similarly, *Pirqe R. El.* 49 A ii–50 B i ("Michael, the angel, descended and took Levi, and brought him up before the Throne of Glory . . . and He [God] put forth His right hand and blessed him [Levi], that the sons of Levi should minister on earth before Him, like the ministering angels in heaven"); 15 Aii ff.; 24 Ai; *Pesiq. R.* 21:8; 28:2 (when the temple of Jerusalem was destroyed, the ministering angels begged God not to destroy the heavenly dwelling place also, on the basis of the correspondence of the earthy with the heavenly); T.B. *Sukka* 29a ("There is no nation which is smitten that its gods are not smitten together with it"); T. B. *B. Bat.* 75b; T. B. *Ta'anit* 5a.

Likewise esoteric Judaism: *3 Enoch* 35:6—The angels in heaven must each time before saying the Thrice Holy "take upon themselves the yoke of the kingdom of heaven," just as Israelites must do every day when they recite the *Shema* (M. *Ber.* 1–2) and when praying generally (T.B. *Ber.* 10b) (Hugo Odeberg, *Third Enoch* [New York: KTAV, 1973] 119n.); and *Hekhalot Rabbati*—the ritual in heaven cannot begin until the prayers of Israel have begun on earth (see Morton Smith, "Observations on Hekhalot Rabbati," in *Biblical and Other Studies*, ed. Alexander Altmann [Cambridge, Mass.: Harvard University Press, 1963], 143).

32. See, e.g., the description from Cylinder B of Gudea in J. Severino Croatto, "The Gods of Oppression," in *The Idols of Death and the God of Life*, by Pablo Richard et al. (Maryknoll, N.Y.: Orbis Books, 1983), 37; and for a thorough discussion, see E. Theodore Mullen, Jr., *The Assembly of the Gods*, HSM 24 (Chico, Calif.: Scholars Press, 1980).

where the legitimacy of the king was being challenged (e.g., 1 Kings 22:19–23). We should rather *regard these gods as the spirituality of the state*, the inner and actual essence of its visible structures. *Of course* the heavenly pantheon would reflect the actual structures of the earthly court; neither could exist otherwise. Far from mystifying power relations, the myth shows by the precise correspondence of earthly and heavenly that it has faithfully and accurately brought to expression the actual power relations at work. The myth is not a disguise at all, but a revelation. Depending on its degree of inclusiveness, it is a relatively true picture of the actual state of affairs in a given society. It does not hide power relations; it reveals them as they really are.

It is not the fact that these power relations are expressed *mythically* that makes them oppressive, but the content and structure of the myth employed. In Israel, God alone was supreme, and no human being could aspire to divinity. In Babylon, the king and royal house were divine and so shared divine supremacy. Both myths legitimated the state, but in Israel the state was instituted by God and under continual judgment, whereas in Babylon the state was a mirror of a static cosmic order, and criticism or rebellion a crime against heaven.

A ruler was expected to live up to the role expectations and values depicted by the myth, and failure to do so could lead to unrest among the priestly caste and even deposition. Thus Akhenaton encountered fierce resistance from the Egyptian priesthood to his novel idea that the sun was the sole god, and Nabonidus, the last king of Babylon, became the derided subject of a political poem and the butt of the hostilities of priests and people for his ten-year absence from Babylon while he rebuilt and adorned shrines to a cult not honored in his capital city. But these were exceptions, and each paid dearly for deviating from the mythic norm.

Such myths of power are by no means fabrications by the ruling classes. They are the unconscious distillate of the actual spiritual quality "exuded," as it were, from the value systems and power relations of the existing state. No fabrication could have been so accurate, so free from idealization, so devoid of "oughts." The myth simply declares what is. "The primitive mentality does not *invent* myths," observed Jung, "it *experiences* them."[33] Court poets and bards need not be written off as sycophants who merely ingratiated themselves to their masters. They had

33. "The Psychology of the Child Archetype," *The Archetypes and the Collective Unconscious*, Collected Works, vol. 9.1, Bollingen Series 20 (Princeton: Princeton University Press, 1971), 154.

simply to shut their eyes and discern the inner spirit of the court; the words would have leaped out all unbidden. Since it is in fact the universal testimony of prophets and seers that their words or visions are "given," we might as well take them seriously and ask rather *who* or *what* is giving them their words. The thesis here is that often it is the "angel" of the institution that does so; the spirituality of the institution itself is there to be "read" by any discerning person. The conflict over true versus false prophecy in Israel gained its peculiar poignancy from the fact that *both* were correct, insofar as each gave voice to a genuine spirituality. False prophets tended to register the "within" of the nation or court in terms of a narrow view of Israel's self-interest as seen from the perspective of those in power. True prophets were those who saw Israel's self-interests as wholly subservient to the will of Yahweh, which transcended and often stood in judgment on Israel's own policies.

Contrast this way of interpreting the "here below" and "up above" perspective with the reductionist sociological explanation given by Peter Berger and Thomas Luckmann.[34] Human beings, they remark, validate their institutions by projecting onto gods or natural law or some divine agency their origins. Berger and Luckmann regard this as a reification in which the human origin of the institution is obfuscated by being withdrawn from sight and hence from criticism.

Their analysis is half right—no doubt human institutions are humanly formed, and it is a great advance to recognize their human origin. But that is only half the truth. These institutions are not simply subject to human fiat. They possess a spirituality, an inwardness, that is highly resistant to change. The heavenly powers are *not* mere projections that mystify the real power relations. They are, quite the contrary, the real interiority of earthly institutions, systems and forces. They can be known only by images projected from the unconscious, to be sure, but what is projected is a more or less accurate depiction of the spirituality actually there. The issue is not whether projection is involved; we humans can know certain aspects of interiority *no other way*. The real issue is the degree to which the spirituality of a specific historical institution is, at any given moment, idolatrous.

It was cynical politicians in the decline of paganism, not those who breathed its vitality in the heyday of Hellenism, who could argue that "the whole belief in immortal gods was invented by wise persons in the

34. *The Social Construction of Reality* (Garden City, N.Y.: Doubleday & Co., 1967), p. 90 and n. 63.

interest of the state," or that "it is for the good of states that men should be deceived in religion."[35] Only as a culture is undergoing radical transformation do the ideological and symbolic underpinnings become fully visible—and only those on the way out.

The rise of the imperial cultus is often cited as an instance of sheer political manipulation through the manufacture of religious ritual. In fact, however, the imperial cultus appears to have arisen spontaneously in the Province of Asia as a manifestation of genuine gratitude for the beneficence Rome had shown to these formerly strife-torn city-states. Only later, sensing the utility of such devotion as a kind of ideological glue to cement together all the disparate parts of the empire, did the politicians consciously exploit it.

It is far from the case, then, that human beings create their gods. The "spirits" of things emerge with the things themselves and are only subsequently divined as their inner essence. The gods, spirits, and demons are not mere personifications or hypostatizations. That is the language of reductionism; it means that these entitites are not regarded as real, but only as poetic fictions or shorthand for speaking about realities the historian knows how to describe more precisely with his analytical tools. Personification means illusion. The Powers we are speaking about, on the contrary, are real. They work on us whether we acknowledge them or not. They do not depend on our belief for their efficacy. Humans cannot even lay claim to creating these Powers indirectly, by virtue of creating the structures, for studies of primates show that most of the hierarchical features that characterized Babylonian society had already been developed in primate societies.[36] To be sure, we do establish new structures and modify old ones. Insofar as we share in the creative process and bring new consciousness to it, we help create the spirituality of things. There is a reciprocity, so we could argue that it is as true to say that the gods create us as to say that we create the gods.

There is no question that the myths of power are used to legitimate, exploit, and oppress. Even "good" myths can be twisted into their opposites by tyrants. But they do not invent the great myths. We know why many have claimed that myths are made by the masters, for if the masters made them, then the oppressed can unmake them and fashion others more

35. Cicero, *De natura Deorum* 1.42, 118; Varro, as quoted by Augustine, *The City of God*, 4.27; 6.5; cited by T. R. Glover, "The Daemon Environment of the Primitive Christian," *HibJ* 11 (1912/13): 153.

36. See George Edgin Pugh, *The Biological Origins of Human Values* (New York: Basic Books, 1977), 227–61.

equitable and just. The intent is well-meant, but the reality is more complex, for we struggle not just with flesh and blood but with principalities and powers as well. Humans *can* change things, but not if they are so naive as to think that they are only changing human things. By virtue of their greater duration in time and their immense magnitude of power, institutions take on a momentum of their own. They are suprahuman, and some of their characteristics are a heritage from the animal kingdom, as I have already remarked. They have their own spirits and tend to preserve themselves through all the shifts of personnel. They can be changed, but genuine change is a function of the change of both structure *and* spirit. It is not pious talk to say that to affect an institution you must touch its soul; it is shrewd advice. Otherwise, the more things change the more they stay the same. There must be a "conversion" of the spirit to the vision of its place in the larger Whole.

In the New Testament the idea of heavenly/earthly correspondence is a part of the background belief of the age and is alluded to in a fashion that assumes the hearer's thorough familiarity with it. When the disciples return from the Lukan mission of the seventy, having successfully cast out demons on earth, Jesus exclaims, "I saw Satan fall like lightning from heaven" (Luke 10:18). Casting out demons on earth casts Satan out of heaven! Or again, Paul's irritation with women who have uncovered heads at worship is prompted by his fear that the angels, also present when the church worships, will be incited to lust (1 Cor. 11:10; see Gen. 6:1–4). And in the Epistle to the Hebrews the believer already participates in heavenly life on earth: "You have come to Mount Zion and to the city of the living God, the heavenly Jerusalem, and to innumerable angels in festal gathering" (12:22).[37]

The Book of Revelation is thoroughly acquainted with this motif. Not only is John permitted access to the divine liturgy through vision (chaps. 4–5), but the prayers of the saints on earth actually constitute an important section of the angelic liturgy in heaven. Rev. 8:1–5 recounts how an angel gathers the prayers that ascend to God and mingles them with incense at the altar before the throne; then when God has, as it were, inhaled them, the angel mixes the prayers with fire from the altar and hurls them on the earth, setting off a chain of physical and historical repercussions in the world. This not only illustrates the unity of heavenly

37. Worship is the moment of heavenly/earthly conjunction par excellence. According to the *Apostolic Constitutions* 7.35, the church on earth, "emulating the heavenly powers night and day," chants its praises just as the heavenly hosts do. So also *1 Clem.* 34:5-7; *Apoc. Paul* 29.

and earthly events but also indicates how the *fatefulness* of that connection can be altered. Left to themselves, the course of things runs to havoc in a world with an infinity of self-worshiping centers, but when any of that number turn from themselves to the Center of the whole, history itself can be changed. "Peals of thunder, loud noises, flashes of lightning, and an earthquake" (v. 5) throw the river of events out of its bed. The unexpected becomes suddenly possible, because humans on earth have evoked heaven, the home of the possibles, and have been heard.

Matthew's community also understood itself to have this capacity to determine things in heaven. Matt. 18:18 reads, "Whatever you bind on earth shall be bound in heaven, and whatever you loose on earth shall be loosed in heaven." The church has been granted "the keys of the kingdom of heaven" (16:19) and can settle matters of eternal consequence. Indeed, if two of you "arrive at an accord on earth" concerning any dispute that they are attempting to arbitrate for members of the church, it shall be ratified "by my Father in heaven" (18:19). Why? Because "where there are two or three convened in my name there I am amongst them."[38] Heaven is near because it is actively pressing both individuals and the group toward those values and goals which were incarnated by Jesus and which are given specific application by the community's own deliberations in the presence of the risen Christ.

So also the Pauline notion of the "body of Christ" can be understood, on the terms being discussed, as the quite literal reality of the Christian community. As the "within" or spirit of the churches, Christ calls them forward toward those transformative human possibilities for liberation, compassion, and love which God presents in each new moment. The "body of Christ" is the human community that has taken on itself as its avowed purpose, however inadequately, the manifestation of Christ's spirit in the world. Put another way, there can be no spirit of Christ apart from its concretions in the world. That is why betrayal of that spirit by the church is such a scandal (Gal. 3:1–5; see Rev. 2:5; 3:16).

The same "as above, so below" theme finds expression in Paul's letter to the Thessalonians: "We wanted to come to you—I, Paul, again and again—but Satan hindered us" (1 Thess. 2:18). Paul probably does not have in mind an actual confrontation with Satan as a figure blocking his path but means simply that circumstances were such as to frustrate his

38. Following the translation of J. Duncan M. Derrett, who sees Matt. 18:19–20 not as a charter of Christ-mysticism but as a guideline for settling legal issues, comparable to 1 Cor. 5:1–5 (" 'Where two or three are convened in my name . . . ': a sad misunderstanding," *ExpTim* 91/3 [Dec. 1979]: 83–86).

attempt to come. What they might have been we can only guess: the arrival of Jewish opponents where he was, or factionalism in the congregation, or public outcry of some sort, or even a recurrence of the chronic affliction that he calls a "messenger (*angelos*) of Satan" (2 Cor. 12:7). The point is simply that he was "hindered" on the earthly plane by the "god of this world" (2 Cor. 4:4); had it been a spiritual sense that the time was not right, he would have said that the *Spirit* hindered him (compare Acts 16:7). Note that this interpretation is not a "modernization" that seeks to dispose of a supernatural reference by reducing it to a human one. Paul believes that the hindrance is from Satan. Earthly and heavenly opposition are one.

Thus when "false apostles" oppose the gospel as Paul understands it, he brazenly brands them servants of Satan (2 Cor. 11:12–15), not as though they had consciously lent themselves out to the devil but because he considered their concrete actions satanic, however sincere they might have considered themselves to be. Again, in 2 Cor. 6:14—7:1, Satan ("Belial") is not "behind" the scenes scheming up idolatry and iniquity. Satan is manifested *in* idolatry, *in* iniquity, *in* the darkness of unbelief and defilement. Satan is, like God, known only in his successive concretions.

This is nowhere clearer than in Rev. 2:13. "Satan's throne" is not in heaven or the lower firmament but on the Acropolis at Pergamum, a forest of Greek temples that might have made an Athenian drool. Satan's throne, in short, is in the addressees' hometown. The threat is not from the sky but from yon sacred hill, not from a malevolent universe bent on their undoing but from the local markets that sell sacrificed meats (Rev. 2:14).[39] For the Seer of the Apocalypse, the satanic is not an abstract force distributed equally throughout the cosmos like a gas. It is the concentrated inner spirituality of idolatrous human structures. And it is as real as they are.

This same macrocosm/microcosm motif animates the vision of Satan incarnating in the Antichrist (2 Thess. 2:9). Here the language itself shows how integrally Satan and his earthly agent are related: "The coming of the lawless one by the activity of Satan." Or again in Revelation 12–13, the Dragon incarnates in the Beast from the Sea (the Roman Empire) and the Beast from the Land (its ideological propaganda machine, the imperial

39. "In Asia, Pergamum led the way in the Imperial cult. Smyrna, Ephesus, and other cities also became centres of this worship. Thus, not unnaturally, Asia became a leading centre of the persecution of Christians" (Paul Keresztes, "The Imperial Roman Government and the Christian Church: I: From Nero to the Severi," *ANRW* II:23.1:272).

cultus). Here Satan constitutes a diabolical trinity, in parody of Godhead. Evil never feels safe unless it wears the mask of divinity.[40]

In all these cases, the simultaneity of heavenly and earthly events witnesses to the perception, mythically couched, that there is more to events than what appears. The physical actors and institutions are only the outer manifestation of a whole field of powers contending for influence. Real change, consequently, will be only that which succeeds in altering both their visible and invisible aspects. "For we are contending not against flesh and blood"—though we most certainly join the battle at precisely that point—"but against the principalities, against the powers," against the spirituality of institutions, against the ideologies and metaphors and legitimations that prop them up, against the greed and covetousness that give them life, against the individual egocentricities that the Powers so easily hook, against the idolatry that pits short-term gain against the long-term good of the whole—all of which is manifested only in concrete institutions, systems, structures, and persons.

I am not arguing for an intrapsychic reductionism in which God, heaven, and the Powers are all conceived as mere projections and hence creations of our own unconscious psychic processes. Quite the reverse. The mind itself, on this reading, is a microcosm of heaven, and thus our own interiority is continuous with and a clue to the interiority of reality itself.

The Way Up Is the
Way Down

The maxim "And as above so on the earth also; for the likeness of that which is in the firmament is here on the earth" (*Asc. Isa.* 7:10) expresses in precise mythic terms the structural dynamic which I have been attempting to explicate by reference to the inner and outer aspects of concrete physical and historical reality. The ancients themselves had

---

40. The idea of Satan incarnating in humans was apparently rife in the first century. Besides the texts already mentioned, *Asc. Isa.* 3:11 refers to Beliar as dwelling "in the heart of Manasseh and in the heart of the princes (*archonton*, G[2]) of Judah." And 4:2–4 describes Beliar, "the great ruler, the king of this world," coming "in the likeness of a man" who is Nero *redivivus.* "This ruler (*archōn*, meaning Satan) *in the form of that king* will come and there will come with him all the powers (*dynameis*) of this world." We can spare ourselves the fruitless debate whether these Powers are earthly or heavenly. They are both, or stated more accurately, they are the outer and inner aspects of one and the same earthly concretions of power. This motif was not confined simply to Antichrist, however. In *NHL 1 Apoc. Jas.* 31:23–26 the "people" that killed Jesus "existed [as] a type of the archons, and it [the people] deserved to be [destroyed] through them [the archons]."

more than just an inkling that the above/below conjunction referred in fact to an inner/outer one. Let me bring forward a few witnesses. The first is *1 Enoch* 43:1–4:

> And I saw other lightnings and the stars of heaven, and I saw how He called them all by their names and they hearkened unto Him . . . and I asked the angel who went with me who showed me what was hidden: "What are these?" And he said to me: "The Lord of Spirits hath showed thee their parabolic meaning [literally, 'their parable']: these are the names of the holy who dwell on the earth and believe in the name of the Lord of Spirits for ever and ever."

Apparently human beings whose souls have answered to God's call cannot just be "on earth"; they must have a "heavenly" counterpart. Hence certain lightnings and stars represent their celestial "dimension," as it were. The author reads the lightnings and stars as *cosmically projected symbols of the spiritual aspect of saints on earth.* The imagery of spatial transcendence is transparently symbolic of inner spirituality as the presence of "heaven" within human personality.

Our second witness is Jewish merkabah ("throne-chariot") mysticism, which flourished within Judaism as a significant but underground movement from some time after Ezekiel right down through medieval cabalism to modern Hasidism. The great historian of this phenomenon in Judaism G. G. Scholem comments almost offhandedly on a shift in the mystics' perception of the nature of the spiritual quest, a shift that took place so inconspicuously that it can only be dated as happening somewhere around 500 C.E. It was the moment when the Jewish mystics no longer spoke of the mystical *ascent* through the seven heavens, and described it rather as a *descent.*[41] This revolution in imagery (and nothing

---

41. G. G. Scholem, *Major Trends in Jewish Mysticism* (New York: Schocken Books, 1941, 1965), 46–47. Perhaps a similar phenomenon happened independently in gnosticism as well. Speaking of the same kind of mystical journey to heaven, the *NHL Steles Seth* says, "The way of ascent is the way of descent" (127:21–22). This echoes an ancient saying of Heraclitus: "The way up and the way down are one and the same" (H. Diels, *Die Fragmente der Vorsokratiker* (Berlin: Weidmannsche Buchhandlung, 1912), 1:89, frag. 60). Perhaps that ancient insight was only now being vindicated. See also *NHL Zost.* 82:23–24 and the *Teach. Silv.* 116:27—117:5; and 117:6–9—"Open the door for yourself that you may know what is. Knock on yourself that the Word may open for you." The *Greater Hekhalot* repeatedly refers to the "descent" into the Merkabah, as do the "Hekhalot Fragments" (cited by Ithamar Gruenwald, *Apocalyptic and Merkavah Mysticism* [Leiden: E. J. Brill, 1980], p. 188). Another way of symbolizing the "descent" to God appears in Re'uyot Yehezkel, where Ezekiel is depicted as "standing on the River Chebar looking down at the water and the seven heavens were opened to him and he saw

is more revolutionary than the transformation of the fundamental metaphors by which we apprehend the world) marked the perception that the
mystic did not in fact journey into heaven but penetrated the soul's own
depths. This shift was the seed that would, after many centuries of drifting,
darkness, nurture, and growth, come to full flower in an inheritor of that
mystical tradition—Sigmund Freud.[42] It is this shift that led finally to the
psychological mind-set of modern times, stripped, however, of a sense
of the divine reality within. It was that shift which enabled Jung, standing
on Freud's shoulders (or toes), to recover a sense of the numinous reality
behind myth and symbol and to redirect us back to these ancient treasuries
of truth, with this one difference: we can now withdraw the unconscious
projections which "change the world into the replica of one's unknown
face,"[43] and locate the cosmic aspect of myth within ourselves—and, I
would wish to add, in the inwardness of the events of our time and the
forces of nature and history and institutional structures that impinge on
us. We are, in short, capable of a "second reading" of the ancient texts,
a reading in which the myth is understood to speak symbolically of the
real but invisible spiritual dimension of personal and corporate earthly
existence.

Why not, then, simply discard the myth in favor of our demythologized
interpretation? The more obvious and general answer is that we cannot
dispense with the myth because it says more than we can tell. It is not
only lucid but opaque. It participates not only in the light of consciousness
and reason but also in the darkness of mystery. It treasures things that
we have not yet learned to comprehend and preserves them for a generation that might. Through a set of powerfully evocative symbols acknowledged as meaningful by a people, it presents an incredibly condensed story that depicts, through the indirect language of narrative, the
nature of ultimate reality, the way things got how they are, the path to
salvation, and the final meanings of life. All our "explanations" of myths

---

the Glory of the Holy One" (cited by Gruenwald, p. 135). The water serves as a mirror
of the things in heaven. But that is tantamount to saying that the heavenly is revealed
through the depths of the unconscious ("water"). See also T. B. *Sanh.* 91b—"So will
the Holy One, blessed be He, bring the soul, [re]place it in the body, and judge them
together, as it is written, *He shall call to the heavens from above, and to the earth, that
he may judge his people: He shall call to the heavens from above*—this refers to the soul;
and to the earth, that he may judge his people—to the body." One could scarcely hope
to find a more explicit equation of heaven with the "within" of a person.

42. If that statement seems extravagant, I recommend a careful reading of David
Bakan's *Sigmund Freud and the Jewish Mystical Tradition* (Princeton: D. Van Nostrand
Co., 1958).

43. C. G. Jung, *Aion. Researches in the Phenomenology of the Self*, Collected Works
9.2, Bollingen Series XX (Princeton: Princeton University Press, 1979), 9.

are dispensable and time-bound and will soon be forgotten, but the myth lives on, fed by its continual interplay with the very reality it "presents."[44] Even myths that justify oppression are "true," in the sense that they faithfully reflect the actual power relations and spirituality of a particular society and its institutions. Insofar as they cease to be accurate reflections of what is and become nostalgic memories of what used to be, they lose their power as descriptions of reality and become art forms. But it is not fruitful to speak of myths as true and false. To function at all, to command assent, they must be true. As societies evolve, their myths evolve with them. When they cease to be true, they are not so much false as antiquated. The real issue, then, is not epistemological but ethical: Are they *unjust*? Do they legitimate oppression? Is the reality they faithfully describe under the judgment of God?

There is a second, more subtle reason that we cannot dispense with the particular mythic language of heaven and the spiritual and the Powers. Henry Corbin suggests that concrete symbolization, such as temples, rituals, and myths, helps us avoid the dangers of a false subjectivity, of introspective self-preoccupation, of narcissistic introversion. "It enables us to find *our interiority outside ourselves*," in contemplation. It unties the binding knot of subjectivity by reestablishing communication between heaven and earth, making the spaces between accessible to all.[45] But this communication takes place in images in the in-between world of the imagination. Ibn 'Arabī speaks of this dimension of awareness, Corbin continues, as the "confluence of two seas," where the world of ideas and the object world of sense perception meet and mingle, producing a third kind of knowing.[46] This "imaginal" realm is not "imaginary," as many moderns have mistakenly thought. It is as real as sensation or thought, as objects or ideas. This intermediate world, "at the confluence of two seas," possesses extension and dimension, figures and colors, but it lacks full materiality and hence cannot be perceived by the senses. In

---

44. Rudolf Bultmann's program of demythologizing the Bible (see his "The New Testament and Mythology," in *Kerygma and Myth*, ed. H. W. Bartsch [New York: Harper & Row, Torchbooks, 1961; London: SPCK, 1953], 1–44), was a move in the right direction but from the wrong foundation. He defined myth as a falsifying objectification of reality and sought to dispense with it through existential interpretation. Had he worked with a more positive understanding of myth, such as we find in the work of Carl Jung, Mircea Eliade, or Paul Ricoeur, his quite proper concern for making the text intelligible and existentially meaningful could have been achieved without sacrificing the myth to the interpretation.

45. Henry Corbin, "The *Imago Templi* and Secular Norms," *Spring* (1975): 185, emphasis his.

46. Ibid., 166.

dreams, for example, the action is perceived *as if* it were staged on the physical plane, but is not. It is the world of images and archetypes. These archetypal images possess extension and dimension in the realm of the imaginal, but not outside it (except meagerly in the functioning brain). They have what Corbin calls an "immaterial materiality" compared to the sensible world, since they possess corporeality and spatiality without substance. The confusion arises when we attempt to speak of the imaginal in sensory terms. We speak of heaven as "up" because it does have its own unique spatial quality *at the symbolic level*. We speak of it as a "place" because it is characterized by a kind of immaterial materiality and is felt as a real, but transcendent, present power and possibility. We speak of it as "spiritual," however, because it cannot be perceived by the senses, since it lacks substance, or by the mind, since it is a felt image not an idea. In short, the intermediate world of the imaginal can be known (as opposed to *thought about*, as we have been doing in this book) only by the "transmutation of inner spiritual states into outer states, into vision-events symbolizing with these inner states." The imagination operates as if it were capable of sensibly perceiving the supersensible.[47]

Is this not also the way we experience our own selves? For centuries philosophers and scientists sought in vain to locate the "seat of the soul" in some physical organ. Today almost everyone agrees that no such organ exists but that the soul or self is the active awareness of the entire living body itself. And yet this "withinness" is experienced as more than simply the sum of its parts, since our bodily parts continually change or can even to a degree be lost without impairing the sense of our selves. In an odd way, we seem to experience our selves as "outside" or "above" or "transcendent" to our bodies, even though the self is clearly the interiority of all that flesh. But this is one of the ways interiority is known. We can discover the self by introspection, reflection, revelation, but some aspects we can find only by projecting that aspect out on other people or things or events and recognizing it "out there" as parts of ourselves. We discover our body as "temple" by going to a temple.

We experience the self as distinct from or outside the body in precisely the same way that we experience the Powers generally. The biblical

---

47. Henry Corbin, "*Mundus Imaginalis* or the Imaginary and the Imaginal," *Spring* (1972): 12. Using different terms, the apocryphal *Gospel of Mary* says almost precisely the same thing. Mary asks Jesus, " 'Lord, now does he who sees the vision see it through the soul or through the spirit?' The Savior answered and said, 'He does not see it through the soul [sensory awareness] nor through the spirit [mind], but the mind [the imaginal] which is between the two—that is what sees the vision' " (Berlin Gnostic Codex 8502; cf. *NHL*, 472).

language describes their spirituality as outside or transcendent to their earthly manifestations—as heavenly, to be exact. But that is only the same convention of language we use to describe our selves (indeed, who is the "my" who says "my self"?). The Powers can no more exist without concretion in an institution or system or officeholder than the self can exist without a body.

Therefore we cannot dispense with the myth, for it will continue to function by throwing up on the screen of consciousness those images that pertain to our wholeness. *We have no other form of access to this realm.* Interpretations such as this one, even when successful, succeed only in describing a process and hinting at its meanings. Experiencing the process is an event of another order altogether. And since one of the basic flaws that the Judeo-Christian myth of salvation seeks to cure is our egocentricity, it is absolutely essential that we "find our interiority outside ourselves." Otherwise we would be certain that we do it all ourselves. The ego would claim all the riches of the self as its own, with no awareness of the larger world in which the self is embedded and of which the ego is utterly unaware.

The journey toward spiritual awareness is not a movement of conquest, but a gift. In the words of the twelfth-century Persian mystic, Sohrawardî, it is like a drop of balsam in the hollow of one's hand, which, when held up against the sun, passes through to the back of the hand. Corbin interprets this as the spiritual path which begins with a movement into the interior to penetrate inward into the mystery of being. Having reached the interior, however, one finds oneself paradoxically on the outside (the back of the hand).[48] We find our interiority outside ourselves. Freed from egocentricity, however partially or briefly, one discovers the *objectivity* of reality for the first time and can now be equipped to perceive the real nature of The Powers That Be.

That is why, in the volumes that follow, we will take with utter seriousness the language of the New Testament when it speaks of angels, powers, demons, gods, and Satan. Since they are neither objects nor ideas, but images whose reality can be experienced only at the imaginal level, we must feel our way into the language about them at their own level of reality in order to speak with any assurance of what they are.

Even the most "irrelevant" details of the myth may, in different times and circumstances, burst afresh with new meaning. Take the picturesque speculations we find in *Jubilees* or the *Enoch* writings or (in part) the

48. Ibid., 4–5.

Book of Revelation, about the various heavens, and which heaven contained the angels in charge of rain, frost, snow, wind, and hail, or where the disobedient angels were imprisoned or the demonic forces allowed to roam. That could be dismissed as simply outdated "science," but the myth has a way of always saying more. And the "more" here may be at least in part an intuitive grasp of the importance of being able to "locate" these transcendent powers *so they do not slip out of sight*. Once they become invisible, these invariant determining forces can no longer be symbolized and thus acknowledged. Driven beneath our wisdom, they operate from concealment, compelling, controlling, and constraining behavior without our understanding the sources of our compulsion.

Our image of heaven as the "inside" of reality is, of course, just another form of spatial metaphor. It takes heaven out of its location in the sky and anchors it firmly on the earth, seen as an integral part of the universe. On this view transcendence is symbolized not by height but by invisibility and withinness. Only by locating the invisible in metaphorical space can we know how to look, and by looking, to discern the spiritual essence and potential of material and cultural phenomena.

In earlier times the myth was lived out unconsciously by projection. It was understood not as a symbolic account of the actual unfolding of psychic or institutional processes but as the drama of supranatural powers enacting the fate of the world in the cosmic realms. That was, and for most people still is, the only way the Powers have been discerned. Visions, auditions, prophetic messages, and the like were the perfectly normal ways of receiving messages from or about these entities in such a context, and only arrogance could have led so-called "modern" interpreters of such phenomena to brand them "hallucinations" and treat them as a form of pathology.

The way of the ancients, however, is closed to most of us today, and even for those who long to recover it, probably regressive. Our way would seem to lie along the path of making the myth conscious, which means withdrawing the projections and identifying the psychic or social reality being indicated. It is not a mistake to project; it is absolutely necessary. That is the only way those mythic contents can be made known. The task is simply to complete the circle by an interpretation that finds their meaning back in the one and only real world characterized by matter and spirit. If we understand "heaven," as has been suggested, as the realm of emergent possibilities, the ecstasy of transcendent realization, and the locus of divine presence, then it is as real within us as it is the inner divine lure in everything. Had not Jesus himself said something to this effect: "the kingdom of God is within [or in the midst of] you" (Luke 17:21)? The *Gospel of Thomas* elaborates on this suggestively: "Jesus said, 'If those who lead you say to you, "See, the Kingdom is in the sky," then the birds of the sky will precede you. If they say to you, "It is in the sea," then the fish will precede you. Rather, the kingdom is inside you, and it is outside of you' " (sec. 3). This saying from the *Gospel of Thomas* reads like a commentary on the previously cited passage from Luke, suggesting that the long controversy over whether to translate *entos* by "within" or "in the midst of, among" is resolvable by affirming both. Once again, the meaning of an ambiguous statement is precisely its ambiguity. The Reign of God cannot just be inner or outer; it must be both or it is neither.

This being the case, the goal of personal individuation becomes inseparable from the goal of cosmic reconciliation: "Jesus said to them, 'When you make the two one, and when you make the inside like the outside and the outside like the inside, and the above like the below, and when you make the male and female one and the same . . . then will you enter [the kingdom].' "[49]

That longing for integration lies at the root of every religion. The marriage of heaven and earth, which the author of Ephesians describes under the image of the marriage of Christ and the church (Eph. 5:21–33) and which the Book of Revelation depicts as a descent of Heavenly Jerusalem to the earth from God (Revelation 21–22), captures the sense of earth's real possibilities and of ours with it. Paul describes the same longing in Rom. 8:18–25, when he speaks of the whole creation as groaning in travail together for the revealing of the children of God. It is nothing less than the desire for what Dorothee Soelle calls "the indivisible salvation of the whole world."[50] *When* God's children will be revealed, and the groaning over, and every tear wiped from their eyes, is not for us to know. What we do know is that we have been handed the task of making known the manifold wisdom of God to the principalities and powers in the heavenly places—now. How we might do so will be the theme of the following volumes.

The Powers are still with us. That is neither a cause for celebration nor despair. It is just a simple fact. The New Testament everywhere

---

49. *NHL Gos. Thom.*, sec. 22. *Gos. Phil.* 67:31–34 reads similarly: "I came to make [the things below] like the things [above, and the things] outside like those [inside. I came to unite] them in that place." The same saying also appears variously in *Acts Pet.* 38, *Acts Thom.* 147, *2 Clem.* 12:2, and Clement of Alexandria, *Strom.* 3.13.

50. *Political Theology* (Philadelphia: Fortress Press, 1971), 60.

assumes them, not as a matter requiring belief but as a problem requiring redemption. So far have we "moderns" grown from awareness of these Powers that we require more than help in simply naming the Powers. We must explore their contours almost from scratch, become familiar with their stratagems, and rediscover what it means, in every concrete circumstance, that Christ is in fact as well as in myth their sovereign.

APPENDIXES AND INDEXES

Appendix 1

Archōn and *Archē*

In the LXX, *archōn* is used more than 630 times, exclusively for an incumbent-in-office. It is applied to spiritual powers in Daniel 10 and 12, both hostile and helpful "princes" or angels (7 times in Theodotion, once in the LXX); otherwise it is focused solely on human affairs. In those passages where the LXX uses *archōn,* the RSV translates prince, leader, ruler, commander, chief, head, governor, official, officer, captain, lord, king, general, chief men; minor uses include chief officer, noble, overseer, magistrate, chieftain, mighty one, quartermaster, and master.

Archē, in its nontemporal usage in the LXX, primarily denotes the *position* of authority: government (11 times), dominion (10), office (5), rule (3). Occasionally it is used, like *archōn,* for the human incumbent in a position: head (5), leader (1).

Josephus uses *archōn* and *archē* exclusively of human agents (although he believes in evil spirits and higher powers). He invariably uses *archōn* of a human incumbent-in-office. (For *archōn* the Loeb translators variously use ruler, head, chief, presiding officer, leader, leading personality, official, magistrate, authorities, commander, governor.) *Archē,* on the other hand, refers to the systems, structures, institutions, and, above all, states that these incumbents rule. Josephus employs *archē* of office, government, and authority in a bewilderingly rich variety of ways. The terms used by the English translators defy any precise categorizations:

rulership	reign	supreme command
authority	throne	rod of empire
government	kingdom	officers of the state
office	crown	royal power
power	dominion	form of government
governorship	province	right to the throne
princedom	empire	kingly title
magistracy	realm	high office
administration	state	forms of rule
post	sovereign power	

All told, Josephus employs the term *archē* over 330 times, all without exception of human political or other power arrangements.

Thirteen times Josephus uses *archē* in the sense of *archōn,* of incumbents-in-office: magistrates (*War* 1.285; *Ant.* 4.220; 5.115; 14:327, 388), chiefs (*Ant.* 3.292), ruler (*Ant.* 4:194; 10.84; 15.76; 18.209), governor (*Ant.* 17.89), king (*Ant.* 17.234), leader (*War* 2.205).

The evidence from Philo is similar. Apart from 18 references to God as *archōn,* all of Philo's uses of *archē* and *archōn* are of human rulers or the structures of power. Once he actually pairs *archais* and *exousiais,* referring to "high offices and posts of authority" in the empire (*Leg.* 71). And although he believes in spirits, Philo never employs these terms to describe them, reserving the term *dynamis* for such entities. *Archōn* in Philo is translated ruler (108 times), magistrate (15), sovereign (15), prince (3), governor (3), official (2), mayor (3), and once "the powers which rule" (*De Somn.* II.136). Of all the writers examined, Philo alone uses *archōn* where we would expect *archē:* rule (3 times) and power (1).

Philo normally uses *archē* for abstract or structural power: sovereignty (41 times), office (35), government (13), authority (9), rule or governance (8), dominion (6), leadership (2), command (2), empire (2), and once each, rulership, reign, throne, magistracy, and queenship. Several times *archē* is used like *stoicheia:* first elements (7 times), ruling principles (2). And it occasionally encroaches on *archōn* in the sense of an incumbent-in-office: ruler (2 times), magistrate (2), emperor (1), princess (1), judge (1). (The translations given here reflect the usage of the LCL translators.)

The following outlines indicate the incidence of usage of *archē* and *archōn* for spiritual powers in the New Testament period. They show at a glance how wide of the mark is Carr's curious assertion that the words for "power" in Jewish literature "are confined to the angels and archangels . . . and never are used of demonic forces."[1]

A. *Archē* and *archōn* used of heavenly powers (ostensibly good)
    1. Pre–New Testament
        a. Dan. 10:13, 20–21; 12:1 (7 times in Theodotion, 1 time in LXX, v. 13)

---

1. *A&P,* 43. In the outlines I have tried to be exhaustive for the pre–New Testament and New Testament periods; for the post–New Testament period the literature is so vast that I have merely given samples.

    b. *1 Enoch* 21:5; 75:1; 80:6–7; 82:7–20; 20:1 (G^{g1})[2]

    c. *Jub.* 10:8[3]

    d. Dead Sea Scrolls—1QS 3: 1QM 13; 1QH 10; 4Q Shir Shab (5 times)[4]

2. New Testament period

    a. Disputed Pauline and deutero-Pauline passages (?)

    b. 1 Pet. 3:22

    c. *Asc. Isa.* 10:11–12; 11:16

    d. *1 Enoch* 61:10–11

    e. *2 Bar.* 59:11

3. Post–New Testament period

    a. Ignatius, *Trall.* 5, *Smyr.* 6

    b. Justin, *Dial.* 36:6

    c. *3 Bar.* 1:8

    d. *Apostolic Constitutions* 7.35.3; 8.12.8

    e. *3 Enoch* (virtually every page)

    f. *Test. Job* 49:2 (50:1–2)

---

2. We must guess at the Greek terms translated into Ethiopic, but our guessing is aided by a few solid clues. The Greek fragment of *1 Enoch* 6:8 reads *archai autōn hoi deka;* R. H. Charles had translated the Ethiopic "chiefs of tens," which conforms precisely to the usage that our survey of the LXX and Josephus would have led us to expect. See R. H. Charles, *The Book of Enoch* (Oxford: Clarendon Press, 1912). *1 Enoch* 75:1 is failsafe, since it has three words that could be translated by *archē* or *archōn:* "And the *leaders* of the *heads* of the thousands [of angels], who are placed over the whole creation and over all the stars" are "inseparable from their *office.*" Here "heads of thousands" must surely reflect the Greek *chiliarchoi.* First Enoch 82:7–20 is even more dense with power terms. For works still extant in part in Latin, like *Jubilees,* we can cross-check the LXX with the Vulgate to get a sense of which Latin terms were used to translate the words for power.

Third Enoch gives us a further clue. It uses the Hebrew *sar* (head, chief, captain, prince) for the higher angels, the very term that the LXX renders most frequently by *archōn.* So there is a high degree of probability that *archōn* would have been used to translate *3 Enoch*'s *sar* as well.

In fact, we do not need to establish anything more than a fair approximation, because we are dealing not with a technical, precise, and systematic terminology but with very inexact and fluid *meaning-clusters* that loosely denote power. The context indicates quite clearly when power is the subject, and we have seen already from the New Testament what a wide range of terms and combinations of terms were used to describe it. When these same phenomena are mentioned in *1 Enoch* or *Jubilees,* then, it is the denotative intent of the passage itself, and not the precise terms it employs, that indicates which Powers are being discussed.

3. See above, note 2.

4. See above, note 2.

    g. *Nag Hammadi Library*
      (1) *Thom.* Cont. 142:31–35. 39–42
      (2) *Tri. Prot.* 41:25
    h. *Apocalypse of Thomas* (*NT Apoc.* 2:800)
B. *Archē* and *archōn* of Satan
   1. Pre–New Testament
    a. *Jub.* 10:7–8
    b. *Testaments of the Twelve Patriarchs*
      (1) *Test. Jud.* 19:4
      (2) *Test. Sim.* 2:7
      (3) *Test. Dan* 5:6
    c. Dead Sea Scrolls: 1QM 17
   2. New Testament period
    a. *2 Enoch* 7:3; 18:3
    b. Mark 3:22; Luke 11:15; John 12:31; 14:30; 16:11; Eph. 2:2
    c. *Asc. Isa.* 4:2–4
   3. Post–New Testament period
    a. Ignatius, *Eph.* 17, 19; *Mag.* 1, *Trall.* 4; *Rom.* 7; *Phil.* 6
    ᴅ. Justin, *Dial.* 124.3
    c. *Acts John* 23, 114 (*NT Apoc.* 2:218, 258)
    d. *Gosp. Phil.* (*NT Apoc.* 1:273)
    e. *The Two Books of Jeu* (*NT Apoc.* 1:261)
    f. *Nag Hammadi Library*
      (1) *Apoc. Adam* 77:3
      (2) *Great Pow.* 41:17, 27, 33
      (3) *Treat. Seth* 54:27
      (4) *Zostrianos* 9:12
    g. *Apoc. Peter* 17 (Ethiopic: *NT Apoc.* 2:683)
    h. *Apoc. Paul* 11 (*NT Apoc.* 2:763)
C. *Archē* and *archōn* of evil powers or fallen angels
   1. Pre–New Testament
    a. Ps. 82:6–7 (LXX) (?)
    b. Dan. 10:13, 20
    c. *Jub.* 10:1–13
    d. *1 Enoch* 80:6–7
   2. New Testament period
    a. Disputed Pauline and deutero-Pauline passages (?)
    b. *Asc. Isa.* 4:2–4; 10:12, 15
   3. Post–New Testament period
    a. Ignatius, *Smyr.* 6:1

b. *Epist. Apost.* 13; 28 (*NT Apoc.* 1:198, 210)
c. *Acts John* 98, 79, 114 (*NT Apoc.* 2:233, 251, 258)
d. Legends from *Pistis Sophia* (*NT Apoc.* 1:402)
e. *Nag Hammadi Library*[5]

The evidence assembled in this outline is by itself quite enough to refute Carr's argument that the terms of power are not used of demonic forces. And this outline deals with only one set of power terms. Once we have laid out all the data for the other terms, there can be no doubt that evil spirits and powers were known by these words.

New Testament usage of *archē* and *archōn* is not all that different from Jewish writings of the period, as the following outline shows.

A. *Archē*
  1. Human
     a. Rulers of the synagogue, magistrates, judges, chief priests, elders, Sanhedrin, etc. (Luke 12:11)
     b. Magistrates, governors, police, church leaders (Titus 3:1)
  2. Structural
     a. Office, position, status, or place of angels (Jude 6)
     b. The authority or legitimate right of a governor to judge (Luke 20:20)
  3. Spiritual and/or human and structural (to be determined)
     a. Rom. 8:38; 1 Cor. 15:24; Eph. 1:21–22; 3:10; 6:12; Col. 1:16; 2:10, 15
B. *Archōn*
  1. Human
     a. A Jewish ruler in Galilee (Matt. 9:18, 23)
     b. The emperor and all kings (Matt. 20:25; see Mark 10:42; Luke 22:25)
     c. Jairus, a ruler of the synagogue (Luke 8:41)

---

5. *Ap. Jas.* 8:35–36; *Ap. John* 10:20—11:24; *Gos. Eg.* 62:23; 63:7; 67:24; *Dial. Sav.* 120:21; 122:14; 138:12; 142:8; 143:15; 145:5, 21; *Apoc. Paul* 19:3; 23:21; *1 Apoc. Jas.* 25:19, 25, 29; 26:23; 31:24, 27; 39:10; *2 Apoc. Jas.* 56:19; *Apoc. Adam* 75:27; *Auth. Teach.* 25:33 (in a series with "authority" and "powers"); *Great Pow.* 41:15; 42:3, 9, 11; 43:29, 35; 44:1, 14; 45:1; 48:8, 11; *Treat. Seth* 51:26–27; 52:14; 53:13; 56:16; 58:21; 59:17; 60:15; 64:18; 68:28; *Apoc. Pet.* 71:5; 74:30; 77:4; *Zost.* 4:29; 10:17(?); 130:11; *Ep. Pet. Phil.* 137:16–17, 21; *Melch.* 2:8; 9:1; 10:10, 29; *Testim. Truth* 29:20; 30:16; 31:4; 32:4–5; 34:8; 42:24–25; 59:14; *Interp. Know.* 6:30–37; 20:22–23; *Trim. Prot.* 35:16; 49:7, 11, 34.

   d. Magistrate or judge (Luke 12:58)
   e. A ruler who belonged to the Pharisees (Luke 14:1)
   f. A ruler with wealth (Luke 18:18)
   g. Rulers who had Jesus crucified (members of the Sanhedrin?)
       (Luke 23:13, 35; 24:20; Acts 3:17; 4:5, 8, 26; 13:27)
   h. Nicodemus, a ruler of the Jews (John 3:1)
   i. The authorities who control Jerusalem (John 7:26, 48; 12:42)
   j. Moses as ruler (Acts 7:27, 35 twice)
   k. Rulers of Iconium (Acts 14:5)
   l. Rulers of Philippi (Acts 16:19)
   m. The chief priest (Acts 23:5)
   n. Magistrates, governors, tax collectors of the Roman Empire
       (Rom. 13:3)
2. Spiritual
   a. Satan as the prince of demons (Matt. 9:34; 12:24; Mark 3:22;
       Luke 11:15)
       (1) The ruler of this world (John 12:31; 14:30; 16:11)
       (2) The prince of the power of the air (Eph. 2:2)
   b. Jesus Christ as the ruler of the kings on earth (Rev. 1:5)
3. Spiritual and/or human
   a. The rulers of this age (1 Cor. 2:6, 8)

Appendix 2

Exousia

The LXX uses *exousia* 59 times,[1] usually in reference to humans, occasionally to God, but never to angels or demons or other spiritual powers.[2] The term is variously translated by the RSV (I am assuming an at least fair degree of congruity between the Greek, Hebrew, and English) as authority, power, permission, control, right, rule, realm, government, dominion. Once it appears in the plural, meaning "positions of authority" in the administration of government (LXX, Esther 8:12e). Cullmann (*Christ and Time* [Philadelphia: Westminster Press, 1964], 194) had argued that the plural of *exousia* in the New Testament always refers to spiritual powers; at least that is certainly not the case in the LXX, and is not even true of the New Testament.

Philo employs *exousia* 31 times, again without reference to spiritual Powers. Most striking is the number of times *exousia* appears in clusters of power terms reminiscent of, yet not identical to, those we have identified in the New Testament.[3] Josephus uses the term far more frequently (151 times), extending the range of the term beyond LXX usage to include the prerogatives of liberty. Josephus uses the plural form for human

---

1. Counting Theodotion's text of Daniel but not that of the LXX. The text of Theodotion, although second century C.E., is clearly based on a manuscript tradition that existed already in New Testament times, since the Dead Sea Scrolls and the Book of Revelation show evidence of familiarity with it. Theodotion's version is generally regarded as superior to the LXX of Daniel (J. W. Wevers, "Septuagint," *IDB* 4: 275).

2. 2 Macc. 3:24 may be the exception: "the Sovereign of spirits (*pneumatōn*) and all authority (*pasēs exousias*)," referring possibly to angelic powers (Werner Foerster, "Exousia," *TDNT* 2 [1964]: 565).

3. E.g., *Leg. all.* III,73—*archei kai hēgemoneuei dynasteia kratous autexousiō . . onoma . . . exousia . . . dynameōs; De cher.* 27–28—*dynameis, exousian, exousia, archein, archonta, archēs, dynameōn.* See also *Leg.* 28; 54; *De spec. leg.* I,294; *De Ios.* 166; *De virt.* 218; *De op.* 17.

157

agents—again, refuting Cullmann—when he places in the mouth of King Agrippa a reference to the procurators of Judea as "the powers that be" (*tas exousias, War* 2.350). In describing the vows of the Essenes, Josephus uses words strikingly reminiscent of Rom. 13:1–7: the initiate swears "that he will for ever keep faith with all men, especially with the powers that be (*tois kratousin*[4]), since no one who rules (*archein*) attains his office save by the will of God, that should he himself bear rule he will never abuse his authority (*exousian*)" (*War* 2.140). Apart from three or so references to the *exousia* of God, all of Josephus's uses of the term refer to human affairs and are often paired with *archai* and other power language.[5]

---

4. *Kratos* is another power term, used 12 times in the New Testament, half of them in doxological strings of terms praising God's "dominion" or "might" (1 Tim. 6:16; 1 Pet. 4:11; 5:11; Jude 25; Rev. 1:6; 5:13). Eleven of the twelve uses refer to God's power. The sole exception, Heb. 2:14, refers to the devil's power.

5. Among many others, *Ant.* 17.231; 18.214, 345; 20.11; *Life* 190.

Appendix 3

Dynamis

The LXX frequently uses *dynameis* to translate *sabaoth* in the expression "Lord of *hosts.*" Ps. 103:21 (102:21, LXX) identifies these powers with angels by synonymous parallelism:

> Bless the Lord, O you his angels,
> you mighty ones (*dynatoi ischui*) who do his word . . .
> Bless the Lord, all his hosts (*dynameis*),
> his ministers that do his will! (vv. 20–21)

Other texts equate these angelic powers with gods. Thus 2 Kings 17:16—Israel forsook the Lord "and worshiped all the host (*dynamei*, LXX) of heaven," that is, stars revered as gods.[1] Isa. 34:4 (LXX) even uses "stars" (*astra*) to translate *saba'*, as does Dan. 8:10 (LXX), while in Dan. 8:10 Theodotion uses *dynameōs*. On the basis of Ps. 29:1 and 89:5–8, B. W. Anderson suggests that these "hosts" or "holy ones" in the skies or "sons of gods" in the heavenly council are the pagan gods, subordinated to Yahweh and bidden to do his will only (Ps. 103:21b), which some have in fact not done and for which they will be judged on the last day (Isa. 24:21–23).[2] The pagan gods are thus depotentiated by sublimation; their terrible powers are turned toward Yahweh in adoration of his superior might, their presence in the heavenly council being marked by the renaming of Yahweh specifically as their master: Yahweh Sabaoth, "Lord of the Powers."[3]

1. So also, using *dynamei*, 2 Kings 21:3, 5; 23:4–5.
2. B. W. Anderson, "Hosts, Host of Heaven," *IDB* 2:658.
3. The phrase "Lord of the Powers" also appears in the LXX of 1 Sam. 4:4 (A, L); 2 Sam. 6:2, 18; 1 Kings 17:1; 18:15; 2 Kings 3:14; 19:20, 31; Isa. 42:13; Jer. 40(33):12, in addition to the passages cited earlier. Some passages seem to distinguish "the powers" from the angels. Ps. 148:2, LXX, reads, "Praise him all his angels, praise him, all his hosts (*dynameis*)." This can scarcely be synonymous parallelism without being sheer redundancy. And the powers are further distinguished from the sun, moon, and stars (v. 3). So also Dan. 3:61 (LXX and Theodotion, but not Hebrew), which is clearly based

The Parables section of *1 Enoch* continues this tradition, using spirits instead of powers to translate *sabaoth* in the Trisagion of 39:12—"Holy, holy, holy, is the Lord of *Spirits*" (where the LXX might have read "Lord of the Powers"), illustrating once again the high degree of interchangeability of these terms for power.[4]

Jubilees refers once to "the powers of the heaven" (1:29), but it is Philo who shows the greatest interest in heavenly "powers." Philo's use of *dynamis* for angelic powers is a synthesis of Jewish monotheism and the Neoplatonic notion of divine emanations.

> God is one, but He has around Him numberless Potencies (*dynameis*), which all assist and protect created being. . . . Through these Potencies the incorporeal intelligible world was framed, the archetype of this phenomenal world, that being a system of invisible ideal forms, as this is of visible material bodies. . . . There is, too, in the air a sacred company of unbodied souls (*psychōn*), commonly called angels in the inspired pages, who wait upon these heavenly powers. . . . Now the King may fitly hold converse with his powers (*dynamesin*) and employ them to serve in matters which should not be consummated by God alone. . . . He allowed His subject powers (*hypēkoois dynamesin*) to have the fashioning of some things, though he did not give them sovereign and independent knowledge for completion of the task. . . . (*De conf.* 171–75)

> . . . The complete whole around us is held together by invisible powers (*aoratois dynamesin*), which the Creator has made to reach from the ends of the earth to heaven's furthest bounds, taking forethought that what was well bound should not be loosened: for the powers of the Universe (*hai dynameis tou pantos*) are chains that cannot be broken. (*De mig.* 181)[5]

---

on Psalm 103. Later speculation created a whole order of *dynameis,* served by angels (*1 Enoch* 20:1 G⁸¹; Philo, *De conf.* 171–75; *3 Bar.* 1:8; *1 Enoch* 61:10; possibly 2 Thess. 1:7 (*A&P,* 37–38). *Test. Abr.* 9 and 14 call Michael the "Commander-in-chief (*archistratēgos*) of the higher powers (*anō dynameōn*)."

4. Compare Heb. 12:9—God is "the Father of Spirits."

5. Philo uses *dynameis* of heavenly powers around 75 times (it is not always possible to distinguish these from its use 80 times as an attribute of God): *De cher.* 20, 27, 28, 51, 106 (deliver Torah!); *De sac.* 59 (3 times), 60 (2 times); *De post.* 20, 167, 168, 169; *Quod deus* 3, 77, 78, 109 (2 times), 110; *De plant.* 14, 129; *De conf.* 137 (twice), 166, 171, 172, 175 (2 times), 182; *De mig.* 181 (2 times), 220; *Quis her.* 166 (2 times), 170, 172, 312; *De fuga* 69, 70, 95, 97, 98, 100, 101; *De mut.* 14, 15, 28, 29; *De som.* I,62, 70, 163, 185, 240; II,254; *De Abr.* 121, 122, 125, 143, 145, 146; *Mos.* II,99 (twice), 291; *De spec. leg.* I,45, 46, 47, (48), 49, 66, 209, 307, 329; II,45; *De virt.* 49. Philo never uses *dynamis* of evil spiritual Powers. Elsewhere he uses the term in a bewildering variety of ways, often idiomatically. Those dealing with the world of power include power as a human attribute (60 times), power as a generic category (94), as force (69—military force 17), strength (39), ability (7), sway or mastery or influence (4), faculty (70), might (9), value (21), function (4), potentiality (16), capacity (17), an attribute of number (12), etc.

By far the most frequent use of *dynamis* in Judaism, however, is for earthly power, especially military "forces." The LXX uses it about 594 times; with the exception of its use to translate "sabaoth" ("hosts" itself having originally been a military term meaning "armies"), all other uses are for attributes of God or for human power. Josephus gives us the clearest idea of the term's range in the first century:

1. *General:* ability, power, vitality, strength, physical ability, good constitution, power of resistance, energy, force, capacity
2. *Military:* armed forces, military power, army, force(s), striking force, garrison, crew, armed following, units, land forces, foot soldiers, infantry
3. *Economic:* wealth, resources, means, assistance, support, help
4. *Spiritual:* miracle-working power
5. *Theological:* God's might, power, rule, authority, providence
6. *Political:* superiority, sovereignty, authority, position of power, influence, office, position, tyranny, political power
7. *Rhetorical:* eloquence, rhetoric, power of speech, descriptive power

In his 535 uses of *dynamis,* Josephus makes no reference to angels, spirits, or demons, although it is clear that he believes in such things.[6]

In the New Testament, aside from its frequent use for "miracle," *dynamis* is used primarily to denote spiritual entities or attributes:

God: Matt. 26:64; Mark 14:62; (Luke 22:69)
Christ: 1 Cor. 1:24
Holy Spirit: Eph. 3:20
Spirit of a dead person: Mark 6:14
Divine attribute: Luke 5:17
Evil spirit: Acts 4:7
Stars: Matt. 24:29; Mark 13:25; Luke 21:26
(Angels: 2 Thess. 1:7?)
A divine man (*theios anēr*): Acts 8:10
Delegated authority over evil spirits: Luke 9:1; 10:19
Delegated authority from evil spirits: Rev. 13:2; 17:12–13
Spiritual powers: Rom. 8:38; 1 Cor. 15:24; Eph. 1:21; 1 Pet. 3:22

There is surprisingly little use of *dynamis* for evil powers in the New

6. Also from the first century c.e., *Life of Adam and Eve* 25:1; 48:4; and *Test. Abr.* 9 and 14. *Second Enoch* 20:1–3A lists "great archangels, incorporeal forces, and dominions, orders and governments, cherubim and seraphim, thrones and many-eyed ones, nine regiments . . . heavenly troops." But version B lacks it; it is probably a Christian interpolation.

Testament, considering its popularity in that sense in the centuries that followed.[7] The only pre-Christian use of *dynamis* for evil powers is *1 Enoch* 20:1, and there only in G^{g1}, which may be an interpolation. *Asc. Isa.* 2:2 says that Manasseh "served Satan and his angels and his powers." The same verse is found in the *Greek Legend* (3:2) and uses *tais dynamesin*. And *Asc. Isa.* 9:16 (L^2), for which no Greek version survives, reads, "And He [the Messiah] will seize the prince (*principem = archōn?*)." These passages are evidence either that *dynamis* was used for evil powers at the time the New Testament was being written or that its use in such passages as 1 Cor. 15:24 and Rom. 8:38 was being interpreted by Christians between the end of the first century and the second half of the second as referring to evil powers.

A special word about the stars as powers. We saw above that the equation "heavenly hosts = powers = angels = stars = gods" was already in place by the time of the LXX. There the stars were powers in their own right, considered as "conscious" beings.[8] In the early sections of the Enoch literature, on the other hand, the sole sovereignty of God is buffered by the appointment of rulers over the stars, whose task is to regulate their movement through the heavens.[9] These *archontes* are the "leaders of the stars" (72:3); they "transgress the order (prescribed)" (80:6) and are worshiped by humanity as gods (80:7), for which the

7. Ignatius, *Eph.* 13:1; *1 Enoch* 41:9; *Martyrdom of Isa.* 2:3; *Apoc. Elij.* (P. Chester Beatty 2018) 2:11, 14; *Acts John* 98, 79, 114 (*NT Apoc.* 2:233, 251, 258); *Apocalypse of Paul* 14 (*NT Apoc.* 2:766); and frequently in Christian writings. The recently published *Nag Hammadi Library* teems with entities designated powers, only a small fraction of which are evil. The context does not always make clear whether the power in question is good or evil, but those that are clearly evil would include *Tri. Trac.* 85:11; 107:10, 12; 109:14, 26; 110:3; *Gos. Eg.* 61:21; *Dial. Sav.* 122:4; 127:14; 129:10; 135:18; *Apoc. Paul* 19:4; *1 Apoc. Jas.* 24:30; 26:18, 24; 27:16, 18; *Apoc. Adam* 64:18, 22; 65:30; 74:19; 75:14, 27; 77:3, 5, 13, 20, 26; 83:6, 19, 24; 84:20; *Great Pow.* 45:31; *Paraph. Shem* 5:4, 34; 6:9; 7:17; 9:32; 10:9; 11:2, 5; 21:26, 34; 22:12, 16, 31; 23:17, 22; 25:34; 27:4, 10, 17–18; 31:34; 34:3, 5; 46:30; *Treat. Seth* 51:28; 56:20; 58:20; *Apoc. Pet.* 77:5; *Teach. Silv.* 91:19; 105:34; 106:3; 109:14; 114:5, 10; *Ep. Pet. Phil.* 135:2, 23, 27; 136:7; 137:10; 42:25; 59:15; 73:29; *Trim. Prot.* 43:16, 19, 27, 32; 47:20, 24; 49:17, 25, 33; *Gos. Mary* 15:11; 16:2, 4, 13.
8. See, in addition, Job 38:7, and, later, *1 Enoch* 18:13–16 and Rev. 9:1–3. Jesus is the "bright morning star," Rev. 2:28; 22:16, a title which Isa. 14:12–15 had historicized from the title of a god in Canaanite myth and applied to the king of Babylon.
9. *1 Enoch* 72:3; 75:1; 80:1, 6, 7; 82:1–20. See also *Apoc. Abr.* 19—"the *powers* of the stars which carry out the commands laid on them." The same idea of "leaders" appointed over the stars, but using the term "angel" instead of what in Ethiopic Enoch appears to be *archōn*, is found in *Asc. Isa.* 4:18; 14:3; *1 Enoch* 43:1–4; 60:15–22; *2 Enoch* 4–6; 11:1–5; 12; 15; 16:7; *3 Enoch* 14:3–4; 17:6

archontes will be punished in the Last Day (80:8; see Deut. 4:19).[10] No hint of astrology finds expression in these passages. This is pure henotheistic astronomy, an attempt to account for the regularity of the heavens and the irregularity of the planets within the context of a belief in one ultimate governing power.

Scholars have attempted since the turn of the century to identify Paul's *stoicheia tou kosmou* ("elements of the universe"; see above, pp. 67–77) with astral spirits, but without success, since the earliest evidence is from the third century C.E.[11] Now we can conclude that the stars were indeed considered within the terms of the language of power, but not as *stoicheia.* The stars were designated as *dynameis,* although in most sources they are rendered innocuous by the appointment of *archontes* as their guardians.

10. Stars are described as "fallen" or evil in Isa. 14:12–15 and 24:21–23. A different reason for the punishment of the stars is given in *1 Enoch* 18:13–16; there it is the failure of the planets to "come forth at their appointed times." So also 21:1–6; 20:4; 90:24. Here the stars themselves are judged, not their "leaders"; but they are not here called *archontes* either. Punishment of the stars is also a feature of Isa. 34:1–5 (esp. the LXX).
11. *Test. Sol.* 8:1–4; 18:1.

Appendix 4

Stoicheia in the Writings of the Early Christian Theologians

Having surveyed the New Testament passages and having seen how *stoicheia*, as a formal category for whatever is constitutive of a thing, can best be taken to mean now one thing, now another, in a specific context, I must confess to a growing suspicion that the early Christian theologians must have known this as well. Reviews of their positions in previous studies have represented them as in conflict over the term's meaning. But in fact the issue does not seem for them to have been much of a matter for debate. What modern scholars have done is assume that what the early theologians said in one context about the *stoicheia* is what they would have said in them all. Tertullian, for example, is reported by exegetes to have regarded the *stoicheia* as the Jewish Law. As far as Gal. 4:3 is concerned, this is largely true, though Tertullian specifically limits his comments to Jewish ceremonial and cultic regulations. But he also notes that "the Romans" speak of the *elementa* as "rudiments of learning" and in passing comments that the reference in Gal. 4:8 to "beings which by nature are no gods" might refer to "the error of that physical or natural superstition which holds the elements to be god," that is, the four physical elements. But he prefers instead to take Gal. 4:10 as the clue and defines *elementa* as "the rudiments of the law" (*Against Marcion* 5.4).

In another context, when Tertullian examines Col. 2:8 he understands by these "elements of the world" neither the Jewish Law nor "the mundane fabric of sky and earth," although in the passage above he also acknowledges the latter as a possible meaning. The context shows that the *stoicheia* here are "traditions of men," which he takes to mean secular literature's worldly learning. "In this sentence . . all heresies are condemned on the ground of their consisting of the resources of subtle speech and the rules of philosophy," especially Epicureanism and Stoicism. Yet in the same paragraph he can speak of the dietary laws and cultic practices of Col. 2:16–23 as references to the Jewish Law, leaving us to infer with fair warrant that he would interpret *stoicheia* in 2:20 as those cultic regulations common to Jews and Gentiles alike (*Against Marcion* 5.19). Such a subtle weighing of the term proves that Tertullian regarded it as a formal category and was searching for the best meaning in the context.

If only we had more extensive sources for the rest of the early theologians, we probably would discover that they too were treating it as a context-determined generic category and, rather than being at odds with one another, were relatively in agreement and largely correct.

Enough can be known to make this more than just a good guess. Thus those who identified the *stoicheia* as earth, air, fire, and water (Clement [in part], Victorinus [in part], and Hilary) were correct regarding 2 Pet. 3:10, 12, though the context of 2 Peter justifies as a variant translation "the heavenly bodies will disappear in fire" (*Living Bible*), since not only the earth but the entire universe would be dissolved (Chrysostom, Theodoret, Victorinus [in part], Theodore of Mopsuestia, and Augustine). However, this astral interpretation probably was late, prompted by the tremendous rise of astrological fatalism. Col. 2:8 does refer to philosophy, as Clement and Origen saw, just as Col. 2:20 refers to religious practices (Eusebius). Gal. 4:3 clearly points to the Jewish law (Jerome), and 4:9 implies worship of *stoicheia* as gods (Theodore of Mopsuestia). One thinks of the parable of the blindfolded sages describing the elephant, but with this caveat: It is not they who were blindfolded but we, with our limited sources and lack of a proper definition.[1]

---

1. Even if further sources that identified the *stoicheia* with stars or angels or demons or personal beings should be discovered—an identification for which we have as yet no evidence prior to the third century C.E.—that would occasion no difficulties for this solution. *Stoicheia* would still be a formal term used in specific reference to these entities. The stars *functioned* as *stoicheia* in Greek thought, even if they may not have been thus named, as did the angels in Jewish apocalyptic. The prologue of *2 Enoch*, in speaking of the orders of angelic powers in heaven, included "the ineffable ministrations of the multitude of the elements." The text is in Slavonic, but *stoicheia* almost certainly lies behind it. One could easily connect this back with the angels set over the physical elements described in *1 Enoch* 82:10–14; *Jub.* 2:2; *Asc. Isa.* 4:18; 4 Ezra 8:20–22; and Rev. 16:5. The early Christian theologians, however, continued to speak, as did Jewish apocalyptic, of angelic powers in charge of the elements (Athenagoras, Hilary of Poitiers), and not of the elements themselves as angelic.

Index of Authors

My debt to other authors vastly exceeds this brief list of those actually cited, but for reasons of economy I have decided not to include a complete bibliography.

166

Index of Passages
with Dates and Abbreviations

Every passage cited has been checked against the standard translations for pertinence and accuracy, and where possible against the original sources. For brevity, abbreviations of biblical books have been omitted, since they are more familiar. The abbreviation "C" stands for century, and the primary references have been placed in italic type.

BIBLE

Genesis
6:1–4—23, 30, 137
10—31, 32 n.53
11:7–8—31 n.52
18:1–33—33 n.57
19:5–16—33 n.57
32:24—33 n.57
39:21—13

Exodus
1:5—26 n.42, 27 n.43

Deuteronomy
4:19—163
17:20—20
32:7—26
32:8–9—26, 27 n.43, 29 n.48

Judges
5:20—131 n.26
13:6, 8—22 n.23, 33 n.57

1 Samuel
4:4—159 n.3
12:16—126

2 Samuel
6:2, 18—159 n.3

1 Kings
17:1—159 n.3
17:18—22 n.23
18:15—159 n.3
22:19–23—134

2 Kings
3:14—159 n.3
17:16—159
19:20, 31—159 n.3
21:3, 5—159 n.1
23:4–5—159 n.1

Esther
8:12e, LXX—157

Job
38:7—162 n.8

Psalms
8:6–7—51
20:1, 5—21 n.20
29:1—17, 159
33:16—126
44:5—21 n.20
44:22—48
54:1, 6—21
62:11—126
68:17—131 n.26
82:6–7—25, 154
89:5–8—17, 159
89:24—21 n.20
103:20–22—17, 159, 160
110:1—51
118:10–12—21 n.20
139:8–9—50
148:2–3—159 n.3
149:5–9—33 n.59

Proverbs
8—64
18:10—21 n.20

Isaiah
6—80 n.93
14:12–15—162 n.8, 163 n.10
24:4–6—131 n.26
24:21–23—28 n.45, 159, 162 n.10
30:15—126
30:27–28—21 n.20
34:1–5—28 n.45, 163 n.10
34:4—17, 159
41–46—27
42:13—159 n.3
44:26—22
45:7—28
48—27

Jeremiah
10:6—21 n.20
40:12—159 n.3
49:38—18 n.12, 91

Daniel
2:47—28 n.47
3:61—159 n.3
7:9—18
7:13—28 n.47
7:22—33 n.59
8:10—24 n.26, 159
8:11—28 n.47
8:15–17—29 n.48
8:25—28 n.47
10, 12—13, 27, 28, 95
10:5–7—29 n.48

168

BIBLE (Continued)

APOCRYPHA (APOT)

APOCRYPHA (APOT) (Continued)

PSEUDEPIGRAPHA[1]

1. *The Old Testament Pseudepigrapha*, Vol. 1, ed. James H. Charlesworth (Garden City, N.Y.: Doubleday & Co., 1983), arrived too late to use in the book proper, but I have cited it in the index (as *OTP*) since it vastly simplifies locating many of the texts.

2. *The Apocalypse of Elijah*, ed. and trans. Albert Pietersma and Susan Turner Comstock, with Harold Attridge (Chico, Ca.: Scholars Press, 1981).

3. *The Books of Elijah*, Parts 1 and 2, collected and translated by Michael Stone and John Strugnell (Missoula, Mont.: Scholars Press, 1979).

4. In R. H. Charles, *Ascension of Isaiah* (London: A. & C. Black, 1900), 141–48.

JOSEPHUS (LCL)
(Jos.); c. 37–100 C.E.

RABBINIC LITERATURE[5]

5. For critical editions and English translations see John T. Townsend, "Rabbinic Sources," in *The Study of Judaism*, Richard Bavier et al. (New York: Anti-Defamation League of B'nai B'rith, 1972), 37–81.

6. English translations in LCL (Apostolic Fathers), ANF *(The Ante-Nicene Fathers)*, ed. A. Roberts and J. Donaldson (Grand Rapids: Wm. B. Eerdmans 1951), or *NPNF*.